CORPORATE INSOLVENCY LAW

CORPORATE INSOLVENCY LAW

A Comparative Textbook

Reinhard Bork

INTERSENTIA
Cambridge – Antwerp – Chicago

Intersentia Ltd
8 Wellington Mews
Wellington Street | Cambridge
CB1 1HW | United Kingdom
Tel: +44 1223 736 170
Email: mail@intersentia.co.uk
www.intersentia.com | www.intersentia.co.uk

Distribution for the UK and Rest of the World (incl. Eastern Europe)
NBN International
1 Deltic Avenue, Rooksley
Milton Keynes MK13 8LD
United Kingdom
Tel: +44 1752 202 301 | Fax: +44 1752 202 331
Email: orders@nbninternational.com

Distribution for Europe
Intersentia Publishing nv
Groenstraat 31
2640 Mortsel
Belgium
Tel: +32 3 680 15 50
Email: mail@intersentia.be

Distribution for the USA and Canada
Independent Publishers Group
Order Department
814 North Franklin Street
Chicago, IL 60610
USA
Tel: +1 800 888 4741 (toll free) | Fax: +1 312 337 5985
Email: orders@ipgbook.com

Corporate Insolvency Law. A Comparative Textbook

ISBN 978-1-78068-983-8
D/2020/7849/93
NUR 820

British Library Cataloguing in Publication Data. A catalogue record for this book is available from the British Library.

FOREWORD

This textbook is a hugely welcome addition to the body of literature on the laws relating to insolvency and restructuring. It comes at a time when the European Union has taken an important step towards harmonisation of insolvency laws of the Member States with the adoption of the Directive on restructuring and insolvency. And undoubtedly there is more to come in the not too distant future.

In a world with strongly interconnected markets, where businesses are not confined to the territory of one single country, it is important to have a comparative outlook on how jurisdictions deal with businesses in financial distress. This is important not only for practitioners, judges, and scholars, but also for students. Notwithstanding that domestic legal systems show considerable differences in this respect, often these different approaches lead to similar solutions in practice. When insolvency looms or is present the questions that arise are in essence similar, regardless of the jurisdiction involved. And these questions are addressed in this textbook in a very structured and illustrative manner. In his book, professor Bork addresses fundamental issues, such as what insolvency actually means, the relationship between the parties involved in the process, how proceedings are commenced and what their effects are on legal relationships that the debtor entered into prior to the opening of proceedings, including transactions avoidance – a topic that has the warm interest of both professor Bork, who is also a close colleague at Radboud University where he holds a chair in Finance, Security Rights and Insolvency Law, and myself as co-chairs of an international working group that has set out to produce a proposal for principle based harmonised rules on transaction avoidance in the EU –, rights and ranking of creditors, and even cross-border implications of insolvency proceedings. In dealing with these (and more) fundamental questions of restructuring and insolvency, he looks at English, French, German, and US law, but only as examples to illustrate the underlying principles and how they may be operationalised.

With professor Bork I agree that law, including the law relating to insolvency and restructuring, is not merely a set of rules. When studying insolvency law on a domestic and, certainly, on a comparative level, it is not sufficient to just know what the rules say and compare them. It is important to understand where those rules come from, what they try to achieve and, therefore, to understand the underlying principles and policy choices that drive those rules. As professor Bork points out, legal rules are only very rarely of a purely technical, valueless nature. More often they link back to basic principles. In order to be able to understand the mechanics of insolvency and restructuring proceedings in any given jurisdiction, it is necessary to analyse those underlying principles. And this is precisely what this textbook does.

The principle based approach taken by Professor Bork, an approach which he already followed in his much acclaimed treatise on the Principles of Cross-Border Insolvency Law, is to be welcomed. I believe that this approach has tremendous added value. As a young scholar I had the distinct privilege of being involved in the project that led to the publication of the Principles of European Insolvency Law. That project strengthened me in my conviction that comparative research is not merely about comparing rules. Unravelling the principles underlying restructuring and insolvency laws is a necessary and very important step in order to understand the restructuring and insolvency regime in any given jurisdiction and essential when attempting to achieve a meaningful degree of harmonisation of laws.

Personally, having studied German insolvency law through professor Bork's much praised "Einführung in das Insolvenzrecht", I welcome his choice for not merely translating his textbook on German insolvency law into English, but for taking it a step further. It is clear that extensive research went into this book and that it is an extremely valuable step forward in learning on the topic. It will be very helpful to all those who embark on a study of insolvency and restructuring law and I have no doubt that it will find its way in academia and practice.

Michael Veder
Professor of private law and vice-dean of research,
Faculty of Law, Radboud University

PREFACE

When I first started to write my German textbook "Einführung in das Insolvenzrecht" (Introduction to Insolvency Law) in 1994, shortly after the German government having published a draft new Insolvency Statute, I did not expect both to become a success. The new German "Insolvenzordnung" was highly appreciated in Germany, pushed both the German Insolvency Law as well as the German insolvency scene to the world's best and was, on the recommendation of – among others – World Bank and International Monetary Fund, adopted by many states, especially in Eastern Europe after the fall of the iron curtain. Likewise, my textbook advanced to the small number of standard references, used by practitioners and students alike.

It was against this background that friends and colleagues from abroad frequently suggested that I have the textbook translated into English. Although I took this as a huge compliment, I hesitated to translate a book which only deals with German insolvency law for foreign readers. Instead, I chose to put the book on a more general level and to rewrite it as a general textbook which deals with insolvency law as such, with the ideas and general features of insolvency law, using national legislation as examples only. In this respect, throughout the book, English, French, German, and US law is considered. I picked these jurisdictions because they represent leading systems internationally as it concerns insolvency law, albeit with typical differences, and their laws are role models for many other states.

I was strongly endorsed in this approach by an invitation as Distinguished Visiting Professor to the College of Law at National Taiwan University in Taipei in 2019. I was asked to hold lectures on insolvency law, putting the general aspects in the foreground. Since I have no knowledge of Taiwanese insolvency law and Taiwanese students are probably only moderately interested in German insolvency law, I offered to deliver the talks on a wider basis. I am very grateful that the College of Law at NTU willingly accepted this concept. It was the initial spark for this book. Occasionally, solutions from other jurisdictions are mentioned, however, without any intention to be exhaustive.

I am deeply obliged to three persons who contributed significantly to this book. First and foremost, Belle Vulto (Nijmegen) must be mentioned who read the whole manuscript from an editor's point of view, highlighting inconsistencies and ambiguities. In my eyes, her contribution made the book better. Lillian Jewell von Seggern controlled my English and added significantly to the perceivability of the text. Last but not least, I am grateful to Marlene Krusemark who controlled the formalities and drafted the lists and tables in a commendably thorough manner.

Insolvency law – as most other fields of law – is subject to constant change, either by legislators or by courts. Hence, it is most likely that this book contains mistakes or refers to outdated legislation. I will therefore be grateful for any hints to new developments, lacunas, or other weaknesses, and I will appreciate any criticism as to design, content, or usability of this textbook.

Reinhard Bork
Hamburg, April 2020

CONTENTS

LIST OF CASES

EUROPEAN CASES

CJEU CASES – SORTED BY NAME

CJEU CASES – SORTED BY CASE NO.

NATIONAL

AUSTRALIA

CANADA

FRANCE

GERMANY

Bundesverfassungsgericht

Bundesgerichtshof

ITALY

UNITED KINGDOM

Supreme Court

House of Lords

Court of Appeal

High Court

Court of Chancery

Court of Exchequer

Privy Council

Scotland

UNITED STATES OF AMERICA

US Supreme Court

Circuit Courts

New York City Supreme Court

District Courts

Bankruptcy Courts

LIST OF ABBREVIATIONS

ABILR	American Bankruptcy Institute Law Review
AC	Law Reports, Appeal Cases (Third Series)
AGS	*L'Association pour la gestion du régime de Garantie des créances des Salariés*
AktG	*Aktiengesetz*
Am. Bankr. LJ	American Bankruptcy Law Journal
arg.	argument ?
Art.	Article (of a statute)
Bankr.	Bankruptcy Court
BAP	Bankruptcy Appellate Panel
BGH	*Bundesgerichtshof*
BGHZ	*Amtliche Sammlung der Entscheidungen des Bundesgerichtshofes in Zivilsachen*
BR	Bankruptcy Rules
B.R.	Bankruptcy Reporter
Bull. civ.	*Bulletin des arrêts des chambres civiles de la Cour de cassation*
CA	Court of Appeal
C.D. Cal.	Central District of California
cf.	*confer*
ch.	chapter
Ch.	Law Reports, Chancery Division (3rd Series)
Cir.	Circuit
CJEU	Court of Justice of the European Union
COMI	Centre of Main Interests
Corp.	Corporation
CRI	Corporate Rescue and Insolvency
D. Del.	District of Delaware

ECLI	European Case Law Identifier
ed.	Editor/edition
E.D.N.Y.	Eastern District of New York
E.D. Pa.	Eastern District of Pennsylvania
E.D. Va.	Eastern District of Virginia
e.g.	*exempli gratia*
EIR	Regulation (EU) 2015/848 of the European Parliament and of the Council of 20 May 2015 on insolvency proceedings
et seq.	*et sequens*
etc.	*et cetera*
EU	European Union
EuInsVO	*Europäische Insolvenzverordnung*
Eur Bus Org Law Rev	European Business Organisation Law Review
EWCA	England & Wales Court of Appeal
EWCA Civ.	England & Wales Court of Appeal, Civil Division
EWHC	England & Wales High Court
EWHC (Ch)	England & Wales High Court, Chancery Division
EWHC (Comm)	England & Wales High Court, Commercial Division
Ex. P.	*Ex parte*
Fed. Appx.	Federal Appendix
fn.	footnote
FS	*Festschrift*
GmbH	*Gesellschaft mit beschränkter Haftung*
GmbHG	*Gesetz betreffend die Gesellschaft mit beschränkter Haftung*
ibid.	*ibidem*
i.e.	*id est*
IER	Immigrant and Employee Rights Section
IILR	International Insolvency Law Review
IIR	International Insolvency Review
InsO	*Insolvenzordnung*

JCLS	Journal of Corporate Law Studies
JIBFL	Butterworths Journal of International Banking and Financial Law
K.B.	Law Reports, King's Bench
Mich. L. Rev.	Michigan Law Review
Minn. L. Rev.	Minnesota Law Review
n.	footnote
NAFTA	North American Free Trade Agreement
N.D. Ill.	Northern District of Illinois
NJW	*Neue Juristische Wochenschrift*
NJW-RR	*Neue Juristische Wochenschrift Rechtsprechungs-Report*
No.	Number
N.Y. Sup. Ct.	New York City Supreme Court
N.Y.S.	New York State Reporter
NZG	*Neue Zeitschrift für Gesellschaftsrecht*
NZI	*Neue Zeitschrift für Insolvenz- und Sanierungsrecht*
OJ	The Official Journal of the European Union
ONCA	Ontario Court of Appeal
ONSC	Ontario Superior Court of Justice
p.	page
para.	paragraph
PEIL	Principles of European Insolvency Law (cf. Literature)
Q.B.D.	Law Reports, Queen's Bench Division
s./sec.	section
Sch.	Schedule
S. Ct.	Supreme Court Reporter
S.D.N.Y.	Southern District of New York
S.D. Ohio	Southern District of Ohio
S.D. Tex.	Southern District of Texas
SSRN	Social Science Research Network
supp.	supplement

UK	United Kingdom
UKHL	United Kingdom House of Lords
UKPC	United Kingdom Privy Council
UKSC	United Kingdom Supreme Court
UNCITRAL Model Law	UNCITRAL Model Law on Cross-Border Insolvency (1997)
Urt.	*Urteil* (judgment)
US/USA	United States (of America)
U.S.C.	United States Code
v.	*vom* (of)
v./vs.	*versus*
VAT	Value Added Tax
ZHR	*Zeitschrift für das gesamte Handels- und Wirtschaftsrecht*
ZIP	*Zeitschrift für Wirtschaftsrecht*

CHAPTER 1
INTRODUCTION

In this first chapter we will learn about the idea of insolvency proceedings. We will be informed on the meaning and purposes of such proceedings as well as the legal resources and their underlying principles. A second part of this chapter deals with the definition of insolvency. We will see that three general approaches – inability to pay debts, likely inability to pay debts, and overindebtedness – can be found in most insolvency laws and how these terms are described and applied. 1.1

I. INSOLVENCY PROCEEDINGS

Let us start with an **example**. A is a highly skilled carpenter. He has organised his business in the shape of a company with limited liability under the law of state X, the D company, with A as its director and only shareholder. D runs the business in small premises owned by itself (which can be valued with 200,000) and has credit facilities of over 100,000 from Bank G which are secured by assignment of all receivables against D's debtors. D has five employees, buys the necessary materials from suppliers H (who delivers on retention of title) and J (who does not insist on securities), pays taxes regularly, and has some other creditors with minor claims, one of them (K) having an enforceable judgment against D. At the beginning of the year, D gets into financial turmoil. The company had accepted and fulfilled a huge order from builder Z who has gone insolvent and has left D with an unsatisfied claim of 40,000. At this point of time, D's other receivables amount to 50,000 (among them 20,000 bank accounts and line of credit), its debts to 270,000, because its credit facilities with G are slightly overdrawn (110,000), the employees have not received their wages for the last months (25,000), D owes 60,000 to its suppliers, 15,000 to tax authorities, and 50,000 to other creditors. K as well as the tax authorities 1.2

threaten to enforce their claims. D's liabilities sum up to 220,000, including a shareholder loan of 10,000 granted by A, yet could be nearly covered if D runs down the business and sells the house. Summed up in a balance sheet, the situation presents itself like this:

Assets		**Liabilities**	
Premises:	200,000	Bank G	110,000
Claim against Z	0[1]	Employees	25,000
Other receivables	50,000	Tax authorities	15,000
		Suppliers	60,000
		Others	50,000
		A	10,000
Total	**250,000**		**270,000**

Hence, several questions arise: first, is D insolvent, and second, should the fulfilment of claims be dedicated to the creditors' initiative, leading to individual enforcement proceedings by every single creditor, or should there be collective insolvency proceedings? These questions arise completely independently from the national law of state X. Instead, they arise as typical consequences of business activities in (at least yet not exclusively) market-oriented economies.[2] While the answers of national laws may diverge, the problems are the same.

A. BASICS

1.3 Insolvency has occurred if the debtor's estate is not satisfactory to pay all their creditors. In this condition, execution by every single creditor would be neither reasonable nor fair. Enforcement proceedings of single

1 Z is insolvent. Hence, the value of the claim of 40,000 against Z must be recorded with 0.

2 It should be noted that from a macro-economic perspective insolvency law is not only aiming at satisfying creditors in the best possible way but also at opening a route to (voluntary or compulsory) exit from the market for market participants who failed and are endangering other participants by creating new debts without a realistic perspective to meet the debts when they are due; cf. *Heese*, Die Funktion des Insolvenzrechts im Wettbewerb der Rechtsordnungen, JZ 2018, 179, 180 et seq.; *Korch*, Insolvenzrecht und Marktgesetze, ZHR 182 (2018), 440, 443 et seq.; *Madaus*, Leaving the Shadows of US Bankruptcy Law, 19 (2018) Eur Bus Org Law Rev 615, 618.

creditors are only tolerable if the debtor's estate is valuable enough to meet all liabilities. If the debtor's assets, with which he or she is liable for all their debts, are insufficient (so that the creditors have a "common pool problem"[3]) execution would lead to a race of creditors after the last remaining assets and would promote the law of the strongest. It would be unjust to allow for full satisfaction of the fastest creditor while others come away empty-handed. It is for this reason that developed nations provide for insolvency proceedings. As opposed to execution by single creditors in single assets, these proceedings are primarily **collective enforcement proceedings**, which aim at a joint satisfaction of all the debtor's creditors.[4] This joint satisfaction is done by seizure and valorisation of all the debtor's assets (the estate) and distribution of the proceeds to the creditors on a *pro rata* basis.[5] In these proceedings all (unsecured) creditors are treated equally which means that they all receive the same share of the proceeds as a percentage of their claims (*pari passu* rule).

An important aspect regards the **ways of valorisation** of the estate. In many 1.4
insolvency proceedings, there is only one way to realise the debtor's assets: *liquidation*. In our example, this would mean that D's business is closed, all assets are sold singly or together for liquidation value and the proceeds are distributed among the creditors on a *pro rata* basis.[6] However, there might be alternatives. Another way of realising the value of the estate is

---

3 Cf. *Eidenmüller*, What Is An Insolvency Proceeding?, working paper available at SSRN 2712628; *Jackson*, The Logics and Limits of Bankruptcy Law, p. 11; *Madaus*, Leaving the Shadows of US Bankruptcy Law, 19 (2018) Eur Bus Org Law Rev 615, 620, 623 et seq.

4 The collectivity requirement is the most important one when it comes to characterising insolvency proceedings; cf. among others *Eidenmüller*, What Is An Insolvency Proceeding? (above fn. 3), p. 14 et seq.; *Madaus*, Leaving the Shadows of US Bankruptcy Law, 19 (2018) Eur Bus Org Law Rev 615 et seq.

5 Accordingly, §1.1 PEIL reads: "In an insolvency proceeding ('proceeding') the assets of an insolvent debtor are collected and converted into money to be distributed among the creditors ('liquidation'), or the liabilities of an insolvent debtor are restructured in order to re-establish the debtor's ability to meet liabilities ('reorganisation'). The proceeding can be a combination of liquidation and reorganisation." See also §12.1 PEIL: "If and to the extent that there is no reorganisation, the administrator converts the debtor's assets into money and distributes it among the creditors. The assets can be realised separately or together, whether or not as a going concern."

6 See below at para. 2.29 and for §12.1 PEIL above at fn. 5. There are exceptions for the receivables assigned to G by way of security and the materials delivered on retention of title. These assets are either not part of the estate and are therefore not sold (retention of title) or they are reserved for G as a secured creditor (assignment). For details, see below at para. 2.21., 2.23.

restructuring (or reorganisation)[7] which means that the estate is deployed in favour of the creditors by reorganising it into a fruitful enterprise and satisfying the creditors' claims from future earnings. A third way, in between liquidation and reorganisation, is restructuring by *asset deal*. Here, the business is restored to productivity and then sold, as a whole, for going concern value[8] which creates much higher proceeds than selling the assets for liquidation value. Both restructuring and restructuring by asset deal have the restructuring of the business as their foundation. However, there is an important difference. "Restructuring" indicates the reorganisation of both the business and its holders, whereas asset-deal restructuring results in the sale of the business, the prorated transfer of the proceeds to the holders' creditors, and the liquidation of the holding company. While restructuring removes debt from the business, asset-deal restructuring removes the business from its debt. Which path is preferable depends on the case at hand. In practice, liquidation is frequently unavoidable. However, in accordance with the principle of optimal realisation of the debtor's assets,[9] asset deals are heavily favoured. This is the case because they are quick, they separate the assets from the liabilities with efficiency and legal certainty, they ensure the realisation of the going concern value and thereby a better outcome for the creditors, and they ultimately rescue the business and the jobs it provides.

1.5 In our **example**, an asset deal is rather unlikely, since there are, except for the house, few assets left which could be sold to another entrepreneur. Hence, restructuring of D's business is the choice at hand, protecting the interests of both debtor and creditors in the best possible way. If A waives the shareholder loan, all other creditors accept a moderate "haircut" (i.e. are content with a reduction of their claims) and the bank extends the credit facilities (against a security right on the premises), restructuring is not unlikely, provided that D has further orders from other customers which can secure liquidity in a mid-term perspective.

---

7 See again §1.1 PEIL (above fn. 5); details below in Chapter 8. – Where restructuring is allocated by national law to a special kind of proceedings (below at para. 1.7), asset deals can be restricted to such proceedings, i.e. are not permissible in liquidation proceedings.

8 See for §12.1 PEIL above in fn. 5.

9 Cf. below at para. 1.11.

Insolvency proceedings are – by their very labelling – **procedures** which bring, alongside insolvency law, procedural law into play. A procedure, defined in a legal sense, is an organised and structured way of coming to a particular legal decision, based on certain principles. Proceedings must provide the requested protection of rights as quickly and comprehensively as possible, which, in the context of insolvency, means that creditors should receive their share of the proceeds as quickly and as comprehensively as possible. Since insolvency proceedings are, at their core, collective enforcement proceedings, they are typically regulated in statute and conducted or at least supervised by a court.[10] They aim at seizing the debtor's assets, deciding on the right way to valorise the estate, transforming this decision, and distributing the proceeds to the creditors. However, national laws can provide for different kinds of insolvency proceedings. Alongside ordinary liquidation proceedings, restructuring proceedings are typically a part of national law. Restructuring can either be a special option within insolvency proceedings or the subject of a completely independent stand-alone procedure, be it ahead of or after the onset of insolvency. 1.6

An **overview** over the different kinds of procedures in the jurisdictions considered in this book should start with Germany because there is currently only one single set of proceedings serving all purposes, leaving it to the parties involved whether the proceedings should aim at restructuring rather than liquidation. As opposed to that, other jurisdictions present a variety of procedures from which the parties have to choose. For example, in England and Wales liquidation proceedings (members' or creditors' voluntary winding up and compulsory winding up by the court, sec. 73-251 Insolvency Act 1986; bankruptcy for individuals, sec. 263H-385 Insolvency Act 1986) must be distinguished from various procedures which aim mainly at restructuring, namely Company Voluntary Arrangement proceedings (sec. 1-7B Insolvency Act 1986), administration proceedings (Sch. B1 Insolvency Act 1986), receiverships (sec. 28-72H Insolvency Act 1986), Scheme of Arrangement proceedings (sec. 895-901 Companies Act 2006) and for individuals debt relief orders (sec. 251A-251X Insolvency Act 1986) and Individual Voluntary Arrangement proceedings (sec. 252-263G Insolvency Act 1986). Similarly, in Book VI of French Code de Commerce various restructuring proceedings are offered (*la mandate ad hoc*, Art. L. 611-3 Code de Commerce; 1.7

10 Cf. below at para. 2.37 et seq.

la conciliation, Art. L. 611-4–611-15 Code de Commerce; *la procédure de sauvegarde*, Art. L. 620–628-3 Code de Commerce; *la redressement judiciaire*, Art. L. 631-1–632-4 Code de Commerce) and contrasted with separate liquidation proceedings (Art. L. 640-1–644-6 Code de Commerce). US law distinguishes liquidation (chapter 7 Bankruptcy Code) from reorganisation (chapter 11 Bankruptcy Code) and provides also for adjustment of debts of municipalities (chapter 9 Bankruptcy Code), family farmers and family fishermen (chapter 12 Bankruptcy Code) and individuals with regular income (chapter 13 Bankruptcy Code). In all these jurisdictions, it is possible to switch from one sort of proceedings to another, yet it is necessary to decide for a certain kind of procedure when commencing insolvency proceedings.

1.8 As mentioned above, insolvency law (including restructuring law) is in most jurisdictions shaped by **statutes**. Even in case law driven countries, insolvency codes exist, the Insolvency Act 1986 of England and Wales being a good example. However, affiliations to legal fields vary. Since insolvency law has its origins in commercial affairs, the relevant rules can be found in many jurisdictions in commercial law. This holds particularly true for the roman legal tradition, as can be illustrated by France, where insolvency law is part of the Code de Commerce. In other jurisdictions, insolvency law is allocated to company law (England and Wales) or procedural law (Germany), picking up the fact that insolvency proceedings are procedures and predominantly collective enforcement proceedings, applicable not only to entrepreneurs but also to consumers.[11] In this book, which starts with the overarching legal phenomena and problems of insolvencies rather than with national legal solutions, statutes are only used as examples. We will learn primarily about the national laws in England and Wales (Insolvency Act 1986[12]), France (Code de Commerce[13]), Germany (Insolvenzordnung[14]) and the USA (Bankruptcy Code[15]) but will also occasionally look at other

---

11 See below at para. 9.28.

12 Available online at http://www.legislation.gov.uk/ukpga/1986/45/contents.

13 English translation at https://www.legifrance.gouv.fr/Traductions/en-English/Legifrance-translations.

14 English translation at https://www.gesetze-im-internet.de/englisch_inso/index.html.

15 Available online at https://www.law.cornell.edu/uscode/text/11.

countries. In addition, we will consider proposals for legislators from the UNCITRAL Legislative Guide on Insolvency Law of 2015[16] and from the Principles of European Insolvency Law, a collection of basic statements for insolvency proceedings and insolvency law, elaborated by three prominent European scholars.[17]

B. PRINCIPLES OF INSOLVENCY LAW

Legal rules are seldom of a purely technical, valueless nature. They instead link back to basic principles, here defined as **core values** and not, like in the Anglo-American linguistic tradition, as meaningful regulatory objects. These principles have a systemising function, as well as a legitimising one. This also applies to insolvency law,[18] the principles of which can be summarised into two groups: procedural principles and substantive principles. 1.9

Since insolvency proceedings are procedures, they are shaped by **procedural principles** which are partly general principles of law and not only underlying insolvency law. The first principle to be mentioned in this context is the principle of efficiency, according to which the proceedings must provide the requested protection of rights as comprehensively as possible, which means that creditors should receive their share of the proceeds as quickly and as comprehensively as possible. The second is the principle of creditors' autonomy: insolvency proceedings are conducted in the interests of the creditors who should be entitled to influence the administration of the proceedings. In addition, there is the principle of transparency: proceedings must be conducted publicly and transparently, so that those affected by them can take part and can bring their legal positions into the discussion. Of particular relevance is the principle of 1.10

16 *United Nations Commission on International Trade Law*, Legislative Guide on Insolvency Law, Part 1 and 2, United Nations Publications, New York 2005.

17 *McBryde/Flessner/Kortmann* (eds.), Principles of European Insolvency Law, Kluwer, Deventer 2003 (new edition 2005). The Principles elaborated in this book are printed on p. 627–634 of the book and are here referred to as "PEIL". They must not be confused with the "principles" referred to below at para.1.9 et seq.

18 I have elaborated this approach extensively for *Cross-Border* Insolvency Law in my book "Principles of Cross-Border Insolvency Law", Intersentia, Cambridge/Antwerp/Portland 2017.

predictability (legal certainty) which means that creditors must be able to foresee (or be reliably advised on) not only their legal position but also on how they can exercise their rights against an insolvent debtor and on how they are expected to contribute to the proceedings. This is closely allied with the principle of procedural justice. Insolvency proceedings, as all procedures, have to be organised and administered in a fair and just way and the procedural rights of both debtor and creditors must be respected. Finally, the principle of priority must be taken into account, according to which a first set of insolvency proceedings excludes the opening of a second set.

1.11 Alongside the procedural principles, a second set of principles is shaping insolvency law: the group of **substantive principles**. Substantive principles reflect the impact of insolvency proceedings on substantive legal positions. The most important example of a substantive principle of insolvency law is the principle of equal treatment of unsecured creditors (the *pari passu* rule) according to which creditors of the same rank are to be treated identically, regarding not only their procedural rights but also their substantive rights. Other substantive insolvency principles are the best possible realisation of the debtor's assets (also known as the principle of optimisation), the protection of the debtor's rights, and the protection of trust, i.e. of the legitimate expectations of (for example) secured creditors or contractual partners. Further, the principle of social protection, e.g. for employees or tenants, is of special relevance here. In some jurisdictions, the fixation principle has been elaborated which supports the distinction between assets, creditors, and creditors' rights that are subject to the insolvency proceedings from those that are not. Finally, the principle of satisfaction must be mentioned in the present context, which has regard to the fact that the main purpose of insolvency proceedings is to satisfy the creditors' claims to the greatest possible extent in accordance with the creditors' out-of-insolvency entitlements and priorities. To some extent, this principle mirrors the principle of best possible realisation of the debtor's assets.

1.12 The **benefit of a principle-based approach** is manifold. Principles – procedural as well as substantive – have systemising force: they can be used as criteria to explain the structure of the law and describe correlations between different rules. We can call such principles "structural principles". Examples are the principles of equal treatment of creditors on the one hand and of protection of trust on the other hand as systemising factors in transactions avoidance law.[19] Principles can also have normative force: they can be used for justifying rules, legitimising the legal consequences of these rules as well as supporting the legal decisions of both legislators and courts, and they can also support the substantive coherence of rules. We can call such principles "substantive principles". Examples are the principle of equal treatment of creditors, the principle of creditors' autonomy and the principle of social protection. Principles in this context can serve as unwritten sources of law. Courts can base their decisions on principles where the written law does not (or does not satisfactorily) address the issue in question, and principles can help judges to fill lacunas or to construe unclear or overly generalised statute properly. Furthermore, principles are imperative to optimising the law, by a demand for principle-oriented decisions from legislators.

C. THEORY

Surprisingly, there is little theory on insolvency law.[20] The most famous approach has been presented by *Thomas H. Jackson*. In his seminal book "The Logics and Limits of Bankruptcy Law", he has suggested the "**creditors' bargain theory**" which, from a law and economics perspective, traces insolvency proceedings back to an assumed contractual *ex ante* consent of all creditors to their enforcement rights being replaced by a collective procedure if the debtor runs into insolvency.[21] However, this theory cannot be built upon. First, it is too creditor-focused and neglects the interests of other persons involved in and affected by the proceedings. Second, since a real consent is not required, it is partly a mere fiction which is first and foremost inadequate to explain the treatment of non-contractual creditors (unless the consent is, diverging from Jackson's proposal, deemed to be 1.13

19 Details below at para. 6.20 et seq.

20 Short overviews are given by *Keay/Walton*, Insolvency Law, at para. 3.4 and *Nsubuga*, Corporate Insolvency and Employment Protection, (2016) 4(1) NIBLeJ 4.

21 *Jackson*, The Logic and Limits of Bankruptcy Law, p. 7 et seq. Opposing among others *Carlsson*, Philosophy in Bankruptcy, 85 (1987) Mich. L. Rev., 134; *Casey*, The New Bargaining Theory, SSRN 3353871, p. 1 et seq.; *Finch*, The Measures of Insolvency, 17 (1997) OJLS 227, 234; *Gross*, Taking community interests into account in bankruptcy; an essay, 72 (1994) Wash. U. L. Rev., 1031 et seq.; *Scott*, Through Bankruptcy with the Creditors' Bargain Heuristic, 53 (1986) U. Chi. L. Rev., 690 et seq.; *Warren*, Bankruptcy Policy, 54 (1987) U. Chi. L. Rev., 775 et seq.

given after the occurrence of insolvency rather than *ex ante*) and of secured creditors (why should they give their consent to collective proceedings if they get their money anyway?). Moreover, referring to an (hypothetical) consent of the unsecured creditors – how would they reasonably answer if they were asked on the onset of insolvency? – is nothing more but applying a rationality test as required for each legal rule.[22] *All* norms should be shaped in a way that the persons affected would reasonably give their consent to this rule. In its heart, the creditors' bargain theory says nothing more than that collective proceedings are a reasonable solution for insolvency cases.

1.14 As a reply to the creditors' bargain theory, the **communitarian theory** has been developed.[23] This theory rightly argues that insolvency proceedings are conducted in the interests not only of the creditors but of all groups affected by the insolvency proceedings, namely those of the employees, suppliers, government, customers, neighbours, and the local and wider community.[24] This does not question the characterisation of insolvency proceedings as collective enforcement proceedings and it does not subordinate the creditors' interests to other interests. But it takes into account that insolvency proceedings, as opposed to normal enforcement proceedings, are not single-dimensional but involve more groups than debtors and creditors and that restructuring is a possible scenario in insolvencies.

---

22 Accurately *Casey*, The New Bargaining Theory (above at fn. 21), p. 1 et seq. However, *Casey's* own theory of insolvency proceedings offering "a framework of bargaining rules for ex post renegotiation" is too much focused in restructuring plan proceedings (cf. below at para. 8.32 et seq.) and is unable to explain normal liquidation proceedings. The contractual approach is avoided by *Buccola* (Bankruptcy's Cathedral, SSRN 3353848, p. 1 et seq.) who considers insolvency law necessary for the shift from property rules to liability rules, i.e. from creditor control to the control of a judicially managed process. However, the author admits that this perception fails to explain the consequences for secured creditors, e.g. by subjugating them to a moratorium. These difficulties can be avoided by a communitarian approach as explained in the next paragraph.

23 A communitarian approach has been founded by *Etzioni*, The Spirit of Community Rights, Responsibilities and the Communitarian Agenda and has been suggested by (among others) *Gross*, Taking Community Interests into Account in Bankruptcy: An Essay, 72 (1994) Wash. U. L. Rev., 1031 et seq. and in: Failure and Forgiveness, p. 193 et seq. Criticism from *Schermer*, Response to Professor Gross: Taking the Interests of the Community into account in Bankruptcy, 772 (1994) Wash. U. L. Rev., 1049 et seq.

24 A similar approach is pleaded by the "multiple value theory"; cf. *Warren*, Bankruptcy Policy, 54 (1987) U. Chi. L. Rev., 775 et seq.

II. INSOLVENCY

A. GENERAL

While insolvency is a common practical phenomenon in all jurisdictions, **terminology** is not, even not within the English speaking world. In the US, for example, the term "bankruptcy" is preferred and used for legal entities (corporate insolvency) as well as for individuals (personal insolvency), both entrepreneurs and consumers. As opposed to that, in England "bankruptcy" is reserved for individuals (sec. 264(1) Insolvency Act 1986) whilst "insolvency" is the legal term for legal entities.[25] "Bankruptcy" is a very old expression which has its origins in the Italian term "*banca rotta*" (the trading bench of an insolvent merchant was broken by his colleagues, signifying that he was no longer worthy of participating as a member of the mercantile community[26]) while the word "insolvency" is even older: it goes back to the Latin word *insolventia* (impossibility to pay). Other languages have this Latin root too (cf. the French *insolvabilité*, the German *Insolvenz* or the Dutch *insolventie*) whereas a further group build upon the Latin *fallere* (to fail or to break a promise) by using *fallimento* (Italian), *fallissement* (French) or *faillissement* (Dutch). 1.15

Determining "insolvency" is an essential task for insolvency proceedings and insolvency law, since this term is of significant **relevance**. It is not only used as a triggering prerequisite for – at least: compulsory[27] – insolvency proceedings[28] but also as a connecting factor to insolvency related legal consequences such as transactions avoidance[29] or directors' liability for wrongful trading.[30] Even in criminal law, "insolvency" can be a requirement for punishability, e.g. for fraudulent bankruptcy, etc. 1.16

---

25 This was quite clear in the original version of the Insolvency Act 1986 which in the Heading of Part I used the phrase "Company Insolvency".

26 Cf. *van Zwieten*, Principles of Corporate Insolvency Law, para. 1-10, fn. 41.

27 In England and Wales as well as in the US insolvency is not required for voluntary proceedings.

28 For details, see below at para. 3.17 et seq.

29 More below at para. 6.21.

30 Cf. below at para. 3.3.

1.17 Insolvency laws typically refer to **three kinds of insolvency**: inability to pay debts, likely inability to pay debts, and overindebtedness.[31] As will be explained in more detail below, all these terms can be found in national insolvency laws, although not all jurisdictions use all these variations and their use is also dependent on the procedure in question.[32] "Likely inability to pay debts", for example, is often used in the context of restructuring proceedings whereas "inability to pay debts" and "overindebtedness" are preferred for liquidation and administration proceedings.

B. INABILITY TO PAY DEBTS

1.18 §1.2 PEIL specifies that "a proceeding can be opened when the debtor is unable or likely to become unable to pay debts as they become due." Accordingly, UNCITRAL Legislative Guide in its Recommendations 15(a)/16(a) states that insolvency proceedings should be commenced if the debtor "is or will be generally unable to pay its debts as they mature."[33] Indeed, most insolvency laws use the words "inability to pay debts" as a definition of insolvency. Debtors are insolvent if they are unable to pay their debts when they fall due. They then lack the necessary financial liquidity, which is why the inability to pay debts is also described as "**illiquidity**". This word refers to the financial means available to the debtor at the point in time when they have to meet their financial obligations. If the liquid means are satisfactory to pay the existing and due debts the debtor is not insolvent (liquidity or cash flow test). Liquid means are cash, bank accounts, credit facilities, and assets alienable on short notice (e.g. listed shares), but not assets which to sell need time, such as real estate or fixed assets. It is for this reason that debtors can become unable to pay their debts although they own valuable assets. If the money is not bound in short-term sellable assets and banks are not prepared to grant additional credit on these assets, inability to pay debts is possible.

---

31 For an overview, see the National Reports in *Faber/Vermunt/Kilborn/Richter*, Commencement of Insolvency Proceedings, each at para. 5.2.

32 An overview on the determination of "insolvency" in the European jurisdictions are given by *McCormack/Keay/Brown*, European Insolvency Law, p. 185 et seq.; *Steffek*, Insolvenzgründe in Europa, KTS 2009, 317 et seq.

33 See also UNCITRAL Legislative Guide, p.46 para. 23 et seq.

The case described above (at para. 1.2) is a good **example**: D owns premises which could be sold and leased back from the buyer in order to gain extra liquidity, but this is not possible in the short term. Hence, D is unable to pay its mature debts and is therefore insolvent. 1.19

A decisive part in the definition of "inability to pay debts" is the addition "**when they fall due**". Most people have debts yet are not insolvent because the debts are not or at least not completely due. Let us illustrate this with an example. When a family buys a house for 500,000 this is typically financed through a bank loan (here of 400,000). In the loan agreement, which runs for five years, the family has obliged themselves to pay a sum of interest (1%) and redemption (3%) of 16,000 p.a. or 1,333.33 per month. Calculated for the duration of the loan, this will amount to payments of 79,999.80 and the remaining debt of the loan will be 338,501.00. "Due" within the meaning of the definition of inability to pay debts are 1,333.33 every month and 338,501.00 at the end of the five years period of time. Hence, as long as the family is able to pay the monthly sums of 1,333.33 (and meet all their other liabilities being mature at this point in time) they are not insolvent. 1.20

The definition "inability to pay debts when they fall due" is frequently amended, either in statute or in case law, by the preceding words "**significant**" and "**sustainable**". Insolvency proceedings are complex and costly procedures. It would not be reasonable to trigger such procedures if the liquidity gap between mature debts and liquid means is either marginal or can be closed within reasonable time. However, which size of the liquidity gap and which duration of illiquidity is reasonable and acceptable may be subject to controversial debate. 1.21

Examples for the aforementioned features of insolvency can be found in many **national laws**. In England and Wales, it is deemed in sec. 123(1)(e) Insolvency Act 1986 that a company is insolvent if it "is unable to pay its debts as they fall due".[34] Included in the cash flow test are liabilities which are due on the date in question or will come due within the reasonably near (foreseeable) future as well as accounts receivable within this time 1.22

34 Extensively on sec. 123(1)(e) Insolvency Act 1986 *BNY Corporate Trustee Services Ltd v. Eurosail-UK 2007-3BL plc* [2013] UKSC 28.

period,[35] yet temporary payment delays are overlooked.[36] In Germany, inability to pay debts (*Zahlungsunfähigkeit*) is a trigger for insolvency proceedings (§§16, 17(1) Insolvenzordnung) and defined in §17(2)(1) Insolvenzordnung with "the debtor shall be deemed illiquid if he is unable to meet his mature obligations to pay". However, according to a groundbreaking albeit not undisputed decision of the *Bundesgerichtshof*, a liquidity gap must be significant and sustainable and a gap of up to 10% is not significant and illiquidity is not sustainable if the liquidity gap (of whichever size) can be closed within three weeks.[37] The French Code de Commerce, however, does not tie on inability to pay debts yet on cessation of payments (*cessation de paiements*), but this term is defined as "being unable to pay its accrued liabilities with its quick assets" (Art. L. 631-1(1)(1) Code de Commerce), which comes very close to the definition of inability to pay debts. US law also does not refer to inability to pay debts. According to §101(32) Bankruptcy Code, the term "insolvent" means, for most debtor entities, "that the sum of such entity's debts is greater than all of such entity's property, at a fair valuation" which aims at overindebtedness (balance sheet insolvency)[38] rather than at illiquidity (in US terminology: equity insolvency). Only a municipality is defined to be insolvent if it is "unable to pay its debts as they become due" (§101(32)(C)(ii) Bankruptcy Code). However, in involuntary cases (applied for by creditors, not by the debtor), insolvency is presumed (among others) if "the debtor is generally not paying such debtor's debts as such debts become due unless such debts are the subject of a *bona fide* dispute as to liability or amount" (§303(h)(1) Bankruptcy Code) which matches the requirements of inability to pay debts. Hence, inability to pay debts is generally recognised as a manifestation of insolvency.[39]

1.23 Inability to pay debts is difficult to **verify**.[40] The most objective way would be to establish a liquidity balance sheet (or liquidity status), presenting the mature debts on the right and the liquid assets on the left side. However,

---

35 *Re Capital Annuities Ltd* [1979] 1 WLR 170; *Sandell v. Porter* [1966] 115 CLR 666.

36 *Hymix Concrete Pty Ltd v. Garrity* [1977] 13 ALR 321; *MacPlant Services Ltd v. Contract Lifting Services (Scotland) Ltd* [2008] CSOH 158; *Sandell v. Porter* [1966] 115 CLR 666.

37 BGH, Urt. v. 24.5.2005 – IX ZR 123/04 = BGHZ 163, 134 = NJW 2005, 3062.

38 See on this below at para. 1.28.

39 Cf. *Burtch v. Opus LLC (In re Opus East LLC)*, 698 Fed. Appx. 711 (3rd Cir. 2017).

40 The UNCITRAL Legislative Guide (p. 50 et seq.) deals extensively with this problem.

the necessary figures are often not available, certainly not for creditors or other outsiders who have no insight in the debtor's financial affairs, but also not for the court or Insolvency Practitioner or even the debtor who has given up proper accounting and has started to collect bills in a laundry basket. It is against this background that many laws draw on (mostly rebuttable) presumptions or use circumstantial evidence. The law of England and Wales, for example, contains fixed presumptions such as (a) the debtor's failure to pay a mature debt of more than 750 £ if payment has been formally demanded at least three weeks prior to the assessment of the inability to pay debts[41] and (b) unsatisfactory execution of a judgment (sec. 123(1)(a)/(b), 268(1) Insolvency Act 1986). However, it is usually not necessary to fall back to these presumptions, since the courts have come to regard mere non-payment of an undisputed claim even without any special demand as a prima facie indicator of inability to pay debts[42] and case law has focused on further indices to determine the debtor's ability to pay.[43] France, as mentioned above (at para. 1.22), refers to "cessation of payments" anyway, albeit as a description of, and not only as a presumption or circumstantial evidence for, insolvency,[44] and in Germany, too, §17(2)(2) Insolvenzordnung presumes debtors to be unable to pay their debts if they have ceased payments which the *Bundesgerichtshof* has concretised with a great bundle of criteria indicating cessation of payments.[45] Similarly, in the USA, the enforcement of a lien suffices under §303(h)(2) Bankruptcy Code.

---

41 On this "statutory demand", cf. *Promontoria (Chestnut) Ltd v. Bell* [2019] EWHC 1581 (Ch).

42 *Cornhill Insurance plc v. Improvement Servives Ltd* [1986] 1 WLR 114; *MacPlant Services Ltd v. Contract Lifting Services (Scotland) Ltd* [2008] CSOH 158; *Re Capital Annuities Ltd* [1979] 1 WLR 170. – See also UNCITRAL Legislative Guide, Recommendation 17 which suggests a presumption for inability to pay debts "if the debtor fails to pay one or more of its mature debts, and the whole of the debt is not subject to a legitimate dispute or offset in an amount equal to or greater than the amount of the debt claimed".

43 The paradigmatic case is *Lewis v. Doran* [2005] NSWCA 243.

44 The same approach is taken by the UNCITRAL Legislative Guide, p. 45 para. 23.

45 Examples are: default to pay a relevant part of the mature debts; heavy increase of arrears; debtor's own declaration of inability to pay; not answering bills and reminders for months; broken payment promises; closing the premises of the company; bounced checks; unsuccessful direct debit; claw back of goods by suppliers with retention of title; increase of enforcement proceedings; enforcement attempts in vain; payment to existential creditors only; default to pay social security or wages for employees; cf. BGH, Urt. v. 12.10.2017 – IX ZR 50/15 = NJW 2018, 396; BGH, Urt. v. 6.7.2017 – IX ZR 178/16 = NZI 2017, 850; BGH, Urt. v. 9.6.2016 – IX ZR 174/15 = NZI 2016, 736.

1.24 **Examples**: According to §64(1) GmbHG, directors of a German GmbH are obliged to reimburse to their company any payments which have been made to creditors of the company after the occurrence of the company's substantial insolvency. The German *Bundesgerichtshof* was confronted with a suit of an Insolvency Practitioner against a director who had induced creditors of the GmbH to be paid. The claim was dependent on the company's inability to pay its debts at the relevant point of time. The Insolvency Practitioner presented a liquidity status which proved a liquidity gap between mature debts, and available liquidity yet also showed that this gap could be closed within the next three weeks because additional payments from third parties could be expected with satisfactory likelihood. The decisive question was therefore whether not only the additional means but also additional debts falling due within the three weeks period of time should be taken into account. The *BGH* decided in the affirmative, reasoning that "insolvency" should be taken seriously and therefore strict standards are appropriate.[46]

1.25 An English debtor company had made payments without consideration to a shareholder. After the commencement of insolvency proceedings, the Insolvency Practitioner challenged the payments as a transaction at an undervalue under sec. 238 Insolvency Act 1986 which could be rejected if the company was not insolvent at the relevant time (sec. 240(2) Insolvency Act 1986). In the case at hand, the company had used new credit facilities to pay off old creditors. The Court of Appeal (by Lewison LJ) found that if the company "was only able to pay its debts as they fall due by taking new deposits, and using them to pay off old debts, in any commercial sense the company was insolvent".[47] However, this can be debated. If a company finds banks who provide the company with fresh money and the company uses this money to pay current debts the bank ultimately takes over the current debts, furnishes them with new maturity and thereby grants the company at least some breathing space if not a fresh start. This can be the beginning of restructuring rather than an indication of insolvency, since it is a conversion rather than an increase of liabilities.

46 BGH, Urt. v. 19.2.2017 – II ZR 88/16 = NJW 2018, 1089.

47 *Re Casa Estates (UK) Ltd.* [2014] EWCA Civ. 383.

In our example above at para. 1.2, D is illiquid (i.e. unable to pay all due debts), since the premises, making up the main part of the assets, cannot be sold on short notice and the receivables against third parties (D's debtors) are conceivably not due or difficult to enforce. Hence, the only liquid means are 20,000 bank account and line of credit. 1.26

C. LIKELY INABILITY TO PAY DEBTS

National laws sometimes do not insist on the debtor's inability to pay debts 1.27 at the relevant point in time yet settle for the likelihood of such inability (imminent or prospective illiquidity/insolvency). This is supported by (among others) §1.2 PEIL[48] and can be useful if legislators wish to enable rescue proceedings or an early dropping out of the market by insolvency proceedings when the debtor's business will probably fail. The main problem is the **definition** of "likelihood". According to German §18(1) Insolvenzordnung, for example, the debtor may apply for insolvency proceedings when inability to pay debts is "imminent", and this is defined in §18(2) Insolvenzordnung with "the debtor shall be deemed to be faced with imminent insolvency if he is likely to be unable to meet his existing obligations to pay on the date of their maturity." The German *Bundesgerichtshof* requires a prognosis as to whether inability to pay debts is "predominantly likely"[49] which proves all the uncertainty connected to imminent or likely insolvency. English law shows no great differences. Under para 11(a) and 27(2)(a) of Sch. B1, Insolvency Act 1986, the law permits it to suffice for administration proceedings that the company is likely to become unable to pay its debts, though what that means is not defined further. According to case law, it is not enough that the company simply has tough times ahead of it; in order to stave off abuse of process, the courts have set the standard at predominant likelihood, too,[50] since "likely" in this context means "more probable than not".[51] "Likely

48 See also UNCITRAL Legislative Guide, p. 48 para. 30. The Guide does not contain any recommendations on likely insolvency.

49 BGH, Beschl. v. 5.2.2015 – IX ZR 211/13 = WM 2015, 931; BGH, Urt. v. 22.5.2014 – IX ZR 95/13 = NZI 2014, 698.

50 *Re AA Mutual International Insurance Company Ltd* [2004] EWHC 2430 (Ch); *Re Colt Telecom Group plc (No 2)* [2002] EWHC 2815 (Ch).

51 *Hammonds v. Pro-Fit USA Ltd.* [2007] EWHC 1998 (Ch); *Re Colt Telecom Group plc* [2002] EWHC 2815 (Ch).

inability to pay debts" is not used in statute in France and in the USA. However, Art. L. 622-10(3) Code de Commerce entitles the court to convert safeguard proceedings into judicial restructuring proceedings "if the adoption of a safeguarding plan is clearly impossible and if the closing of the proceedings would certainly and shortly lead to the cessation of payments" which comes close to the concept of likely or imminent insolvency. In the USA, transaction avoidance is possible under §548 (a)(1)(B)(ii)(II) Bankruptcy Code if the transaction leaves the debtor with "an unreasonably small capital", which is the case where the debtor is "technically solvent but doomed to fail",[52] which also is comparable to imminent insolvency.

D. OVERINDEBTEDNESS

1.28 A third way to establish insolvency is the reference to overindebtedness, also known as **balance sheet insolvency**. An entity is overindebted if the amount of all of its debts exceeds the value of all of its assets. As opposed to inability to pay debts, in the balance sheet test, all of the debtor's financial obligations are taken into account, including those which are not due, and all of the debtor's assets are regarded, including those which are not alienable on short notice. However, the devil is in the detail. First, the business of a natural person is frequently not coined by its assets. Its most valuable entrepreneurial "assets" of which its economic success decisively depends – such as ingenuity, creativity or bargaining power – cannot be valuated and not be placed on a balance sheet. Hence, such balance sheet would not be very informative. It is for this reason that some jurisdictions restrict the overindebtedness test to legal entities (companies) where personnel is changing permanently where balanceable assets are of greater importance for the business' value. Second, much depends on how the value of the assets is assessed. If they are evaluated on going concern basis then overindebtedness is less likely than under evaluation on liquidation basis.[53] Hence, national laws should commit themselves to one of these assessment methods. Third, some sort of prognosis is necessary, since (a) a balance sheet assessment delivers a snapshot only which says nothing

52 *MFS/Sun Life Tr.-High Yield Series v. Van Dusen Airport Servs. Co.*, 910 F. Supp. 913, 944 (S.D.N.Y. 1995).

53 Cf. above at para. 1.4.

about the development in the nearer or more distant future and (b) there is no need to open insolvency proceedings if the company is overindebted but able to meet all its obligations in a medium-term perspective.

In our **example** (above at para. 1.2), D‘s debts slightly exceed the value of the disposable assets, even if the shareholder loan is neglected. However, for ascertaining D's overindebtedness, much depends on the prognosis for the foreseeable future. 1.29

Against this background, it does not come as a surprise that **national** 1.30
laws offer a colourful picture.[54] Although UNCITRAL Legislative Guide advises, albeit reluctantly,[55] in its Recommendations 15(b)/(16b) to commence insolvency proceedings if the debtor's "liabilities exceed the value of its assets", many states do not follow this proposal. France, for example, does not refer to overindebtedness for entrepreneurs but offers special proceedings for overindebted consumers.[56] As opposed to that, a balance sheet test can be applied in England and Wales according to sec. 123(2) Insolvency Act 1986 in order to verify inability to pay debts yet this is only to find out whether, on the balance of probabilities, the company can or cannot reasonably be expected to be able to meet its liabilities.[57] The word "overindebtedness" is not in use and the balance sheet test has a supporting function rather than an autonomous one; a clear distinction between inability to pay debts and overindebtedness is not visible. The German §19 Insolvenzordnung recognises overindebtedness explicitly as a relevant and autonomous kind of insolvency albeit in relation to legal entities (companies) only. Assets must be assessed on a liquidation basis. However, if this leads to overindebtedness a continuation prognosis is due, asking for the company's predominant likelihood of continued operation of the business which is measured by the ability to pay debts which fall due in a medium-term perspective (current and next financial year).[58] In the US, overindebtedness (balance sheet insolvency)

54 A comprehensive overview is given by *Piekenbrock*, Die Überschuldung als Eröffnungsgrund in Europa, KTS 2017, 333 et seq.
55 Cf. UNCITRAL Legislative Guide, p. 46 para. 25 et seq., 29.
56 For details, see below at para. 9.28.
57 *BNY Corporate Trustee Services Ltd v. Eurosail-UK 2007-3BL plc* [2013] UKSC 28.
58 BGH, Urt. v. 26.1.2017 – IX ZR 285/14 = BGHZ 213, 374 = NJW 2017, 1611; BGH, Urt. v. 7.3.2013 – IX ZR 64/12 = NZI 2013, 438.

is the main form of insolvency according to §101(32) Bankruptcy Code, albeit without using this word.[59] Statute defines insolvency with the words "that the sum of such entity's debts is greater than all of such entity's property, at a fair valuation". Which valuation is fair depends on the market conditions; courts tend to utilise going concern values.[60] Hence, as the UNCITRAL Legislative Guide puts it, "a fair market value is generally considered to be the value that reasonably can be expected to be obtained in an 'arm's-length' sale between a buyer and a seller, where neither party is under a compulsion to buy or sell."[61]

1.31 **Examples:** C has been injured in a car accident. The car was insured with insurer X who filed for insolvency proceedings one year after the accident. C applied for compensation from public funds, claiming that a car which is insured with an insolvent insurer is an "uninsured car". Although this position meets the wording of the terms and conditions of the public funds, C's application was rejected. The court held that X's application for insolvency proceedings was not sufficient. Instead, substantive insolvency was necessary and X was neither unable to pay its debts nor overindebted.[62]

1.32 In our example (above at para. 1.2), D is not only unable to pay its debts as they fall due but also overindebted, since the total value of its assets (250,000) does not cover the total amount of all debts (270,000).

1.33 ***For further reading***: *Bork*, Einführung, §§1, 10; *Bork*, Rescuing Companies, para. 801 et seq.; *Fletcher*, Law of Insolvency, para. 1-001 et seq., 20-013 et seq.; *Saint-Alary-Houin*, Droit des enterprises en difficulté, para. 1 et seq., 439 et seq., 1086 et seq.; *Tabb*, Law of Bankruptcy, §1.1. et seq.; *van Zwieten*, Principles of Corporate Insolvency Law, Chapter 1-4.

59 However, it is used in case law, cf. *Burtch v. Opus LLC (In re Opus East LLC)*, 698 Fed. Appx. 711 (3rd Cir. 2017).

60 See for a transactions avoidance case *In re Imagine Fulfillment Services, LLC* 489 B.R. 136, 144 et seq. (Bankr. C.D. Cal. 2013).

61 UNCITRAL Legislative Guide, p. 46 fn. 10.

62 *Murray v. American Family Mutual Insurance Co.*, 429 F.3d 757 (8th Cir. 2005).

CHAPTER 2

PARTIES INVOLVED

In the second chapter we will be informed about the parties involved in the insolvency proceedings and their affected legal interests and procedural roles. We will see that the main participant is the debtor and will discuss who is eligible for insolvency proceedings. We will also learn that creditors, too, play an important role. We will deal with different types of creditors and specifically learn about creditor classes and creditors' self-administration. Finally, insolvency proceedings are managed by official – typically state authorised – bodies which is why also the institutional framework – courts and first and foremost Insolvency Practitioners – have to be discussed. 2.1

I. DEBTOR

Insolvency proceedings are not imaginable without a debtor. Since insolvency proceedings are basically enforcement proceedings, debtors are necessarily **involved in three capacities**. First, they are the persons who have the enforceable liabilities against their creditors; they – literally – are the ones who are in debt. Second, debtors hold the assets which are to be executed in the insolvency proceedings, the assets with which the debtor is liable for their debts. And third, debtors are subjects of the proceedings; they have procedural rights (e.g. to challenge decisions of the court) and are addressees of procedural obligations (e.g. to furnish information to the Insolvency Practitioner or the court). 2.2

Strictly speaking, defining the legal term "debtor" is not necessary because it follows from the procedural role of who is the main subject of the insolvency proceedings: it is the person against whose estate the proceedings are conducted. It is for this reason that national insolvency laws typically do not contain definitions, yet rather answer to the question 2.3

who is *allowed* to have the role of a debtor in insolvency proceedings. The first aspect to be treated here concerns the distinction between **natural and legal persons**. Although insolvency law in some jurisdictions stems from company law,[1] it is supported by Recommendation 8 of the UNCITRAL Legislative Guide[2] and nowadays generally accepted in national laws[3] that also human beings may be debtors in insolvency proceedings.[4] In the US, for example, §109(b) Bankruptcy Code simply states that for insolvency proceedings "a person" may be a debtor (and then excludes certain entities like railroad companies, insurance undertakings, and banks from this rule because they are subject to special statutes). The term "person" is defined in §101(41) Bankruptcy Code which expressly mentions individuals, partnerships, and corporations, excluding (with some exceptions) governmental units.[5] In Germany, a slightly different approach has been chosen, albeit with comparable results: §§11, 12 Insolvenzordnung enumerate the entities eligible for insolvency proceedings, starting with a general rule according to which insolvency proceedings may be opened for the assets owned by any natural or legal person, and then mentioning special entities, especially those which under German law are companies but not legal persons. In English law, it follows indirectly from the heading preceding sec. 1 Insolvency Act 1986 ("company insolvency") and directly from sec. 386(1) Insolvency Act 1986 ("individual") that both natural and legal persons are comprised. The same is true for France where Art. L. 611-1 Code de Commerce refers to all persons registered in the commercial and companies register or the trade register, and according to Art. L. 620-2 Code de Commerce regular insolvency law is applicable to individuals who are engaged in a retail activity or artisanal trade, farming, or an independent professional activity.

---

1 Cf. above at para. 1.6.

2 See also the definition in the Glossary of the UNCITRAL Legislative Guide, p. 3 at para. 11. – The PEIL are silent on this matter.

3 For an overview, see the National Reports in *Faber/Vermunt/Kilborn/Richter*, Commencement of Insolvency Proceedings, each at para. 3.4.

4 Historically, bankruptcy proceedings for individuals are much older than insolvency proceedings for legal entities, the reason being that the legal autonomy of companies and other entities has not been recognised before the 19th century; cf. for the UK *Fletcher*, The Law of Insolvency, para. 1-012-1.026.

5 For the latter see below at para. 2.9. – For some types of proceedings, individuals must meet additional special requirements; cf. §§109(e)/(h), 707(b) Bankruptcy Code.

Example: D, a law firm organised as a partnership of solicitors, applies for insolvency proceedings. Partnerships are recognised in many jurisdictions as eligible debtors, e.g. Germany (§11(2)No. 1 Insolvenzordnung) and the USA (§101(41) Bankruptcy Code[6]). In England and Wales, however, a special statutory instrument was necessary to reach this result (sec. 420 Insolvency Act 1986 with the Insolvent Partnerships Order 1994). The situation is different in France where an association is only eligible if it is legal person. Since a partnership is not a legal person, the lawyers and not the partnership are debtors in insolvency proceedings. 2.4

Groups of companies are, in most jurisdictions, not debtors themselves, but rather consist of a conglomerate of debtors, each member of the group being subject to its own insolvency proceedings. Hence, the insolvency of a group member does not necessarily entail the insolvency of other or all group members. As a consequence, there are separate insolvency proceedings for each insolvent group member ("one enterprise – one insolvency – one procedure"). However, most national laws[7] offer a joint forum for all these proceedings and provide for rules on coordination of proceedings and cooperation of Insolvency Practitioners and courts ("administrative consolidation"; cf. for France Art. L. 662-8 Code de Commerce, for Germany §§3a et seq., 56b, 269a et seq. Insolvenzordnung, for the USA rule 1015 Bankruptcy Rules[8]). Beyond this, in some jurisdictions,[9] the estates of various group members, whether insolvent or not, can be united ("substantive consolidation"), albeit in special cases only. The leading jurisdiction is the USA,[10] but it also holds true for France where the commenced proceedings, but only as an exception, may be 2.5

---

6 See also *Milavetz, Gallop & Milavetz, P.A. v. United States*, 559 U.S. 229, 130 S. Ct. 1324, 176 L. Ed. 2d 79, 78 U.S.L.W. 4197 (2010).

7 Cf. the National Reports in *Faber/Vermunt/Kilborn/Richter*, Commencement of Insolvency Proceedings, each at para. 10.1. See also UNCITRAL Legislative Guide p. 276 para. 82 et seq.

8 In England and Wales, this is accomplished by appointing the same Insolvency Practitioner for various group members or by factual cooperation of various Insolvency Practitioners.

9 See the National Reports in *Faber/Vermunt/Kilborn/Richter*, Commencement of Insolvency Proceedings, each at para. 10.2.

10 See *Tabb*, Law of Bankruptcy, §2.24.

extended to one or more other persons where their assets are intermingled with those of the debtor or where the legal entity is a sham (Art. L. 622-2(2) Code de Commerce). Similarly, "piercing the corporate veil" is regularly declined by English courts and only possible in rare cases (e.g. fraud, intermingling of assets, or where the parent company acted as "shadow director").[11]

2.6 **Example:** M Holding plc, the mother company of a group of companies, has granted a loan to its subsidiary D Ltd. Shortly before commencing insolvency proceedings, D pays the loan back. I, the Insolvency Practitioner of D, challenges the payment under transactions avoidance law. In most jurisdictions, this is possible, since M is treated as a separate legal entity and has to repay the money to D's estate according to the rules on preferences[12] or shareholder loans.[13] This is also true if M is insolvent itself. Only where "substantive consolidation" is admissible, is transactions avoidance between D and M not necessary, since the estates of both debtor companies are available for all creditors of both companies.

2.7 The fact that natural as well as legal persons are eligible for insolvency proceedings makes it necessary to highlight the distinction between insolvent companies (and other legal entities) on the one hand, and their **directors and shareholders** on the other hand. Where insolvency proceedings are conducted for companies, the debtor is the company and it is represented by its directors. The directors are not debtors themselves and neither are the company's shareholders.[14] This does not exclude that the company's insolvency might lead to personal insolvency proceedings for a shareholder or director as a debtor, e.g. due to a liability for the company's debts or for wrongful trading, but this is a second set of proceedings, dealing with the estate and the debts of the shareholder or director. These proceedings are to be considerably distinguished from the company's insolvency.

---

11 The leading case here is *Adams v. Cape Industries plc.* [1990] Ch 433; see also *Re BCCI (No 3)* [1992] BCC 715.

12 Below at para. 6.20 et seq.

13 Details below at para. 6.46.

14 Cf. *Bork*, Rescuing Companies, para. 9.03.

A second question concerns the distinction between **entrepreneurs and consumers**. Insolvency law has its origins in commercial affairs. Traders realise profits and losses and where the losses prevail, insolvency looms. Hence, it does not come as a surprise that all insolvency laws are at least addressed to entrepreneurs.[15] However, it is a more recent development that consumers are also eligible for insolvency proceedings and not all countries follow this lead.[16] While in England, Germany, and the USA insolvency law has always been applicable to both entrepreneurs and consumers (although consumer insolvency proceedings were quite rare in Germany before the *Insolvenzordnung* came into force in 1999), in France insolvency proceedings were reserved for entrepreneurs for a long time and it was only in 2016 when consumers were included, albeit in a special chapter of the *Code de la consommation* (Art. L. 711 et seq.). We will deal with insolvency proceedings for consumers in more detail below in Chapter 9. Against this background, it is slightly surprising that the UNCITRAL Legislative Guide recommends the eligibility of debtors only if they engage in economic activities.[17] There is no need to exclude individuals not engaged in economic activities from the application of insolvency law if they are insolvent because (e.g.) they issued a surety or guarantee for the debt of a relative, caused huge damages in an (uninsured) car accident or bought a private home, subsequently lost their jobs and are now unable to pay their debts. On the contrary, such exclusion is undesirable. 2.8

A difficult subject is the insolvency of **public bodies** (entities under public law). There is general agreement that states are not eligible for insolvency proceedings,[18] although it is broadly discussed whether procedural solutions for the accomplishment of (often hopelessly) overindebted states should be established.[19] On a lower level, the UNCITRAL Legislative 2.9

---

15 Typically excluded are banks and insurance companies, since there are normally special legal regimes for the insolvency of such institutions. See the National Reports in *Faber/Vermunt/Kilborn/Richter*, Commencement of Insolvency Proceedings, each at para. 4.2.

16 Cf. UNCITRAL Legislative Guide, p. 38 para. 2 and the National Reports in *Faber/Vermunt/Kilborn/Richter*, Commencement of Insolvency Proceedings, each at para. 4.4.

17 UNCITRAL Legislative Guide, Recommendation 8 and p. 38 et seq.

18 See BVerfG, Beschl. v. 3.7.2019 – 2 BvR 824/15 = NJW 2019, 2761 and for Germany §12(1)No. 1 InsO: "Insolvency proceedings may not be opened for the assets owned by 1. the Federation or a Land; (…)."

19 See for first guideline *Buckley*, The Bankruptcy of Nations: An Idea Whose Time Has Come, 43(3) The International Lawyer, 2009, 1189 et seq.; *International Monetary Fund*, Legal and Policy Development and Review Departments, "Proposed Features

Guide recommends to include state-owned enterprises.[20] However, some jurisdictions go further and extend the scope of their insolvency law to subnational public entities, especially municipalities.[21] For example, this holds true for Germany, where a legal person under public law which is under the supervision of a *Land* is eligible unless the law of the *Land* exempts such legal person from insolvency proceedings (§12(1)No. 2 Insolvenzordnung). In the US, §101(41) Bankruptcy Code excludes governmental units from the scope of insolvency law yet provides for an exception for municipalities in chapter 9 Bankruptcy Code (adjustment of debts of a municipality). In France however, insolvency law is only applicable to private entities[22] which excludes all public bodies. Similarly, it follows from the heading of "The First Group of Parts: Company Insolvency" that the Insolvency Act of England and Wales confines itself to "companies", which excludes all public bodies.

2.10 Finally, insolvency law is frequently applied to **marked out estates** without an own legal personality, especially to the estate of a deceased person.[23] In these cases, there is, legally speaking, only one debtor with one estate (which consists of the assets owned by the heir before the event of death and of the inherited assets). However, economically speaking, there are two partial estates held by the same person: the personal estate of the holder (heir) and the second estate which this person has inherited. If the holder's personal estate is sound but the second, inherited estate is insolvent, insolvency proceedings must be restricted to the insolvent part of the estate. This is arranged for in many jurisdictions, for example in England and Wales as well as in France and Germany for the insolvent estate of a deceased person (sec. 421 Insolvency Act 1986; Art. L. 621-14

---

of a Sovereign Debt Restructuring Mechanism", 2003, available at http://www.imf.org/external/np/pdr/sdrm/2003/021203.pdf; *Krueger*, A New Approach to Sovereign Debt Restructuring, 2002, available at http://www.imf.org/external/pubs/ft/exrp/sdrm/eng/index.htm; *Paulus* (ed.), A Debt Restructuring Mechanism for Sovereigns – Do We Need a Legal Procedure?; *Rault*, The Legal Framework of Sovereign Debt Management, p. 198 et seq.; *Rogoff/Zettelmeyer*, Bankruptcy Procedures for Sovereigns: A History of Ideas, 1976–2001, IMF Staff Papers 49 No. 3, p. 20 et seq.

20 UNCITRAL Legislative Guide, Recommendation 8 and p. 40.

21 For an overview see the National Reports in *Faber/Vermunt/Kilborn/Richter*, Commencement of Insolvency Proceedings, each at para. 4.1.

22 Cf. above at para. 2.3.

23 A further example are domestic assets in cross-border cases which can be subject to domestic secondary insolvency proceedings, cf. below at para. 10.9 et seq. For trusts, see §109(A)(v) Bankruptcy Code and *Brady-Morris v. Schilling (In re Kenneth Allen Knight Trust)*, 303 F.3d 671 (6th Cir. 2002).

Code de Commerce; §11(2)No. 2 Insolvenzordnung).[24] However, on closer look, this is not a matter of eligible debtors – the debtor is the holder of the insolvent estate[25] – but rather of restricting the effects of insolvency proceedings to one of the two estates as a delimitable part of the debtor's assets.[26]

II. CREDITORS

Insolvency proceedings, at least liquidation proceedings,[27] are collective enforcement proceedings, primarily conducted in order to protect the rights and interests of the creditors. Creditors are **holders of claims against the debtor.**[28] Substantively (and mostly also procedurally[29]), they are necessarily involved. The creditors' rights (claims) are the flipside of the debtor's debts (liabilities). A debtor with no creditors is not insolvent. If no claims exist, proceedings to enforce such claims are not necessary. Hence, in insolvency proceedings, the group of creditors plays an important role, although this group is not a homogenous one. Different types of creditors have to be distinguished (ordinary, secured, preferential, and subordinated creditors) and their rights have to be balanced against each other. All national laws address these topics, albeit in quite divergent ways when it comes to details.[30] 2.11

A. TYPES

In insolvency proceedings, typically **four groups of creditors** are involved. 2.12
The first group comprises the ordinary, unsecured creditors who are

24 Differently in the USA where a decedent's estate is excluded from bankruptcy relief because the state probate process provides for mandatory collective proceedings which cover all claims against this estate, cf. *Tabb*, Law of Bankruptcy, §2.2 and *Goerg v. Parungao (In re Goerg)*, 844 F.2d 1562 (11th Cir. 1988).

25 Different, however, French law where the deceased is supposed to be the debtor which is why such proceedings are labelled as "*procédure sans débiteur*" (procedure without a debtor); cf. *Le Corre*, Droit et pratique des procédures collectives, para. 211.71.

26 For details, see below at para. 4.20.

27 See above at para. 1.4.

28 Cf. the definition in the Glossary of the UNCITRAL Legislative Guide, p. 4 at para. 12(j).

29 See below at para. 7.6.

30 See the National Reports in *Faber/Vermunt/Kilborn/Richter*, Commencement of Insolvency Proceedings, each at para. 15.1.

primarily concerned, in whose interest insolvency proceedings are conducted and who at the end receive their share of the proceeds of the estate on a *pro rata* basis. The second group is made of the secured creditors who are fully paid as far as their security right is valid and recoverable (as for the rest they are ordinary creditors). The third group consists of the preferential creditors who are fully paid out of the proceeds of the estate because they have either acquired their claims after the commencement of the insolvency proceedings or enjoy special protection through preferential statutory treatment (e.g. for outstanding wages) without which they would be ordinary creditors as well. Finally, the fourth group comprises subordinated creditors who rank behind the ordinary creditors and normally get no payments out of the proceeds as these do not even suffice to satisfy the ordinary, let alone the subordinated creditors.

1. Ordinary Creditors

2.13 The first and mostly largest group comprises ordinary creditors. In principle, an **ordinary creditor** is "a natural or legal person that has a claim against the debtor that arose on or before the commencement of the insolvency proceedings."[31] Several features follow from this definition and some others have to be added.

2.14 First, the term **claim** needs explanation. Most creditors are entitled to payment from the debtor, i.e. their claim is targeted at money and it is due. However, this is not necessarily the case. Hence, two questions need to be answered. The first question concerns rights to payment which are *contingent or not due*. National insolvency laws regularly ignore the lack of maturity and recognise the holders of contingent claims also as ordinary creditors.[32] For example, §101(5)(A) Bankruptcy Code defines a claim as a "right to payment, whether or not such right is reduced to judgment, liquidated, unliquidated, fixed, contingent, matured, unmatured, disputed, undisputed, legal, equitable, secured, or unsecured" and includes a "right to an equitable remedy for breach of performance if such breach gives rise

[31] UNCITRAL Legislative Guide, p. 4 at para. 12(j). Cf. also §3.3 PEIL: "A claim against the debtor existing at the time of the opening of the proceedings ('insolvency claim') …".

[32] See §10.4 PEIL: "An unmatured insolvency claim is admitted for its discounted value. An illiquid insolvency claim is admitted for its assessed value. A conditional insolvency claim is admitted for its discounted value or conditionally for its full amount. A non-monetary insolvency claim is converted into a monetary claim for its assessed value."

to a right to payment".[33] Similar provisions on not mature or contingent claims are available in other jurisdictions (e.g. sec. 382(3) Insolvency Act 1986, rules 14.1(5), 14.2(1) Insolvency Rules 2016; Art. L. 643-1 Code de Commerce; §§41, 42 Insolvenzordnung). The second question concerns claims which are *not targeted at money*. In many jurisdictions, creditors with such other claims are eligible too, provided their claims can be converted into money.[34] For example, where customers have ordered and already paid for new cars to be delivered by a car-salesman, on the vendor's insolvency the customers are ordinary creditors, since their claims are – depending on national law – either directly targeted at money (if the customer is entitled to terminate the contract and reclaim their payment) or convertible into money (if the customer's claim for delivery of the car still exists). Many insolvency laws state this expressly. For example, in Germany §45(1) Insolvenzordnung holds that "non-liquidated claims or contingent claims shall be filed at the value estimated for the date when the insolvency proceedings were opened." Similar rules apply in England and Wales (rules 14.1(5), 14.2(1) Insolvency Rules 2016). US law, however, does not recognise claims which are not targeted at money[35] and the same holds true for France.[36]

Example: S, shareholder of D Ltd., has granted a loan to the company. 2.15
Upon the opening of insolvency proceedings against D, S files the loan with the Insolvency Practitioner. This is correct, since S has a claim and is therefore a creditor.[37] Shareholders as such are not creditors of the debtor company. However, shareholder claims can result from contracts with the company, from company law, or from other legal bases. If so, they are treated in the same way as other creditors unless national insolvency or company law subordinates shareholder claims.[38]

33 *Secure Leverage Grp., Inc. v. Bodenstein*, 558 B.R. 226 (N.D. Ill. 2016). Cf. also §502(c) Bankruptcy Code.

34 As opposed to this, the Glossary of the UNCITRAL Legislative Guide (p. 4 para. 12(g)) restricts the term "claim" to rights to payment.

35 Although the term "claim" is given the broadest possible definition, *In re Dubois*, 834 F.3d 522 (4th Cir. 2016).

36 *Le Corre*, Droit et pratique des procédures collectives, para. 663.14.

37 Cf. *Ray v. City Bank & Trust Co. (In re C-L Cartage Co.)*, 899 F.2d 1490 (6th Cir. 1990).

38 For the latter, see below at para. 7.31 et seq.

2.16 Second, the creditors' claims must be **directed at the debtor**. Claims against third parties – e.g. guarantors, sureties, directors, or shareholders – must be distinguished from the secured debt and are not recognisable in insolvency proceedings against the debtor. The debtor's estate is liable for the debtor's debts, not for third parties' debts, since third parties have their own estate into which execution is possible. Third parties can go insolvent as a result of the debtor's insolvency because it leads to the creditors' enforcing their liability rights against the third party. However, this second set of insolvency proceedings against the third party is to be properly distinguished from the insolvency proceedings against the debtor.[39]

2.17 Third, a very important **time bar** for ordinary creditors must be observed. Principally, creditors are only entitled to participate in insolvency proceedings where their claims have been established before the commencement of insolvency proceedings.[40] The idea of such proceedings is to realise the debtor's estate existing when proceedings are opened[41] for the benefit of the creditors entitled when proceedings are opened. This is based on the fixation principle[42] and comprehensibly expressed in German §38 Insolvenzordnung which reads "The insolvency estate shall serve to satisfy the well-founded claims held by the personal creditors against the debtor on the date when the insolvency proceedings were opened". Similar rules apply in England and Wales,[43] France,[44] and in the US.[45] And §3.3 PEIL defines an "insolvency claim" with "a claim against the debtor existing at the time of the opening of the proceeding". Creditors who acquire their claims after the commencement of the proceedings are either preferential creditors (because they have delivered their counter-performance in the interests of the proceedings)[46] or they are new creditors of the debtor who do not participate in the proceedings at all and instead

---

39 Cf. above at para. 2.7.

40 Even if the claims are not due or contigent, see above at para. 2.14.

41 More on this below at para. 4.5.

42 See above at para. 1.11. This principle is best elaborated in Dutch law, see *Boekraad*, Over fixatie en verificatie van vorderingen, Tijdschrift voor Insolventierecht 2019/4, 18 et seq.; *Franken*, Het Insolventiepassief, p. 34 et seq.; *Snijders*, in: Fixatiebeginsel en partijautonomie, Een kwart eeuw, p. 367 et seq.

43 Cf. rule 14.1(3) Insolvency Rules 2016.

44 Art. L. 621-43(1) Code de Commerce.

45 §101(10) Bankruptcy Code restricts relevant claims to pre-commencement claims. Exceptions for several post-commencement claims can be found in §502(f)–(i) Bankruptcy Code.

46 See below at para. 2.24.

can pursue their claims against the debtor's new estate (if any) after the termination of the proceedings. However, sometimes the legal basis for a claim has been laid before the opening of insolvency proceedings, but the claim itself has come into full existence after this point in time. In such cases, the legal basis is decisive. To allegorise it: If the claim is compared to a flower, it is important that the bulb was planted before the relevant point in time, whereas it is not necessary that the flower has already blossomed.

Example: In 1977, the claimant bought products which contained asbestos from the defendant company. In 1997, insolvency proceedings were opened for the seller which ended with a reorganisation plan discharging the company of all debts not entitled in the plan. At this time, the seller knew that he had sold products which contained asbestos but neither the claimant nor the seller knew of any claims or lawsuits. In 2007, the claimant was diagnosed with cancer and filed a lawsuit against the defendant who invoked the discharge. Since the discharge only applied to ordinary creditors and their pre-petition claims, the question arose whether the claimant's tort law claim was a pre-petition claim or not. The US Court of Appeal (3rd Circuit) held that a claim is a pre-petition claim if the individual was exposed to the product (or other conduct) giving rise to the injury even though neither the debtor nor the creditor was aware of the injury.[47] 2.18

Fourth, ordinary creditors are, as such, **unsecured**. If creditors have security rights they can seek satisfaction of their claims from the collateral and are not referred to the proceeds of the estate. Hence, they are not obliged to lodge their claims with the court or Insolvency Practitioner and they enjoy priority over all unsecured creditors, no matter whether preferential, ordinary, or subordinate.[48] They are fully paid as far as their security right is validly established and economically recoverable. Only for the part of their debt that is not covered by the collateral they are ordinary creditors. We will come to the details below at para. 2.21, 7.13 et seq. 2.19

Ordinary creditors are **paid collectively** from the proceeds of the estate on a *pro rata* basis. That means that they have to lodge their claims with 2.20

47 *In re Grossman's Inc.*, 607 F.3d 114 (3rd Cir. 2010).
48 See for England and Wales *Buchler v. Talbot* [2004] UKHL 9 (meanwhile slightly reversed by sec. 176ZA Insolvency Act 1986).

the court or the Insolvency Practitioner. All creditors whose claims have not been rejected participate in the distribution of the proceeds of the debtor's assets and finally receive the same proportion of their claims.[49] This leads to partial satisfaction while the rest of the claim remains unsatisfied and can either be enforced against new assets (which the debtor receives after the opening or termination of the insolvency proceedings[50]) or be subject to a discharge.[51]

2. *Secured Creditors*

2.21 As described in para. 2.19, secured creditors are satisfied from the collateral.[52] Which **security rights** are at stake depends on the applicable law. Into consideration come all sorts of securities or – as Art. 8(1) EIR puts it – "rights *in rem* of creditors or third parties in respect of tangible or intangible, moveable or immoveable assets, both specific assets and collections of indefinite assets as a whole which change from time to time, belonging to the debtor". This definition rightly highlights, on the one hand, that the assets encumbered with the security right must belong to the debtor. Otherwise they are not part of the estate and therefore not affected by the insolvency proceedings. On the other hand, it is not necessary that secured parties are creditors in the insolvency proceedings. They can also be "third parties", meaning that the secured claim is directed against another debtor, not the debtor of the insolvency proceedings at stake.

2.22 **Example:** where a father grants a security right over his property for the benefit of a bank which has granted a loan to his daughter, in the father's insolvency proceedings the bank is involved as a secured creditor and may enforce its security right, at least if the daughter is in default.[53] However, if the daughter pays the interest rates, etc. when they fall due the security right cannot be enforced in the father's insolvency proceedings yet is still to be respected by the father's Insolvency Practitioner until the loan has been paid back or the daughter defaults.

---

49 Extensively below at para. 7.39 et seq.

50 See below at para. 4.5 et seq.

51 Cf. below at para. 7.41, 9.2 et seq.

52 See for details below at para. 7.13.

53 Under which exact prerequisites the security right is enforceable depends on the security agreement and the national substantive law applicable to the security right.

Security rights must be distinguished from the **right to separation**. Where a person claims that certain assets do not belong to the debtor and are therefore not part of the insolvency estate, it alleges a right to separation, meaning that the object in question has to be separated from the debtor's assets and to be handed over to the entitled person. Dependent on national substantive laws, a typical right to separation is the right of a landlord to get the leased item back after termination of the lease contract, because the lease object belongs to the landlord and not to the debtor. Other examples are claims for surrender of lent objects or in many jurisdictions claims of a vendor based on retention of title. We will deal with this subject in more detail below at para 7.22 et seq. 2.23

3. *Preferential Creditors*

When preferential creditors are discussed, **classes of creditors** come into play. All jurisdictions know at least two classes of creditors: ordinary and preferential creditors. One class ranking ahead of another means that the proceeds of the estate are primarily paid to the higher ranking creditors until they are all paid in full. Only then can the remaining proceeds be distributed to the lower ranking creditors on a *pro rata* bases (unless the proceeds suffice to pay both classes in full). More generally speaking: equal treatment of creditors takes place only among equal-ranking creditors, not among classes. 2.24

Preferential creditors are creditors with claims which rank ahead the ordinary unsecured creditors (priority claims[54]). Two types of preferential creditors are common. The first group consists of those who have delivered their **counter-performance for the benefit of the proceedings** after the commencement of the insolvency proceedings. They are sometimes called "creditors of the estate", since through their delivery they have enriched the estate and can therefore expect to receive their remuneration from the estate in full.[55] For example, where the Insolvency Practitioner seeks to rescue the debtor company and therefore continues the business, deliveries from suppliers (including energy, water, and other goods), work activity of employees, and keeping the rented premises is necessary. All these persons 2.25

54 Cf. the Glossary of the UNCITRAL Legislative Guide, p. 6 para. 12(hh).

55 See §5.1(1) PEIL: "Obligations incurred by the administrator during the proceeding and the administrator's fees are to be funded from the debtor's assets and satisfied as they fall due, in priority to insolvency claims."

will not cooperate if their remuneration is paid on a *pro rata* basis only. Hence, they need to be paid in full. The same holds true for the official bodies. Courts and Insolvency Practitioners are paid from the estate which therefore finances the proceedings. No Insolvency Practitioner is prepared to manage the proceedings unless they can expect to be paid in full. Hence, insolvency proceedings cannot be operated without granting preferential satisfaction to the "expenses"[56] of the proceedings, and all national laws researched here contain pertinent rules.[57]

2.26 The second group of preferential creditors is marked by the fact that priority is given to certain **ordinary creditors**. Their claims have been established before the commencement of insolvency proceedings and they are therefore, in the abstract, ordinary creditors.[58] However, legislators frequently decide to grant privileges to certain groups of ordinary creditors by upgrading their ordinary claims to priority claims, be it for social reasons (privileges for outstanding wages or maintenance claims), or be it for fiscal reasons (privileges for outstanding taxes). We can call these groups "false estate creditors", since their claims have been established before the commencement of the proceedings and they have not delivered for the benefit of the proceedings. Although they are supported by §7.2 PEIL ("An employee has a preferential ranking in respect of certain insolvency claims for wages and other sums due under the contract of employment or arising from its termination"[59]), such privileges are highly debatable. They are at least a systematic disruption and in many cases difficult to justify. This is why some states – e.g. Germany – have relinquished this type of privilege completely whereas others are busy in developing even more groups of preferential creditors. In England and Wales, for example, sec. 386 with Schedule 6 Insolvency Act 1986 establishes five classes of preferential debts[60] and in the US currently ten classes of priority claims are recognised in §507 Bankruptcy Code.

---

56 This term is used, for example, in sec. 115, 156 Insolvency Act 1986 and §503 Bankruptcy Code.

57 See sec. 115, 156, 176ZA, 324 Insolvency Act 1986 and rule 10.149 Insolvency Rules 2016; Art. L. 622-17, 641-13 Code de Commerce; §§53–55 Insolvenzordnung; §503 Bankruptcy Code.

58 Cf. above at para. 2.17.

59 See, however, also §7.3 PEIL: "A public fund is available to meet certain insolvency claims of employees for wages and other sums due under the contract of employment or arising from its termination. If the public fund pays the employee, it is subrogated in the rights of the employee."

60 English courts are also prepared to treat certain pre-commencement claims as expenses of the proceedings if they incurred before the commencement of the

This leads to the subject of **ranking among various classes of preferential creditors**. Where national laws provide for more than one class of preferential creditors (e.g. by distinguishing between ordinary and secondary preferential debts, preferential and pre-preferential debts, or contractual and other preferential debts) they have to decide in which order these classes participate in the proceeds. Typically, a clear order of classes is established, §507 Bankruptcy Code ("the following expenses and claims have priority in the following order") being a good example.[61] This means that the proceeds of the estate are distributed to the highest ranking class until all creditors of this class are satisfied, then the second class is served and so further until the class of ordinary creditors is reached (subject to the sufficiency of the proceeds). Again, equal treatment is only granted among equal ranking creditors within a class, not among classes. 2.27

4. Subordinated Creditors

Occasionally, jurisdictions put certain groups of creditors **behind the ordinary creditors**. Such subordinated classes almost always receive no payments at all. Since the proceeds of the estate are regularly not sufficient to pay the ordinary creditors in full, nothing remains for the subordinated creditors. Examples for this class are shareholder loans. Where shareholders are free under national company law to help their struggling company with a loan instead of fresh equity capital, this loan would be an unsecured claim and the shareholder – similar to a bank – would be an ordinary creditor in the insolvency proceedings unless insolvency law ranks this claim inferior to ordinary creditors. Such subordination can be found in Germany where §39(1)No. 5 Insolvenzordnung subordinates "claims for restitution of a shareholder loan or claims resulting from legal transactions corresponding in economic terms to such a loan". However, this is not a general doctrine and other jurisdictions subordinate claims only which arise by virtue 2.28

proceedings in respect of property afterwards retained by the Insolvency Practitioner for the benefit of the estate. The leading case is *In re Lundy Granite Co* [1870–71] LR 6 Ch App 462; see also *Kahn & Anr v. Commissioners of Inland Revenue* [2002] UKHL 6; *Pillar Denton Ltd & ors v. Jervis* [2014] EWCA Civ. 180; *Shinners & Anr v. London Trocadero (2015) LLP* [2019] EWHC 2932 (Ch).

61 For England and Wales, cf. sec. 175, 328 Insolvency Act 1986 and *Re Nortel GmbH* [2013] UKSC 52; for France see Art. L. 622-17641-13 Code de Commerce; for Germany §§54, 55, 209 Insolvenzordnung.

of the statutory contract.[62] Typical subordinated creditors are further – dependent on the details of national insolvency law – creditors who voluntarily stepped back and postponed their claims until all ordinary creditors are paid in full, beyond creditors who did not file their claims in time, who are entitled to fines or gifts or who have claims for payment of post-petition interest on pre-petition claims or for reimbursement of the expenses arising from the participation in the proceedings (sec. 328(4) Insolvency Act 1986 and rule 14.23 Insolvency Rules 2016, §§39(1) No.1-4 Insolvenzordnung, §726 Bankruptcy Code[63]).[64]

2.29 In our **example** described at para 1.2. the proceeds of D's estate will be distributed as follows: Bank G is secured by assignment of D's receivables, among them the claim against Z which is worthless, since Z is insolvent himself. Let's assume that G can be satisfied from the other receivables in the amount of 50,000. The rest is part of the unsecured liabilities (220,000). The Insolvency Practitioner sells the house for 200,000. Fees are 5,000 for the court and 20,000 for the Insolvency Practitioner. The five employees have outstanding wages in the amount of 25,000 which are privileged by national law, as A's shareholder loan (10,000) is subordinated. Hence, from the proceeds (200,000), 50,000 are paid to preferential creditors (fees, employees) and 150,000 to the ordinary creditors (whose claims amount to 185,000) which leads to an (unusually high[65]) proportion of 81.08%. A receives nothing, since nothing is left for subordinated creditors.

---

62 See for England and Wales *Soden v. British & Commonwealth Holdings Plc* [1997] UKHL 41.

63 See also §510 Bankruptcy Code which even gives the court discretion to subordinate other claims "under principles of equitable subordination" (§510(c) Bankruptcy Code).

64 It is debatable whether creditors with claims for payment of post-petition interest on pre-petition claims or for reimbursement of the expenses arising from the participation in the proceedings would be ordinary creditors were it not for the subordination. Although these claims can be linked to a pre-petition contract, they arise after the commencement of the proceedings, i.e. are post-commencement claims, and their holders are new creditors, not ordinary creditors. See for new creditors above at para. 2.17.

65 In almost all countries, the average share for ordinary creditors is 3–5%, since the major part of the proceeds is distributed to secured and preferential creditors.

B. ORGANISATION

Creditors are involved in the proceedings not only by filing their claims and receiving their share of the proceeds but also by participating in the formation of the proceedings. As main economic stakeholders, they are keen on articulating and coordinating their interests and at least influencing – if not rendering – the key decisions in the proceedings. The UNCITRAL Legislative Guide therefore deals extensively with creditors' participation[66] and states in Recommendation 126 that "insolvency law should specify that creditors, both secured and unsecured, are entitled to participate in insolvency proceedings and identify what participation may involve in terms of the function that may be performed". This can be based on the principle of creditors' autonomy.[67] Typically, creditors are organised in **two procedural bodies**, creditors' meetings and creditors' committees,[68] which in national laws have quite diverse tasks and quite diverse influence.[69] 2.30

1. *Creditors' Meeting*

Most jurisdictions provide for one or more creditors' meetings.[70] They open the chance for creditors' participation by assembling all creditors in a general meeting where they are informed about and get the chance to discuss and influence the course of the proceedings. However, national laws differ widely from each other when it comes to the details. The main reason for these differences is that creditors' participation by creditors' meetings is costly and cumbersome. In a small insolvency case with some ten or twenty creditors, convening and holding a meeting of all creditors is not a problem. However, if in big cases, especially where the debtor is an investment company, 50,000 or 100,000 creditors are involved, creditors' meetings are burdensome to organise. Hence, jurisdictions restrict such assemblies in number and responsibilities. As regards the **number** of meetings, most national laws provide for at least one creditors' meeting at an early stage of 2.31

---

66 UNCITRAL Legislative Guide, p. 190 et seq.

67 Cf. above at para. 1.10.

68 Cf. §2.4 PEIL: "The creditors' collective interests may be represented by a meeting of creditors, a creditors' committee or a creditors' representative."

69 See the National Reports in *Faber/Vermunt/Kilborn/Richter*, Commencement of Insolvency Proceedings, each at para. 15.2.

70 Cf. UNCITRAL Legislative Guide, p. 195 et seq. para. 91-98 with Recommendations 127 et seq.

the proceedings where the creditors are informed about the main aspects of the case and possible solutions. However, in England and Wales, sec. 379ZA Insolvency Act 1986 states that, in individual insolvencies (bankruptcies), a creditors' meeting is only convened if a qualified minority of 10% in value or number or ten creditors request in writing that the decision be made by a creditors' meeting. Additionally, Part 15 of the Insolvency Rules permits the replacement of a physical meeting through correspondence, electronic voting or a virtual meeting for all kinds of insolvency proceedings. In Germany, three (physical) creditors' meetings are mandatory: a "report meeting" six weeks to three months after the opening of the proceedings where the Insolvency Practitioner reports on the case; an "examination meeting" three weeks to five months after the opening of the proceedings where the claims of the creditors can be discussed; and a final meeting at the end of the proceedings where the Insolvency Practitioner delivers their final report (§§29, 156, 176, 197 Insolvenzordnung). In the US, one mandatory creditors' meeting is provided for in §341 Bankruptcy Code yet further meetings are possible (rule 2003(f)/(g) Bankruptcy Rules). In France, however, creditors' meetings are unknown. The creditors' interests are attended to by the Insolvency Practitioner (Art. L. 622-20 Code de Commerce) who is supervised by up to five creditors as controllers (Art. L. 621-10 Code de Commerce).[71]

2.32 As regards the **responsibilities** of creditors' meetings, legislators are reluctant to give too much power to creditors' meetings. In some jurisdictions, they have the right to be informed but no competence to make binding decisions. In other jurisdictions, only essential decisions with significant impact on the general body of creditors are reserved for a creditors' meeting. Such essential decisions of a creditors' meeting include, for example, appointment or substitution of the court- or company-appointed Insolvency Practitioner (sec. 139, 298(4)(c), para. 97(2) Sch. B1 Insolvency Act 1986; §57 Insolvenzordnung; §§702(b), 703, 1104(b)(1) Bankruptcy Code), decisions on liquidating or continuing the debtor's business (para. 51 Sch. B1 Insolvency Act 1986; §157 Insolvenzordnung), on the sale of the debtor's enterprise to an insider (person with specific interests, §162 Insolvenzordnung) and on an insolvency/restructuring plan (sec. 4, 258 Insolvency Act 1986, sec. 899 CA 2006, para. 51 Sch. B1 Insolvency Act 1986; §235 Insolvenzordnung; §§1129, 1325 Bankruptcy Code).

[71] Cf. below at para. 2.43.

Much depends on how the **voting** in creditors' meetings is organised. Typically, the voting power of a creditor is related to the amount of money their claim accumulates to. This means that only creditors with filed and undisputed (or preliminarily admitted) claims are entitled to vote[72] and that a motion is only adopted if the sum of the claims held by backing creditors exceeds one half of the sum of claims held by those present and voting (majority in value). Examples can be found in English (rules 15.31, 15.34 Insolvency Rules 2016), German (§§76, 77 Insolvenzordnung) and US law (rules 2003(b)(3), 2007(b)(1) Bankruptcy Rules, §702(c)(2) Bankruptcy Code). However, in some cases a majority in value is either replaced or amended by a majority of creditors. 2.33

2. *Creditors' Committee*

Of significantly more importance is the creditors' participation by creditors' committees.[73] Creditors' committees are small and efficient entities, normally compiled of three to ten members, which represent the general body of creditors. They are regulated in most national laws,[74] are established either by the court, by the Insolvency Practitioner, or by a creditors' meeting, and are typically involved in most insolvency proceedings of a relevant size. **Members** can be (and in some jurisdictions must be) creditors, but national laws frequently permit representation by external experts (either as members or as proxy for creditors as members) who advocate the interests of certain creditor groups, e.g. an insolvency expert of a union representing the interests of employees or an agent of a credit insurer enforcing the interests of suppliers. Some national laws try to ensure that the most important creditor groups are represented, typically main creditors (mostly banks, but also tax authorities), secured creditors, and employees,[75] while others leave it to the creditors to decide on the composition of the committee[76] and restrict themselves to demand 2.34

---

72 See for US law *In re Lupo*, Case No. 09-21945-JNF., 2011 BL 28300 (Bankr. D. Mass. Feb. 03, 2011).

73 Extensively UNCITRAL Legislative Guide, p.197 et seq. para. 99-114 with Recommendations 129 et seq.; see on a comparison between German and English law *Bork*, Creditors' Committees, Int. Insolv. Rev. 21 (2012), 127 et seq.

74 Sec. 49, 68, 101, 141, 301, para. 57 Sch. B1 Insolvency Act 1986; Part 17 Insolvency Rules 2016; Art. L. 626-29 et seq. Code de Commerce; §67 Insolvenzordnung; §§705, 1102 Bankruptcy Code.

75 Cf. §67(2) Insolvenzordnung.

76 See rule 17.4 Insolvency Rules 2016, §§705(a), 1102(a) Bankruptcy Code.

that adequate representation of creditors is ensured.[77] A special case is France where two creditors' committees are provided for, one for banks and one for suppliers, but they are only involved in the implementation of restructuring plans (Art. L. 626-29 et seq. Code de Commerce).[78]

2.35 The **responsibilities** vary. Typically, creditors' committees are tasked with supervising, supporting, and/or cooperating with the Insolvency Practitioner (or the debtor where self-administration or debtor-in-possession proceedings are permitted[79]). This is at least enforced by rules which oblige the Insolvency Practitioner to provide the committee with necessary information and to attend the committee's meetings. Beyond this, some jurisdictions bind acts of the Insolvency Practitioner to the consent of the creditors' committee. For example, according to the German §160(1) Insolvenzordnung the Insolvency Practitioner "shall obtain the consent of the creditors' committee if he intends to engage in transactions which are of particular importance to the insolvency proceedings."[80] Similar provisions can be found in English law (sec. 314 Insolvency Act 1986[81]). However, in the USA, creditors' committees are restricted to chapter 11 (debtor-in-possession) proceedings.[82] They are tasked with negotiating with the debtor over the restructuring plan[83] and generally supervising the debtor (§1103(c) Bankruptcy Code). A creditors' committee may also be elected by a creditors' meeting in liquidation cases yet is not

---

77 Cf. §1102(a)(4) Bankruptcy Code.

78 See below at para. 8.36.

79 On them, see below at para. 8.21 et seq.

80 This is explained in §160(2) Insolvenzordnung: "Consent under subsection (1) shall be required in particular

1. if such transaction purports to sell the enterprise, plant, the entire stock, a part of real property to be disposed of by private sale, the debtor's shares in another enterprise if such shares are intended to bring about a permanent affiliation to such other enterprise or the entitlement to receive recurring earnings;
2. if such transaction purports to enter into a loan contract with considerable burdens on the insolvency estate;
3. if such transaction purports to bring or join a court action amounting to a considerable value in dispute, to refuse the bringing of such action, or to negotiate a settlement or compromise to settle or avoid any such action."

81 However, there is no similar provision for administration proceedings where creditors have to seek the help of the court, *Fletcher*, The Law of Insolvency, para. 16-080.

82 Cf. *In re Caesars Entm't, Operating Co*, 526 B.R. 265 (Bankr. N.D. Ill. 2015).

83 On this, see below at para. 8.32 et seq.

involved in decisions but rather a "mouthpiece" for the creditors' interests (§705 Bankruptcy Code). In France, the two creditors' committees are only involved in the implementation of a restructuring plan (Art. L. 626-30-2 Code de Commerce).

III. PROCEDURAL BODIES

Insolvency proceedings are state-organised formal procedures which are governed by two main bodies: courts and Insolvency Practitioners. 2.36

A. COURT

Since insolvency proceedings are at their core collective enforcement proceedings, court involvement is almost unavoidable.[84] In nearly all jurisdictions courts have their role in insolvency proceedings which is supported by the UNCITRAL Legislative Guide[85] as well as by §2.1.(1) PEIL.[86] Which courts are competent for dealing with insolvency cases is a matter of national insolvency and procedural law. However, insolvency law is a much specialised subject and it is therefore important that states assign insolvency proceedings to experienced judges in **specialised courts**. In some jurisdictions (Germany, USA) special insolvency or bankruptcy units within the courts[87] are established, in others (England and Wales, France) insolvency proceedings are administered by commercial or company courts,[88] but there are also states where insolvency proceedings 2.37

---

84 Occasionally, insolvency proceedings are managed by specialised administrative bodies, albeit under supervision of a court. Cf. for England and Wales sec. 124A Insolvency Act 1986; for Ireland *In re Irish Bank Resolution Corp. Ltd.* 538 B.R. 692, 697 et seq. (D. Del. 2015); for French consumer insolvencies Art. L. 712-1 et seq., 741-1 Code de la Consommation (below at para. 9.33).

85 Cg. UNCITRAL Legislative Guide, p. 3 para. 7: "The Legislative Guide assumes that there is reliance on court supervision throughout the insolvency proceedings, which may include the power to commence insolvency proceedings, to appoint insolvency representatives, to supervise its activities and to take decisions in the course of the proceedings."

86 §2.1(1) PEIL reads: "The proceeding is opened and supervised by the court."

87 Amtsgericht, §2 Insolvenzordnung; district court, 28 USC §§151–159, 1334.

88 High Court (chancery division/companies court) or county court (for minor cases), sec. 117, 373 Insolvency Act 1986; Art. L. 610-1, 621-2, 631-7, 641-1, Art. R 600-1 Code de Commerce.

are in the hands of general civil courts without any specialisation.[89] However, it is decisive that such proceedings are managed by judges who are experienced in commercial affairs.[90] Otherwise it is difficult to deal with the insolvency and possibly the restructuring of companies and other market participants. A judge who is not able to interpret a balance sheet is not sufficiently prepared for adjudicating in insolvency cases.

2.38 The **tasks** of courts are, at a minimum, to supervise the adequate conduct of the proceedings within the given procedural framework and to decide if actions of other participants, particularly those of the Insolvency Practitioner, are challenged by other parties.[91] Beyond this, courts are – dependant on jurisdiction and kind of proceedings – frequently commissioned with certain milestone decisions, e.g. to formally open insolvency proceedings,[92] to appoint, control and – if need be – dismiss the Insolvency Practitioner,[93] and to deliver judgments on grave matters, e.g. confirmation of restructuring plans.[94] Courts shall guarantee the efficient valorisation of the debtor's assets yet are not tasked to execute this valorisation. This is a commercial business which courts are not suitable for and which is therefore assigned to the Insolvency Practitioner.

2.39 A controversially debated matter is the ***vis attractiva concursus***. It concerns actions which derive directly from the insolvency proceedings and are closely linked with them. For example, where an Insolvency Practitioner challenges performances of the debtor under transactions avoidance law[95] or takes the position that a security right is invalid, the question arises which courts are competent for litigation. In some

---

89 For an overview, see the National Reports in *Faber/Vermunt/Kilborn/Richter*, Commencement of Insolvency Proceedings, each at para. 13.

90 See UNCITRAL Legislative Guide, p. 33 para. 1 et seq.; also Art. 25(1) Directive (EU) 2019/1023 of the European Parliament and of the Council of 20 June 2019 on preventive restructuring frameworks, on discharge of debt and disqualifications, and on measures to increase the efficiency of procedures concerning restructuring, insolvency and discharge of debt, and amending Directive (EU) 2017/1132 (Directive on restructuring and insolvency, OJ 2019 L 172/18): "Member States shall ensure that members of the judicial and administrative authorities dealing with procedures concerning restructuring, insolvency and discharge of debt receive suitable training and have the necessary expertise for their responsibilities."

91 Cf. below at para. 2.44.

92 More on this below at para. 3.3.

93 See below at para. 2.41.

94 Details below at para. 8.38.

95 Cf. below at para. 6.2 et seq.

jurisdictions, all actions which derive from the insolvency proceedings and to which the Insolvency Practitioner is party are assigned to the insolvency or bankruptcy courts. We call this "*vis attractiva concursus*" because the insolvency proceedings have "attracting force", since they attract litigation from the general courts to the insolvency courts. This is – at least to some extent – the case under US law which in 28 USC §1334(b) assigns "all civil proceedings arising under title 11, or arising in or related to cases under title 11" originally but not exclusively to the district courts where either bankruptcy judges or district judges decide.[96] Similar rules can be found in French law (Art. R 662-3 Code de Commerce).[97] In England and Wales, statute refers variously to competences of "the court" (e.g. for transactions avoidance in sec. 238(2), 239(2) Insolvency Act 1986). It follows from (among others) sec. 373, 436 Insolvency Act 1986 that this court is the court competent for administrating insolvency proceedings which boils down to the *vis attractive concursus*. As opposed to this, Germany does not recognise any *vis attractive concursus* and assigns actions which derive from the insolvency proceedings to the general jurisdiction of civil courts.

B. INSOLVENCY PRACTITIONER

The key player in insolvency proceedings is the Insolvency Practitioner 2.40
(also referred to as insolvency representative, liquidator, administrator, administrative receiver, official receiver, nominee, trustee, supervisor – depending on jurisdiction and kind of proceedings[98]). Hence, it does not come as a surprise that the UNCITRAL Legislative Guide deals extensively with the insolvency representative.[99] All jurisdictions provide for an

96 This is supplemented by 28 USC §157 which empowers the district judge to refer bankruptcy matters to the bankruptcy judge. However, this section has been seen critically by the US Supreme Court in *Stern v. Marshall*, 131 S. Ct. 2594 (2011); see also *Executive Benefits Ins. Agency v. Arkison*, 134 S. Ct. 2165 (2014); *Wellness Int'l Network Ltd. v. Sharif*, 135 S. Ct. 1932 (2015).

97 Cf. Cour de Cassation (chambre commerciale) – 7.4.2009 – 08-16884 = Bull. civ. 2009, IV, no. 51.

98 A collection for all kinds of Insolvency Practitioners in the EU can be found in Annex B to the European Insolvency Regulation. See also for England and Wales sec. 388 Insolvency Act 1986 and comprisingly *Bork/Wiese*, Die Rechtsstellung des Insolvency Practitioner.

99 UNCITRAL Legislative Guide, p. 174 et seq. See also §2.2(1) PEIL: "An administrator is appointed in order to carry out the liquidation or the reorganisation."

Insolvency Practitioner as the main procedural body.[100] In most kinds of proceedings, the main **task** of this institution is the valorisation of the debtor's assets, be it through sale of every single asset, be it through asset deal or restructuring of the debtor company.[101] The Insolvency Practitioner therefore has to take the assets in possession, administer the estate (e.g. by collecting debts from third parties, selling perishable goods, insuring valuable assets, or – more generally – by continuing the debtor's business), valorise the estate and finally pay the proceeds proportionally to the creditors.[102] In accomplishing their duties, Insolvency Practitioners are neither state authorities nor civil servants. They are private persons which are commissioned by the court, the company, or the creditors[103] to administer the proceedings in the interests of all stakeholders (debtor as well as creditors)[104] as a "representative of the estate" (§323(a) Bankruptcy Code) or "agent of the company" (para. 69 Sch. B1 Insolvency Act 1986). They are sometimes devolved the competences of an "officer of the court" (para. 5 Sch. B1 Insolvency Act 1986), but generally speaking they do not act sovereignly as a government body. They run a private business, are not paid by the government but from the estate and act on the basis of private law, not public law.

2.41 Many states endeavour to ensure the quality of the Insolvency Practitioner by rules on **eligibility**. Two points are important: independence and competence.[105] First, Insolvency Practitioners must take the interests of all

---

100 Cf. the National Reports in *Faber/Vermunt/Kilborn/Richter*, Commencement of Insolvency Proceedings, each at para. 12.

101 Cf. above at para. 1.5.

102 More details are listed in UNCITRAL Legislative Guide, p. 178 et seq.

103 See below at para. 2.42.

104 Cf. *Koch Ref. v. Farmers Union Cent. Exch., Inc.*, 831 F.2d 1339 (7th Cir. 1987); *Nat'l Am. Ins. Co. v. Ruppert Landscaping Co.*, 187 F.3d 439 (4th Cir. 1999).

105 Cf. Art. 26(1) Directive (EU) 2019/1023 of the European Parliament and of the Council of 20 June 2019 on preventive restructuring frameworks, on discharge of debt and disqualifications, and on measures to increase the efficiency of procedures concerning restructuring, insolvency and discharge of debt, and amending Directive (EU) 2017/1132 (Directive on restructuring and insolvency, OJ 2019 L 172/18): "Member States shall ensure that: (a) practitioners appointed by a judicial or administrative authority in procedures concerning restructuring, insolvency and discharge of debt ('practitioners') receive suitable training and have the necessary expertise for their responsibilities; (b) the conditions for eligibility, as well as the process for the appointment, removal and resignation of practitioners are clear, transparent and fair; (c) in appointing a practitioner for a particular case, including cases with cross-border elements, due consideration is given to the practitioner's experience and expertise, and to the specific features of the case; and (d) in order to avoid any conflict of

parties into account and must therefore not be biased; hence, independence from debtor and creditors is key. Second, insolvency proceedings can be rather different in size, complexity, and challenge and it is important for an optimal result of these proceedings that the Insolvency Practitioner is fit for the task to manage the individual case assigned to them (which includes not only legal knowledge but also economic experience). There are different ways to reach this goal. Some jurisdictions require the choice of an appropriate person in each individual case. For example, German §56 Insolvenzordnung states that "from among all those persons prepared to take on insolvency administration work the insolvency court shall select and appoint as insolvency administrator an independent natural person who is suited to the case at hand, who is particularly experienced in business affairs and independent of the creditors and of the debtor". Similarly, US law requires the Insolvency Practitioner to be chosen from a panel established by the US trustee[106] (§586(a) Bankruptcy Code), to be disinterested and "competent to perform the duties of trustee" (§321(a)(1) Bankruptcy Code).[107] French law, too, insists on independence and competence of the Insolvency Practitioner (Art. L. 621-5, 811-1 et seq. Code de Commerce). In a more general approach, other national laws require the Insolvency Practitioner to be a certificated member of a recognised professional body which includes the authorisation to act as an Insolvency Practitioner, England and Wales with sec. 390, 390A Insolvency Act 1986 being a good example.

In each insolvency case a concrete member of the group of eligible persons has to be chosen. Selection can be subject to a creditors' vote. However, the **appointment** is typically assigned to courts or state authorities but also to debtors or creditors, depending on jurisdiction and kind of proceedings. For example, in England and Wales the court is only occasionally involved in choosing and appointing the Insolvency Practitioner. In most alternatives, 2.42

interest, debtors and creditors have the opportunity to either object to the selection or appointment of a practitioner or request the replacement of the practitioner." See also Recommendations 115 et seq. of the UNCITRAL Legislative Guide, p. 188 et seq. and §2.2(2) PEIL: "The administrator must be independent and must act impartially." See also *Fletcher*, Spreading the Gospel, (2014) J.B.L., 523, 528 et seq.

106 The US trustee is a governmental official, appointed and supervised by the Attorney General, 28 USC §§581, 586(c).

107 Cf. *In re Natl. Store Fixture Co.*, 37 B.R. 481 (Bankr. W.D. Mo. 1984).Even appointment by e-filing is permissible, see *Re All Star Leisure (Group) Limited* [2019] EWHC 3231 (Ch); *Re Keyworker Homes (North West) Limited* [2019] 3499 (Ch).

the Insolvency Practitioner is either appointed[108] or at least chosen (and then court-appointed)[109] by the person commencing the proceedings which is either the company (by resolution of its shareholders or its directors[110]) or a – where applicable: secured – creditor. In the USA, the trustee is elected by the US trustee (§§702(d), 1302(a) Bankruptcy Code) or a creditors' meeting (§702(b) Bankruptcy Code). As opposed to this, in Germany the Insolvency Practitioner is always appointed by the court (§27(1) Insolvenzordnung) which is only bound to unanimous proposals of a preliminary creditors' committee (§56a(2) Insolvenzordnung) or to a proposal of the not cash-flow insolvent debtor in self-administration proceedings (§270b(2)(2) Insolvenzordnung).[111] However, the court-appointed Insolvency Practitioner can be replaced by a different person through a vote of the creditors' meeting (§57 Insolvenzordnung). In France, the Insolvency Practitioner may be proposed by the debtor but is chosen and appointed by the court (Art. L. 611-6, 621-4, 641-1 Code de Commerce).

2.43 In performing their duties, Insolvency Practitioners act rather independently. They have therefore a huge responsibility and it is important to counterbalance this by adequate rules on **control and liability**. On the one hand, Insolvency Practitioners are supervised by the courts or state authorities as well as by the creditors,[112] particularly the creditors' committees,[113] which have no commanding powers but can approach the court if they find the Insolvency Practitioner to act deficiently. In severe cases, Insolvency Practitioners can be removed and replaced by another person.[114] On the other hand, Insolvency Practitioners are personally liable for damages they cause in the conduct of their duties.[115] Typically, compensation for damages has to be paid to the estate (the company), not directly to creditors.

108 Sec. 1, 91, 100, 139, 292, para. 14, 22 Sch. B1 Insolvency Act 1986.

109 Para. 13 Sch. B1 Insolvency Act 1986.

110 See below at para. 3.2.

111 More on debtor-in-possession proceedings below at para. 8.21 et seq.

112 In France, the IP is supervised by up to five creditors as controllers (Art. L. 621-10 Code de Commerce).

113 Cf. above at para. 2.35.

114 Sec. 108(2), 171(2), 172 (2), 298(1), para. 88 Sch. B1 Insolvency Act 1986; §59 Insolvenzordnung; §324 Bankruptcy Code; cf. *In re Natl. Store Fixture Co.*, 37 B.R. 481 (Bankr. W.D. Mo. 1984). In France, liability is based on the general rules in Art. 1382 Code Civil.

115 Sec. 212 Insolvency Act 1986, §60 Insolvenzordnung.

Challenging the decisions of the Insolvency Practitioner is not possible in a technical sense, since he or she is not a member of the court whose decisions could be subject to appeal. Whilst court decisions can be challenged – regularly according to general national civil procedure law[116] –, decisions or acts of the Insolvency Practitioner can mostly not.[117] However, it is in most cases possible to file a complaint to the supervisory judge (or even a lawsuit against the Insolvency Practitioner) and ask for interfering measures.[118] 2.44

For further reading: *Bork*, Einführung, §§5–8; *Bork*, Rescuing Companies, para. 9.01 et seq.; *Fletcher*, Law of Insolvency, para. 2-007 et seq., 5-001 et seq., 4-018 et seq., 6-085 et seq., 7-035 et seq., 7-075 et seq., 10-001 et seq., 16-067 et seq., 21-023 et seq.; *Saint-Alary-Houin*, Droit des enterprises en difficulté, para. 416 et seq., 475 et seq., 505 et seq., 735 et seq., 1225 et seq.; *Tabb*, Law of Bankruptcy, §1.16 et seq., §2.2 et seq.; *van Zwieten*, Principles of Corporate Insolvency Law, para. 2-26 et seq., 8-55 et seq., 11-45 et seq. 2.45

---

116 In some jurisdictions, appeals against decisions of the insolvency court are restricted in order to enhance the efficiency of the proceedings; cf. §6 Insolvenzordnung.

117 Exceptions are possible, e.g. in the Netherlands Art. 69 Faillissement Wetboek.

118 See also above at para. 2.38.

CHAPTER 3

COMMENCEMENT OF PROCEEDINGS

The third chapter is dedicated to the initial phase of insolvency proceedings. We will be informed on various ways of commencing the proceedings and will learn how national laws try to protect the estate with preliminary measures against further diminution through acts of the debtor or grasp by creditors. We will see which prerequisites are foreseen for the opening of insolvency proceedings and how it is ensured that the costs of such procedures are covered. 3.1

I. INITIATION

Rules on the commencement of proceedings vary according to jurisdiction and kind of procedure.[1] §1.3 PEIL suggests: "The debtor or a creditor or a public authority can apply for the opening of the proceeding." However, insolvency proceedings are regularly commenced **by the debtor or its creditors.** It is only in rare cases for the court or a state authority to initiate the procedure.[2] Even tax authorities are normally not entitled to commence proceedings unless they are involved as creditors. If the debtor is a natural person it is qualified to start the procedure on its own behalf.[3] Debtor companies are represented by their directors,[4] but some national laws also 3.2

1 See the National Reports in *Faber/Vermunt/Kilborn/Richter*, Commencement of Insolvency Proceedings, each at para. 5.1.
2 Cf. sec. 137, 264(1)(d) Insolvency Act 1986; Art. L. 631-5, 640-5 Code de Commerce; further UNCITRAL Legislative Guide, p. 52 et seq.
3 See sec. 264(1)(b) Insolvency Act 1986; §13 (1)(2) Insolvenzordnung; §301 Bankruptcy Code.
4 This follows from general company law. However, some national laws entitle directors explicitly to commence insolvency proceedings, see for England and Wales sec. 1(1), 124(1), para. 12 (1)(b) Sch. B1 Insolvency Act 1986.

allow for a decision of the shareholders (e.g. sec. 91(1), 100, para. 22(1) Sch. B1 Insolvency Act 1986). Debtors can initiate both liquidation and restructuring proceedings. In most jurisdictions, creditors are also entitled to commence insolvency proceedings,[5] be it singly or jointly.[6] However, their commencement rights are sometimes restricted to liquidation proceedings[7] which is criticised by the UNCITRAL Legislative Guide.[8] Exceptions are in England and Wales the creditor's application for an administration order (para. 12(1)(c), 35 Sch. B1 Insolvency Act 1986) and a Scheme of Arrangement (sec. 896(2)(b) Companies Act 2006), in France for judicial restructuring proceedings (Art. L. 631-5 Code de Commerce) and in the US for chapter 11 proceedings (§303 Bankruptcy Code). German law does not distinguish between liquidation and reorganisation proceedings, hence creditors can apply for insolvency proceedings regardless of their aims or likely outcome (§13(1)(2) Insolvenzordnung).

3.3 Typically, there are **two ways** to commence insolvency proceedings. The first possibility is the direct appointment of an Insolvency Practitioner, sometimes combined with a notice given to the court or with the filing of a restructuring proposal, which can be found in many rules on voluntary (liquidation or reorganisation) proceedings initiated by the debtor.[9] The second possibility is the filing of an application or petition for a decision of the court to formally open insolvency proceedings. This is the only way to commence insolvency proceedings in France (Art. L. 611-3, 611-6, 621-1, 631-4, 640-4 Code de Commerce), Germany (§13(1)(1) Insolvenzordnung) and the USA (albeit for involuntary cases applied for by creditors only,

---

5 This is a frequently used option in Germany where nearly one-third of all applications are creditor applications (2018: 6,012 by creditors, 13,290 by debtors), mostly filed by tax authorities or social insurance carriers. As opposed to that, in the USA, only 0.05% of all applications emanate from creditors, although the application fee (28 U.S.C. §1930) for involuntary petitions is 335 $ only; see for details and proposals for incentives *Hynes/Walt*, Bankruptcy Bounties, SSRN 3275490. In Germany, application costs are born by the estate if proceedings are opened; otherwise it is for the applying person to bear the costs (which are dependent on the value of the estate or of the creditor's claim, reaching from 180 € minimum to 54,868 € maximum).

6 In most jurisdictions, every single creditor may commence the proceedings. However, US law requires a joint application of three creditors with a qualified amount of claims where the debtor has twelve or more creditors, §§303(b), 104 Bankruptcy Code; cf. *Mont. Dep't of Revenue v. Blixseth*, 581 B.R. 882 (D. Nev. 2017).

7 Cf. sec. 100(1A), 124(1) Insolvency Act 1986; Art. L. 611-3, 611-6, 620-1, 640-5 Code de Commerce; §§301, 303 Bankruptcy Code.

8 UNCITRAL Legislative Guide, p. 54 para. 48.

9 Partly in England and Wales, sec. 1(2), 86, 91, para. 22 Sch. B1 Insolvency Act 1986.

§303 Bankruptcy Code, whereas in voluntary cases applied for by the debtor, the filing of the debtor's petition suffices, §301(b) Bankruptcy Code). It is also a frequently used option for the commencement of liquidation proceedings by debtors[10] as well as creditors[11] in other jurisdictions, e.g. England and Wales. Additionally, in this country some restructuring proceedings also depend exclusively or alternatively on an application for a court order. For example, the Scheme of Arrangement is compulsively commenced by an application for a court order (sec. 896(1) CA 2006), administration proceedings can be started either by the appointment of an Insolvency Practitioner (para. 14, 22 Sch. B1 Insolvency Act 1986) or by the application for a court order (para. 12 Sch. B1 Insolvency Act 1986) and the same holds true for individual voluntary arrangements (sec. 253, 256A Insolvency Act 1986).

Controversially discussed are rules which contain an **obligation to file for insolvency proceedings** for the directors of the debtor company.[12] Such duties are sceptically discussed by the UNCITRAL Legislative Guide[13] but can be found in French law where Art. L. 631-4, 640-4 Code de Commerce state that the commencement of judicial restructuring or liquidation proceedings must be requested by the debtor at the latest within the 45 days following the cessation of payments if the debtor has not, within this time limit, requested the commencement of a *procédure de conciliation*.[14] Similarly, under German law, the directors of an insolvent legal person are obliged by §15a(1) Insolvenzordnung to apply for the opening of proceedings without culpable delay, at the latest, however, three weeks after the commencement of cash-flow-insolvency or overindebtedness. As opposed to this, English law does not contain such provisions yet trusts in rules on directors' liability[15] for fraudulent or wrongful trading (sec. 212 et seq. Insolvency Act 1986) to deter directors from waiting too long to file for insolvency.[16] US law contains no duty to file but wrongful trading is covered by "deepening insolvency" under 3.4

---

10 Cf. sec. 86, 124(1), 129(1), 264(1)(b) Insolvency Act 1986.

11 See fn. 6.

12 For a comparison between German and English law, see *Bork*, Rescuing Companies in England and Germany, para. 7.22 et seq.

13 UNCITRAL Legislative Guide, p. 49 et seq.

14 Details below at para. 8.13.

15 Once the company is insolvent, directors have to take the interests of the creditors into account (§172(3) Companies Act 2006); cf. *Burnden Holdings (UK) Ltd v. Fielding* [2019] EWHC 1566 (Ch).

16 For an example, see *McTear v. Eade* [2019] EWHC 1673 (Ch).

tort law.[17] This diversity of laws is difficult to assess. On the one hand, it is a fact that many insolvency proceedings are commenced far too late. It should be in the best interests of all stakeholders that companies in financial distress enter either rescuing or insolvency proceedings as early as possible in order to maintain the estate before it is completely wasted, to ensure a satisfaction of creditors which is as high as possible, and to preserve restructuring chances. Hence, it makes sense to put some pressure on the management to file for insolvency proceedings in time once substantive insolvency has occurred. On the other hand, most sanctions for not filing in due time are not very effective. In many jurisdictions, companies are frequently substantively insolvent for a long time – one or two years of delayed filing for insolvency is quite common in practice – before insolvency proceedings are commenced which proves the sanctions for late filing vain. However, this is not only a result of ineffective law but also a psychological phenomenon, since it is generally agreed that debtors and managers are the last to realise that their company is in distress and the point of no return has been reached.

3.5 **Example**: R, director of D Ltd., is aware of D's inability to pay debts but continues D's business for three years. This leads to liability for damages (to be paid to the estate) under English,[18] French,[19] and German[20] insolvency law whereas in the US, liability follows from tort law.

II. PRELIMINARY MEASURES

3.6 Where insolvency proceedings are commenced by an application for an opening decision of the court, an interim phase between the application and the court decision may occur during which the debtor's assets are not yet seized so that the debtor is able to further diminish the estate and to

---

17 *Smith v. Arthur Andersen LLP*, 421 F.3d 989 (9th Cir. 2005); *Gourian Holdings, Inc. v. DeSantis, Prinzi, Springer, Keifer & Shall (In re Gourian Holdings, Inc.)*, 165 B.R. 104 (E.D.N.Y. 1994), cf. *Konstantinov*, Wrongful trading, BRICS Law Journal 2 (2015), 100 et seq.; *Schillig*, Deepening Insolvency, 30 (2009) Company Lawyer 298 et seq.

18 Sec. 212 Insolvency Act 1986; see *Re HCL Environmental Projects Ltd* [2013] EWHC 2876 (Ch).

19 Art. L. 631-4, 640-4 Code de Commerce.

20 §15a Insolvenzordnung.

expand the liabilities. During this period of time, individual creditors are still able to enforce their claim through execution of the debtor's assets. In this situation the **need** for preliminary measures, which aim at preserving the estate to the benefit of the general body of creditors against harmful acts of the debtor or single creditors, may arise.[21] Typical preliminary measures available in national insolvency laws[22] are, among others, a moratorium (or stay) against creditors, the appointment of a preliminary Insolvency Practitioner, and restraints against the debtor.

A. MORATORIUM

Since insolvency proceedings are collective enforcement proceedings, they have the effect of prohibiting individual enforcement claims by single creditors.[23] This effect is preponed in many national laws[24] to the **application stage** by a moratorium (or stay) which primarily is an enforcement ban for the time span between application for and opening of insolvency proceedings. However, it should be stressed that under English law the word "moratorium" is occasionally used in a different way, especially where directly – i.e. without court involvement – commenced restructuring proceedings have no seizing effect but the debtor needs special protection against not cooperating creditors. In such cases the law occasionally[25] effectuates such a moratorium by statute (para. 42, 43 Sch. B1 Insolvency Act 1986 for court ordered administration) which imposes similar effects to the estate as the opening of liquidation proceedings. This sort of moratorium, which must be distinguished from the free-standing moratorium as provided for in Part A1 Insolvency Act 1986 and a *preliminary* moratorium as discussed here (which is also known to English 3.7

21 Cf. §3.5 PEIL: "Between the filing of the application and the opening of the proceeding, the court can take interim measures to preserve the debtor's assets."

22 See the National Reports in *Faber/Vermunt/Kilborn/Richter*, Commencement of Insolvency Proceedings, each at para. 17. No preliminary measures are regulated in French law.

23 Cf. below at para. 5.16.

24 See the National Reports in *Faber/Vermunt/Kilborn/Richter*, Commencement of Insolvency Proceedings, each at para. 18.

25 There is no moratorium in the Scheme of Arrangement proceedings, neither from the statute, nor available by court order. However, the High Court decided in the unpublished judgment *Sea Assets Ltd v. PT Garuda Indonesia* to protect scheme negotiations by putting a single creditor under an enforcement ban. See *Moss*, Scheme of arrangement: a recent example, Insolv. Int. 2003, 6 et seq.

law, sec. 1A Sch. A1, sec. 252 Insolvency Act 1986[26] and para. 44 Sch. B1 Insolvency Act 1986[27]), will be considered later in this book.[28]

3.8 In order to prevent creditors from achieving last-minute advantages by enforcing their claims after the application for insolvency proceedings the main **effect** of a moratorium is therefore an enforcement ban against all creditors. Affected are not only ordinary creditors but also secured creditors.[29] The idea is to preserve the debtor's estate as it is at the time and to protect it against exploitation and divestiture by single creditors. This is also a prerequisite for successful restructuring, since reorganisation is only possible if the enterprise is not prematurely destructed by creditors' execution of claims. However, the effects of a stay are not always restricted to an enforcement ban. It sometimes has further consequences such as a restraint on terminating contracts,[30] commencing or continuing litigation directed at collecting pre-insolvency claims,[31] or set-off.[32]

3.9 As a preliminary protection of the estate, a moratorium is imposed **either by statute or by court decision**. For example, in Germany, it is for the court to decide on preliminary measures. According to §21(1)(1) Insolvenzordnung, the court "shall take all measures appearing necessary in order to avoid any detriment to the financial status of the debtor for the creditors until the insolvency court decides on the request" (i.e. for opening proceedings) which includes an enforcement ban (§21(2)(1)No. 3 Insolvenzordnung). As opposed to this, US law provides for immediate protection from the collection efforts of creditors by an automatic stay which is triggered by the filing for insolvency proceedings without any court decision (§362(a)(2) Bankruptcy Code).[33] The same holds true for

---

26 Here, the moratorium covers the time between the proposal for a CVA and the shareholders' and creditors' meeting deciding on this proposal; cf. sec. 1A, para. 4(1)(d) Sch A1 Insolvency Act 1986 and for the IVA sec. 253 Insolvency Act 1986.

27 This interim moratorium covers the time span either between application and court decision or between filing a copy of notice of intention to appoint an administrator and the appointment taking effect, para. 44(1)/(2) Sch. B1 Insolvency Act 1986.

28 Below at para. 8.27.

29 Sec. 1A, para. 12(1)(e)–(g), 13, 14 Sch. A1; para. 44(5), 43(2)–(4) Sch. B1 Insolvency Act 1986; §21(2)(1)No. 3/5 Insolvenzordnung; §362(a)(3)/(4)/(5) Bankruptcy Code.

30 However, see for para. 44(5), 43 Sch. B1 Insolvency Act 1986 *Re Pan Ocean Ltd.* [2014] EWHC 2124 (Ch).

31 Sec. 1A, para. 12(1)(h) Sch. A1 Insolvency Act 1986, sec. 252(2)(b), para. 44(5), 43(6) Sch. B1 Insolvency Act 1986; §362(a)(1) Bankruptcy Code.

32 §362(a)(7) Bankruptcy Code. Different for English law *Electro Magnetic(s) Ltd. v. Development Board of Singapore Ltd.* [1994] 1 SLR 734.

33 *FDIC v. Hirsch (In re Colonial Realty Co.)*, 980 F.2d 125 (2nd Cir. 1992).

the interim moratorium in English administration proceedings (sec. 1A, para. 44(1) Sch. B1 Insolvency Act 1986). An intermediate position is taken by English law for the CVA moratorium:[34] here the directors must apply for the moratorium to the court but it enters into effect without a court decision by force of law as soon as the court receives the application (sec. 1A, para. 8(1) Sch. A1 Insolvency Act 1986) whereas the IVA moratorium[35] needs a court order (sec. 252(1) Insolvency Act 1986).

There are various ways of **termination** of the stay. The effects of the moratorium cease upon the decision of the court either to open or not to open insolvency proceedings,[36] but in the former case they are superseded by the effects of the opening decision.[37] Another possibility is the removal of assets from the estate, e.g. through disposal by the debtor or a preliminary insolvency practitioner.[38] Finally, a creditor may ask the court for relief from the moratorium, which is particularly foreseen for secured creditors.[39] 3.10

Example: Debtor company D files for insolvency and creditor G wants to enforce claims against D and S, D's main shareholder who has granted a surety. Enforcement against D is prohibited by the moratorium unless the court grants relief from the stay. However, the effects of this moratorium are restricted to the estate of D. Hence, enforcement against third parties (S) is possible unless it is interdicted by statute[40] or court decision.[41] 3.11

B. PRELIMINARY INSOLVENCY PRACTITIONER

Many jurisdictions allow for the appointment of a preliminary Insolvency Practitioner during the application stage, who will eventually become 3.12

34 On this, see below at para. 8.9, 8.27.
35 Details below at para. 9.32.
36 Cf. para. 44(1)(a) Sch. B1 Insolvency Act 1986; §362(c)(2) Bankruptcy Code.
37 Cf. below at para. 5.17.
38 See §362(c)(1) Bankruptcy Code.
39 Examples are para. 44(5), 43(7) Sch. B1 Insolvency Act 1986; §362(d) Bankruptcy Code.
40 E.g. §1301 Bankruptcy Code.
41 Made available under §105 Bankruptcy Code.

the final Insolvency Practitioner after the opening of the proceedings.[42] Their **task** is at least to supervise the debtor, but also to have the assets of the debtor at their disposal where the debtor is restricted in its disposal powers[43] or to control the debtor's post where interception of the mail has been ordered by the court[44] for the time span between the application for and the opening of insolvency proceedings. Examples can be found in German law where §§21(2)(1)No.1, 22 Insolvenzordnung provide for a provisional Insolvency Practitioner who has the functions and powers assigned to him by the court. Similarly, in English law, sec. 135 Insolvency Act 1986, rule 7.33 et seq. Insolvency Rules 2016 enable the court to appoint a provisional liquidator and confer on him functions and powers at the court's discretion. US law also contains rules on interim trustees. According to §§303(g), 701 Bankruptcy Code, the court, on request of a party in interest, may appoint an interim trustee promptly after the filing for bankruptcy proceedings if it is necessary to preserve the property of the estate or to prevent loss to the estate. The interim trustee has the powers of the (final) trustee (§701(c) Bankruptcy Code).[45]

C. RESTRAINTS AGAINST THE DEBTOR

3.13 Another set of preliminary measures regards the debtor's **power of disposal**. It is a typical consequence of the opening of insolvency proceedings that the debtor's assets are seized and the debtor's power of disposal is transferred to an Insolvency Practitioner. Given that this effect is frequently bound to the opening decision of either the court or a creditors' meeting, the interests of creditors and other parties can be severely tarnished by debtors who use the time span between application for and opening of insolvency proceedings for disposing of their assets, be it by selling goods to third parties, paying creditors who are exercising pressure upon the debtor, or transferring money to off-shore accounts. If such dispositions are to be feared, a provisional interference in the debtor's rights is due. German law provides for such interference in

---

42 The latter is foreseen by statute in the USA (§701(d) Bankruptcy Code). Typically, this is subject to a decision of the creditors or the court; cf. above at para. 2.42.

43 See below at para. 3.13.

44 Cf. below at para. 3.16.

45 This includes the bringing of avoidance actions, *Fogel v. Shabat (In re Draiman)*, 483 B.R. 338 (Bankr. N.D. Ill. 2012). In other jurisdictions, transactions avoidance is only possible after the opening of insolvency proceedings, cf. below at para. 6.2, 6.13 et seq.

§21(2)(1)No. 2 Insolvenzordnung which enables the court to "impose a general prohibition on making dispositions on the debtor or order that the debtor's dispositions shall require the consent of the provisional Insolvency Practitioner in order to become effective". The disposal power is accordingly transferred to a preliminary Insolvency Practitioner who either receives the power of disposal himself or can foreclose the debtor's disposal by withholding his or her consent. In England and Wales, the CVA moratorium comes with restraints for the debtor's competence to obtain credit and for the powers of disposal in para. 17 et seq. Sch. A1 Insolvency Act 1986 yet these disposal powers are not transferred to the Insolvency Practitioner (nominee). Similar rules are missing for the administration moratorium, but para. 13(1)(d) Sch. B1 Insolvency Act 1986 enables the court to make interim orders, which covers restraining measures against the debtor, including interference in the disposal powers and even the appointment of an interim manager (para. 13(3)(a) Sch. B1 Insolvency Act 1986). In the USA, restrictions to the disposal powers are closely intertwined with the appointment of an interim trustee who has the duties and powers of the (final) trustee (cf. §§303(g), 701(c) Bankruptcy Code) which includes the power of disposal of assets (§704(a)(1) Bankruptcy Code).

It should be noted, however, that even if the debtor keeps its right 3.14
of disposal, all transfers executed in the interim phase between the application for and the opening of insolvency proceedings can be subject to **transactions avoidance law**. These rules – which we will learn about later on in this book[46] – enable the Insolvency Practitioner to revoke pre-commencement transactions and they frequently cover the time span between the application and the opening decision.[47]

Example: D, being confronted with an application for the opening of 3.15
insolvency proceedings, transfers the money on her bank account to her spouse. This is either invalid, since D lost her power of disposal as a consequence of a statutory or court ordered interim moratorium. Or it is voidable as a transaction at an undervalue according to the rules of transactions avoidance law.[48]

46 Below at para. 6.1 et seq.
47 See below at para. 6.14.
48 More below at para. 6.29 et seq.

D. OTHERS

3.16 Some national laws give the courts a broad discretion regarding preliminary measures. For example, according to the German §21(1) Insolvenzordnung "the court shall take all measures appearing necessary in order to avoid any detriment to the financial status of the debtor for the creditors" which includes – among others – the appointment of a preliminary creditors' committee (§21(2)(1)No. 1a Insolvenzordnung) and the provisional interception of the debtor's mail (§21(2)(1)No. 4 Insolvenzordnung) which is frequently used in order to receive information about hidden assets. A wide discretion is also granted in England and Wales by para. 13(1)(d) Sch. B1 Insolvency Act 1986 which entitles the court to all preliminary measures the court deems necessary, among others, the appointment of an interim manager or other restrictions to the directors' powers (para. 13(3) Sch. B1 Insolvency Act 1986). However, in France and the USA no such authorisation of the court is available.

III. PREREQUISITES FOR THE OPENING OF INSOLVENCY PROCEEDINGS

3.17 National laws are regularly not content with an admissible application of an entitled person to open insolvency proceedings but require the debtor to be **substantively insolvent.**[49] We have dealt with the term "insolvency" extensively earlier in this book; hence, reference can be made to para. 1.15 et seq. above. However, legislators offer a quite colourful picture in this regard. First, many national laws treat liquidation proceedings differently from restructuring proceedings. And second, not all kinds of insolvency are always relevant.

3.18 For the opening of **liquidation proceedings** most laws require substantive insolvency of the debtor regardless of whether the procedure is initiated by the debtor or a creditor. For example, under the German §16 Insolvenzordnung, a "reason" to open insolvency proceedings is necessary. Such reasons are inability to pay debts (§17 Insolvenzordnung)

---

49 For substantive insolvency as a prerequisite see the National Reports in *Faber/Vermunt/Kilborn/Richter*, Commencement of Insolvency Proceedings, each at para. 5.2.

and in the case of a legal person overindebtedness (§19 Insolvenzordnung).[50] Likelihood of insolvency is only sufficient if it is the debtor who applies for the opening of insolvency proceedings (§18 Insolvenzordnung). Similarly, in France, liquidation proceedings applied for by the debtor or a creditor can only be opened if the debtor has ceased payments (Art. L. 640-1 Code de Commerce). In England and Wales, winding up by the court for which the debtor and any creditor can apply is permissible if the company is unable to pay its debts (sec. 122(1)(f) Insolvency Act 1986), but this is only one out of eight circumstances which admit liquidation proceedings and which do not refer to the debtor's substantive insolvency; hence, substantive insolvency is a possible but not a contingent prerequisite for compulsory liquidation proceedings. Beyond this, voluntary winding up is possible as long as the debtor company is solvent (sec. 84, 89 Insolvency Act 1986). In the US, substantive insolvency is only required if the application comes from a creditor (involuntary case) whereas insolvency is irrelevant in voluntary cases (§301 Bankruptcy Code). For involuntary cases, §303(h)(1) Bankruptcy Code refers to cash-flow or "equitable" insolvency ("if the debtor is generally not paying such debtor's debts as such debts become due")[51] which comes close to inability to pay debts yet surprisingly diverges from the definition in §101(32) Bankruptcy Code.[52]

As opposed to liquidation proceedings, most – but not all – **restructuring proceedings** can be commenced without any reference to the debtor's insolvency.[53] However, national laws do not show a clear line. For example, in the US, reorganisation proceedings are permissible under chapter 11 Bankruptcy Code regardless of the debtor's insolvency, yet only for voluntary cases on application of the debtor whereas for involuntary cases §303(h)(1) Bankruptcy Code applies, requiring "equitable insolvency" (inability to pay debts). In France, restructuring proceedings are generally not bound to the debtor's insolvency with the judicial restructuring proceedings being an exception. Here, Art. L. 631-1 Code de Commerce requires the cessation of payments regardless of whether the application for such proceedings 3.19

50 This meets Recommendation 15 and 16 of the UNCITRAL Legislative Guide, p. 64 et seq.

51 E.g. *Hayden v. QDOS, Inc. (In re QDOS, Inc.)*, 607 B.R. 338 (B.A.P. 9th Cir. 2019); *In re On-Site Fuel Serv., Inc.*, No. 18-04196-NPO, 2019 BL 191363, 2019 Bankr Lexis 1596 (Bankr. S.D. Miss. May 24, 2019).

52 Cf. above at para. 1.22.

53 See on this UNCITRAL Legislative Guide, p. 53 et seq. para. 47; for details below at para. 8.7 et seq.

has been made by the debtor or by a creditor. Under English and Welsh law,[54] neither Scheme of Arrangement nor CVA or IVA proceedings have substantive insolvency as a trigger. However, the situation is different for administration. This procedure requires inability to pay debts either to have arisen or to be imminent in the sense of sec. 123 Insolvency Act 1986, whether for out-of-court (para. 27(2)(a) Sch. B1 Insolvency Act 1986) or in-court administration (para. 11(a) Sch. B1 Insolvency Act 1986). In all, it is only in Germany, where the unitary proceedings cover liquidation as well as restructuring (§1 Insolvenzordnung), that the debtor's insolvency is always a prerequisite (§§16 et seq. Insolvenzordnung). Even the "protective umbrella proceedings" – which are designed to grant the debtor breathing space for preparing a restructuring plan[55] – are only admissible if the debtor is imminently insolvent or overindebted (§270b(1) Insolvenzordnung).

IV. COSTS

3.20 An important question for all insolvency proceedings concerns the costs of the procedure. In almost all jurisdictions the expenses of the proceedings are **paid from the estate**.[56] This means that the debtor has to finance the insolvency proceedings from the proceeds of his assets and that creditors who apply for the proceedings are not obliged to pay for the court or the Insolvency Practitioner. In consequence, the costs and expenses of the proceedings are usually classified as preferential claims ranking ahead of the claims of ordinary creditors.[57]

3.21 Another consequence frequently used by national legislators is to bind the opening of insolvency proceedings to the **sufficiency of assets** for covering the costs. This is possible without any further problems where the opening of insolvency requires a court decision, since the court can examine the sufficiency of assets and reject the application for the opening of the procedure if the estate is not valuable enough to cover the necessary expenses (and the expenses are not advanced by a creditor or the state). It is more difficult where proceedings are commenced by filing

---

54 For a comparison between the laws of Germany and England, see *Bork*, Rescuing Companies in England and Germany, Chapter 8.

55 More below at para. 8.8.

56 See the National Reports in *Faber/Vermunt/Kilborn/Richter*, Commencement of Insolvency Proceedings, each at para. 8; for application costs above at fn. 5.

57 Extensively above at para. 2.25 and below at para. 3.22.

for insolvency proceedings or by appointing an Insolvency Practitioner. Beyond this, much depends on the definition of "costs of the proceedings". If only the remuneration for the court, the Insolvency Practitioner, and the members of a creditors' committee needs to be covered, a less large estate is necessary than it would be if also other expenses of the proceedings (e.g. remuneration for employees)[58] were included.

Despite consensus on the principle, **national laws** differ widely on the details.[59] A lean and straightforward solution can be found in German law. §26(1) Insolvenzordnung states that "the insolvency court shall refuse a request to open insolvency proceedings if the debtor's assets will probably be insufficient to cover the costs of the proceedings. Such refusal shall be excluded if a sufficient amount of money is advanced, or the costs have been deferred in accordance with section 4a." To understand this provision it is necessary to know that (1) the term "costs of the proceedings" is defined in §54 Insolvenzordnung with the remuneration for the court, the preliminary and the final Insolvency Practitioner, and for the members of a creditors' committee (which excludes other expenses of the proceedings) and that (2) natural persons who apply for a discharge of the residual debt[60] may also apply for deferment until such time as discharge of residual debt is awarded (§4a(1) Insolvenzordnung). However, many laws do not follow this line.[61] For example, in the USA, expenses of the proceedings enjoy priority over ordinary creditors, second only to domestic support obligations (§§726(a)(1), 507(a)(2) Bankruptcy Code). Expenses of the proceedings include not only the compensation for the trustee (§§503(b)(2), 330(a)(1)(A) Bankruptcy Code) but also other expenses such as costs of preserving the estate, taxes, expenses of creditors, etc.[62] However, the commencement of the proceedings does not depend on these priority claims being covered by the estate and no advance is required, except for a (relatively low) filing fee.[63] The same holds true for England and Wales. 3.22

58 Cf. above at para. 2.25.

59 See the National Reports in *Faber/Vermunt/Kilborn/Richter*, Commencement of Insolvency Proceedings, each at para. 8 and for consumer proceedings below at para. 9.30.

60 Cf. below at para. 9.6.

61 A sceptical view is also taken by the UNCITRAL legislative Guide, p. 61 et seq.; but see also Recommendation 26 (at p. 67).

62 See for details §503(b) Bankruptcy Code.

63 See for the filing fee above at fn. 5 and 28 U.S.C. §1930 which can be reduced or waived by courts for a debtor unable to pay the fee, 28 U.S.C. §1930(f). However, under §303(e) Bankruptcy Code the court may in involuntary cases require the petitioner to file a bond to indemnify the debtor for their expenses.

Here, the expenses of the proceedings, which cover the remuneration for the official bodies as well as other expenses caused in the process of the proceedings,[64] enjoy first class priority (sec. 115, 175(1A)/(2)(b), 176ZA, 324, para. 65(2), 99 Sch. B1 Insolvency Act 1986) but in insolvencies (for companies) they may not be considered at the commencement stage, neither as a prerequisite for the commencement (sec. 125(1) Insolvency Act 1986 expressly interdicts refusing to make a winding-up order on the ground that the company has no assets) nor as an amount to be advanced by the person commencing the proceedings.[65] However, in bankruptcies (for individuals) the court may dismiss a bankruptcy petition under sec. 266(3) Insolvency Act 1986 where it is convinced that there are no assets distributable to the creditors or that such assets would be extinguished by the proceedings.[66] Similarly, in France, the costs, including the fees for the Insolvency Practitioner, enjoy preferential treatment (Art. L. 622-17(II) Code de Commerce) but no advance is necessary and the opening of the proceedings does not depend on the sufficiency of the estate.

3.23 ***For further reading***: *Bork*, Einführung, §§9–13; *Bork*, Rescuing Companies, Chapter 7, 8, 10; *Fletcher*, Law of Insolvency, para. 4-003 et seq., 4-045 et seq., 6-002 et seq., 10-004 et seq., 15-011 et seq., 15-054 et seq., 16-025 et seq., 16-046 et seq.; 16-151 et seq., 19-009 et seq., 21-001 et seq., 22-001 et seq.; *Saint-Alary-Houin*, Droit des enterprises en difficulté, para. 464 et seq., 1217 et seq.; *Tabb*, Law of Bankruptcy, §2.1 et seq.; *van Zwieten*, Principles of Corporate Insolvency Law, para. 8-35 et seq., 11-54 et seq., 11-98, 12-40.

64 See also rules 3.50, 3.51(2), 6.42(4), 7.108(4), 10.149 Insolvency Rules 2016.

65 However, the not court-appointed Insolvency Practitioner may conclude a private arrangement with the appointing person or may ask for voluntary creditors' indemnity, cf. *Re Exchange Travel (Holdings) Ltd (in liq) No 3* [1997] 2 BCLC 579.

66 Details at *Fletcher*, The Law of Insolvency, para. 6-108.

CHAPTER 4
THE ESTATE

The fourth chapter will explain the term "estate". We will learn which assets of the debtor are objects of the insolvency proceedings and which are not. The chapter will start from the characterisation of insolvency proceedings as collective enforcement proceedings and will explain that the seizability of assets is decisive. We will also be informed on the importance of the principle of social protection for the debtor when exemptions from the general definition of the estate are at stake. 4.1

I. ASSETS OF THE DEBTOR

The main and most important effect of the opening of insolvency proceedings is the seizure of the estate which – at least in liquidation proceedings – means that the right of administration and disposal is transferred from the debtor to the Insolvency Practitioner.[1] Hence, it is important for all parties involved to determine composition, size, and value of the estate.[2] Having in mind that insolvency proceedings are at its core collective enforcement proceedings,[3] one can start from the thesis that the estate consists of all assets which are **objects of enforcement proceedings**. If single creditors can have an asset seized – regardless of whether moveable (e.g. machines, cars, paintings) or immoveable (real estate), tangible (be it moveable or not) or intangible (e.g. claims, 4.2

1 See for details below at para. 5.3 et seq.
2 See also UNCITRAL Legislative Guide, p. 75 para. 1 et seq.
3 Cf. above at para. 1.3.

receivables, patents, licenses, etc.), situated inland or abroad[4] –, then, in individual enforcement proceedings, the same asset should be object of insolvency proceedings and therefore be part of the estate.

4.3 However, assets are only part of the estate if they **belong to the debtor.**[5] Debtors are liable with their assets for their debts yet only with *their* assets. Assets belonging to a third party are not included in the debtor's insolvency proceedings unless this third party has granted a security right over this asset, covering a creditor's claim against the debtor or a debtor's claim against one of his or her debtors. Without such a security right the third party has a right to separation[6] which entitles the third party to claim surrender of its unencumbered property from the Insolvency Practitioner if he or she is in possession of this asset. However, where assets belonging to the debtor are burdened with a security right to the benefit of a creditor, the collateral is typically[7] still part of the estate. Security rights – even where transfer of title or assignment by way of security is concerned – do not exempt the collateral from the estate. They entitle the creditor to separate satisfaction from the proceeds of the collateral as far as this is necessary to cover the debt. If the proceeds exceed the debt the surplus value is distributed to the ordinary creditors, which proves that the collateral is part of the estate. To put it more generally, where the debtor has a legal interest to assets belonging to or separated for third parties, this legal interest is also part of the estate.[8]

4.4 **Example:** Vendor V has delivered goods to debtor D under retention of title. In D's insolvency proceedings, the goods are not part of the estate, since the owner is still V, not D. V has a right to separation, i.e. he or she may require surrender of the goods from the Insolvency Practitioner, at least after having terminated the sales contract.[9]

---

4 For the latter, see below at para. 10.10.

5 Cf. §3.1 PEIL: "Assets belonging to the debtor at the time of the opening of the proceedings and assets acquired thereafter are included in the proceeding. When the debtor is a natural person certain assets are excluded from the proceeding." Further UNCITRAL Legislative Guide, p. 77 para. 10 et seq.

6 See above at para. 2.23. and below at para. 7.22.

7 For exceptions, see below at para. 7.13 et seq., particularly for England and Wales at para. 7.17.

8 See the wording of §541(a) Bankruptcy Code and *McCarthy, Johnson & Miller v. N. Bay Plumbing, Inc. (In re Pettit)*, 217 F.3d 1072, 24 EBC 2695 (9th Cir. 2000).

9 For details, see below at para. 7.17.

However, where V has transferred the title (ownership[10]) to D and D has passed it on to bank B by way of security, the encumbered assets are, in most jurisdictions, still part of the estate and subject to the rules on security rights.[11]

It has already been pointed out that the idea of insolvency proceedings is to realise the debtor's estate existing when proceedings are opened for the benefit of the creditors entitled when proceedings are opened.[12] This **time bar**, based on the fixation principle,[13] is also important for determining the concrete size of the estate.[14] Typically, only those assets are part of the estate which belong to the debtor at the point in time when insolvency proceedings are commenced.[15] Unless national laws provide otherwise – and many jurisdictions follow this path by including "new acquisition" in the estate[16] –, assets which the debtor acquires after this point in time (e.g. by succession or by spending unseizable income) do not pertain to the estate. They are not realised by the Insolvency Practitioner and their proceeds are not distributed to the creditors. Instead, the debtor is entitled to dispose of these assets and deal with them at will. However, two important exceptions must be mentioned. The first concerns assets that replace parts of the estate after the commencement of the proceedings,[17] e.g. an insurance claim which replaces a house destroyed by fire or a car damaged in a traffic accident (and later on the money paid by the insurance company which 4.5

10 In the Anglo-American legal system, the concept of "ownership" is to some extent different from other, particularly continental, legal systems. Here, the word "ownership" is frequently replaced by "legal title". In this book, both will be used equivalently.

11 For them, see below at para. 7.13 et seq.

12 Above at para. 2.17; for §3.1 PEIL see above at fn. 5.

13 CF. above at para. 1.11 and 2.17.

14 See also UNCITRAL Legislative Guide, p. 81 para. 22 et seq.

15 Cf. UNCITRAL Legislative Guide, p. 82 Recommendation 37.

16 In accordance with UNCITRAL Legislative Guide, p. 82 Recommendation 35(b), national laws contain exceptions for assets *acquired* during the proceedings but not for assets acquired after the termination of the proceedings. However, this must not be confused with assets acquired before the commencement of (or during, as the case may be) the proceedings but *discovered* after this point in time. In those cases, a reopening and continuance of the proceedings may be due; cf. for Germany §203 Insolvenzordnung; for England and Wales *Fletcher*, The Law of Insolvency, para. 8-037; for the US §350(b) Bankruptcy Code and *Kane v. Nat'l Union Fire Ins. Co.*, 535 F.3d 380 (5th Cir. 2008); see also §13.3 PEIL: "Assets discovered after the closure of a liquidation may give rise to a further liquidation."

17 Cf. §541(a)(6) Bankruptcy Code.

replaces the insurance claim). The second exception regards claims against third parties which are triggered by the commencement of the insolvency proceedings.[18] This primarily concerns claims arising from transactions avoidance law which entitle the Insolvency Practitioner to claw-back from the recipient assets transferred or payments performed by the debtor prior to the opening of insolvency proceedings[19] but also – depending on national liability law – claims against directors or shareholders for wrongful trading, etc.

4.6 The aforementioned principles are reflected in most national laws, albeit with some modifications.[20] For example, in **Germany,** §35 Insolvenzordnung defines the term "insolvency estate" with "the insolvency proceedings shall involve all of the assets owned by the debtor on the date when the proceedings were opened and those acquired by him during the proceedings". This definition confirms that only assets of the debtor form the estate but also includes assets acquired by the debtor in the time span between the commencement and the termination of the proceedings (so-called "new acquisition"). This includes wages and income from self-employment but also assets which are inherited, received as a gift or lottery win, or acquired otherwise (e.g. by erroneous payment of a third party on the debtor's bank account or by enforcing transactions avoidance claims). Also embraced is collateral, since security rights entitle the secured creditor to separate satisfaction[21] but do not remove the collateral from the estate.

4.7 In **France**, the estate is not expressly defined by statute. However, according to Art. L. 641-9 "the order commencing or pronouncing the judicial liquidation proceedings shall also give rise, from its date of issue, to the divestment of the debtor from the management and the right to dispose of its assets, including even those acquired by any means, until the closing of the judicial liquidation proceedings." It follows from this rather indirect definition that – similar to German law – only the debtor's assets are part of the estate and that "new acquisition" is included.[22] This also

---

18 Cf. §541(3) Bankruptcy Code and UNCITRAL Legislative Guide, p. 82 Recommendation 35(c).

19 For details, see below at para. 6.1 et seq.

20 See the National Reports in *Faber/Vermunt/Kilborn/Richter*, Commencement of Insolvency Proceedings, each at para. 19.

21 Details below at para. 7.19.

22 See for the debtor's salary Cour de Cassation (chambre commerciale) – 13.4.2010 – 08-19074 = Bull. civ. 2010, IV, no. 78.

holds true for payments to the Insolvency Practitioner on claims triggered by the opening of insolvency proceedings (cf. Art. L. 622-20, 651-2 Code de Commerce). Further, the estate comprises assets charged with security rights, since the secured creditor has a right to separate satisfaction only which does not exclude the collateral from the estate.

In the **USA**, "property of the estate" is extensively regulated. According to §541(a)(1) Bankruptcy Code, the estate comprises of "all legal or equitable interests of the debtor in property as of the commencement of the case", wherever located and by whomever held. Assets acquired after the commencement of the proceedings are therefore not part of the estate.[23] This excludes remuneration for services performed by an individual after the commencement of the proceedings from the estate. However, §541(a)(6) Bankruptcy Code assigns "proceeds, product, offspring, rents, or profits of or from property of the estate" to the estate which crosses the time bar described above, since rents, for example, are fruits of the property grown and harvested after the commencement of the proceedings. In addition, §541(a)(7) Bankruptcy Code captures "any interest in property that the estate acquires after the commencement of the case". However, both rules aim at including the "fruits" of property into the estate, provided the property itself is part of the estate.[24] Apart from this, the definition is very broad and includes real and personal property, tangible and intangible property, regardless of whether the asset is held by the debtor or by a third party (which has to return the asset to the Insolvency Practitioner), and also collateral which serves as a security for a creditor.[25] 4.8

The law in **England and Wales** is less precise. It follows from sec. 107, 144(1), 145(1), 148(1), 234(2) Insolvency Act 1986 that in liquidation and administration proceedings the debtor's "property" or "assets" constitute the estate, even if the assets are held by third parties (sec. 234(2) Insolvency Act 1986). It is clear from sec. 234(3) Insolvency Act 1986 that property owned by third parties is not part of the estate. This includes collateral, since, under English law, assets covered with a security right are not property of the debtor to whose estate not the collateral but only the 4.9

23 However, there is a "grace period" of 180 days after the filing of the petition. It covers assets acquired (A) by bequest, devise, or inheritance; (B) as a result of a property settlement agreement with the debtor's spouse, or of an interlocutory or final divorce decree; or (C) as a beneficiary of a life insurance policy or of a death benefit plan, §541(a)(5) Bankruptcy Code.

24 *McLain v. Newhouse (In re McLain)*, 516 F.3d 301 (5th Cir. 2008).

25 Cf. §363(f) Bankruptcy Code.

equity of redemption belongs.[26] The term "estate" is defined in sec. 283(1) Insolvency Act 1986, albeit for individual bankruptcies only, with "(a) all property belonging to or vested in the bankrupt at the commencement of the bankruptcy, and (b) any property which by virtue of any of the following provisions of this Part is comprised in that estate or is treated as falling with the preceding paragraph." Further, according to the general definition in sec. 436 Insolvency Act 1986 "property includes money, goods, things in action, land and every description of property wherever situated and also obligations and every description of interest, whether present or future or vested or contingent, arising out of, or incidental to, property". It follows also from this definition and from sec. 306(2), 307 Insolvency Act 1986 that assets acquired after the commencement of the proceedings are part of the estate, and this includes the proceeds of transactions avoidance claims and other claims triggered by the commencement of insolvency proceedings.

4.10 **Examples**: D, a bankrupt barrister, has worked for some "clients" on a non-contractual basis. The Insolvency Practitioner demands from D surrender of fees which were paid to D after the opening of insolvency proceedings as remuneration for her efforts for these "clients". This claim is justified in most jurisdictions, since money received from third parties is "new acquisition" and as such part of the estate, regardless of the existence of estate-appendant pre-commencement claims. However, the High Court of England and Wales decided differently, arguing that payments of non-contractual obligations cannot be seen as "arising out of property" within the meaning of sec. 306 Insolvency Act 1986.[27]

4.11 D owns a house which she has let to her tenant T. After the opening of insolvency proceedings against D in April 2020, T wants to know to whom he should pay the rent for May 2020. Rents are frequently (depending on national law) not contingent claims which are collectively created by signing the tenancy contract but future claims which originate from the contract anew every month. Hence,

26 *Re Pyle Works Ltd* [1890] 44 Ch. D. 534. An exception is the "prescribed part" (percentage of the value of assets subject to a floating charge, sec. 176A Insolvency Act 1986), see below at para. 7.17.

27 *Gwinnutt v. George* [2018] EWHC 2169 (Ch). However, the court did not decide whether the money was "after-acquired property" within the meaning of sec. 307 IA 1986 which would put a different complexion on this matter.

since rents for future months do not exist at the point in time when insolvency proceedings are opened, they are in themselves not part of the estate. Nonetheless, in Germany, the rent is part of the estate as "new acquisition" and must therefore be paid to the Insolvency Practitioner. The same holds true in France and also in the US, where §541(a)(6) Bankruptcy Code includes rents into the estate, and England and Wales, where assets acquired after the commencement of the proceedings are part of the estate. In the end, this is the only reasonable solution because it might be difficult to liquidate a company which continues to acquire assets outside the insolvency proceedings.

II. EXCEPTIONS

The rather broad definition of the estate ("all assets belonging to the debtor") is subject to some important restrictions.[28] The first exception regards **not commercialised assets**, especially personal rights of the debtor. For example, if the debtor can claim the withdrawal of a libellous statement from a third party this right is not part of the estate and therefore not executed by the Insolvency Practitioner. It is granted to protect the personality of the debtor and is not a property right destined for creditor satisfaction.[29] Another example is the debtor's manpower. Debtors cannot be forced by the Insolvency Practitioner to work after the opening of insolvency proceedings for the benefit of the creditors. There is only indirect pressure on debtors who wish to apply for a discharge.[30] 4.12

Example: Debtor D is subject to insolvency proceedings. After the opening of the proceedings M, D's mother, dies and leaves her daughter D as the only heir. D rejects the succession. The Insolvency Practitioner thinks that this decision is void because D lost her right of disposal. However, the transfer of the disposal right from the debtor to the Insolvency Practitioner is restricted to the estate. 4.13

---

28 In the US, exemptions are regulated by state law and only alternatively in §522 Bankruptcy Code which will exclusively be dealt with in the following paragraphs.

29 Cf. for England and Wales *Hayes v. Butters* [2014] EWHC 4557 (Ch); for the US §522(d)(11)(D) Bankruptcy Code.

30 See below at para. 9.13 et seq.

The right to accept or reject a heritage is a personal right, which is as such not part of the estate and cannot be executed by the Insolvency Practitioner. Hence, the inherited assets can also not become part of the estate unless the debtor has accepted the legacy. This is expressly stated in German law (§83(1) Insolvenzordnung: "If the debtor prior to the opening of the insolvency proceedings succeeded or during the insolvency proceedings succeeds to a decedent's estate or to a legacy, only the debtor shall be entitled to accept or disclaim such estate or legacy") but is also recognised in other jurisdictions, for example by the courts in France.[31] In England and Wales, however, the heritage belongs to the estate[32] and the same holds true for the USA unless the debtor has acquired the heritage before or within 180 days after the filing of the bankruptcy petition (§541(a)(5)(A) Bankruptcy Code).

4.14 The second exemption regards **unseizable assets**. Since insolvency proceedings are, at their core, collective enforcement proceedings, the creditors as a whole cannot be satisfied from the proceeds of goods which they could not seize in individual enforcement proceedings. In other words, the commencement of insolvency proceedings does not enlarge the pool of assets with which debtors are liable for their debts. This rule can be found in German §36(1) Insolvenzordnung which states: "Objects not subject to execution shall not form part of the insolvency estate" and it is also recognised in other jurisdictions.[33] In most cases it is the principle of social protection for debtors being natural persons which justifies such exemptions.[34] An illustrative example is the income (or the pension) of the debtor. In many jurisdictions a minimum part of the income/pension is declared unseizable by law (or by court order) in order to guarantee the debtor's living. Creditors cannot seize this part of the income/pension

---

31 Cour de Cassation (chambre commerciale) – 3.5.2006 – 04-10115 = Bull. civ. 2006, IV, no. 109; but cf. also Art. L. 641-9(4), L. 643-11(1)No. 1 Code de Commerce.

32 *Hunt v. Fripp* [1898] 1 Ch. 675.

33 See for France Cour de Cassation (chambre commerciale) – 5.2.2002 – 99-11903 = Bull. civ. 2002, IV, no. 28.

34 Cf. for §3.1 PEIL above in fn. 5; further UNCITRAL Legislative Guide, p. 80 para. 18 et seq.

in individual enforcement proceedings and it is therefore not part of the estate in insolvency proceedings. The debtor may dispose of this protected part at will and the Insolvency Practitioner is not entitled to collect it from the employer or the pension institution.[35]

A third category of goods exempted from the estate are **non-transferable assets.** However, these assets are mostly either not commercialised (above at para. 4.12) or not seizable (above at para 4.14) and to this extent a separate group is not necessary. However, occasionally the debtor owns assets which are not transferrable yet can be commercialised for the benefit of the creditors. For example, in many jurisdictions the moral right of an author is part of his or her personality rights and as such neither transferable nor seizable. But it can be realised for the benefit of the creditors by licensing, at least if the debtor gives their consent (as demanded by some national copyright laws). Hence, non-transferable assets can be part of the estate if they have commercial value realisable for the benefit of the creditors. 4.15

Example: Prior to the opening of insolvency proceedings, debtor D was injured in a car accident. He was granted damages for pain and suffering which the Insolvency Practitioner claimed for the estate. This was successful under German law, since the German legislator abolished the rule that claims to such damages are not transferable and therefore not seizable and thus not part of the estate. However, in England,[36] France,[37] and the USA[38] these claims are judged as personal rights of the debtor and therefore not part of the estate.[39] 4.16

35 Cf. for England and Wales sec. 283(2), 310, 310A Insolvency Act 1986, sec. 11 et seq. Welfare Reform and Pensions act 1999; for France Art. 698 Code de Procédure Civile; for Germany §§850 et seq. Zivilprozessordnung. In the USA, postpetition earnings of an individual are expressly excluded from the estate (cf. §541(a)(6) Bankruptcy Code and above at para. 4.8), unless the debtor files for chapter 11 or chapter 13 proceedings; this is supplemented by §§522(d)(10)/(12), 1325(b)(2) Bankruptcy Code.

36 *Wilson v. United Counties Bank Ltd.* [1920] AC 102 (HL).

37 Cour de Cassation (chambre commerciale) – 5.2.2002 – 99-11903 = Bull. civ. 2002, IV, no. 28.

38 §522(d)(11)(D) Bankruptcy Code.

39 See above at para. 4.12.

4.17 On the other hand, realisable value is not a contingent prerequisite for affiliation to the estate. Even **worthless assets** are part of the estate if they are as such commercialised, transferable, and seizable. For example, an outmoded and rotten machine located in the debtor's factory may only have scrap value and conceivably the costs for negotiating a sale and carrying the machine to the buyer consume the scrap value; nevertheless the machine is part of the estate and the right of disposal is assigned to the Insolvency Practitioner. The same holds true for real estate covered exhaustingly with mortgages; it is part of the estate even though it has no commercial value for the creditors.

4.18 However, many national laws enable the Insolvency Practitioner to **release** such assets from seizure and transfer the right of disposal back to the debtor. For example, in England and Wales sec. 178, 315 Insolvency Act 1986 permits the liquidator, by giving the prescribed notice, to disclaim any onerous property, notwithstanding that he or she has taken possession of it, endeavoured to sell it, or otherwise exercised rights of ownership in relation to it. "Onerous property" is defined in sec. 178(3), 315(2) Insolvency Act 1986 with "(a) any unprofitable contract, and (b) any other property of the company which is unsaleable or not readily saleable or is such that it may give rise to a liability to pay money or perform any other onerous act". In Germany, release from seizure for worthless assets[40] is generally recognised[41] which finds its expression in §§32(3), 35(2),[42] 85(2) Insolvenzordnung. The Insolvency Practitioner can waive the rights assigned to him for single assets, thus extricating himself from the burdensome duty to dispose of such assets. The same holds true for the US, where §554 Bankruptcy Code entitles the Insolvency Practitioner to abandon burdensome property of the estate or property that is of inconsequential value and benefit to the estate.

---

40 For contracts, see below at para. 5.25 et seq.

41 Example: BGH, Urt. v. 27.4.2017 – IX ZB 93/16 = NZI 2017, 608 (release of real estate).

42 This rule entitles the Insolvency Practitioner to release "the assets from the non-dependent employment" where the debtor is self-employed, e.g. the complete office of an insolvent doctor or lawyer. The idea is to give an incentive for the debtor to continue their business, the release mostly being under the condition of transferring a share of the new income to the estate.

Example: Debtor company D is obliged by environmental law to clean-up contamination at its plants. D lacks the necessary financial means and files for insolvency proceedings. The Insolvency Practitioner abandons the polluted real estate in order to escape the clean-up costs. This attempt is successful in Germany[43] but not in the USA where the Supreme Court held that an Insolvency Practitioner is not entitled to evade environmental law by using the power to abandon burdensome property.[44] 4.19

Whilst the estate is regularly composed of all the debtor's assets,[45] in some exceptional cases only a part of the debtor's assets are subject to the insolvency proceedings. The technical term for such proceedings is **particular insolvency proceedings**, because they deal with a partial estate only. Examples are insolvency proceedings that concern the inherited assets of a deceased[46] and proceedings which are restricted to domestic assets (whereas all other assets of the debtor are subject to foreign insolvency proceedings).[47] 4.20

For further reading: *Bork*, Einführung, §14 A.; *Fletcher*, Law of Insolvency, para. 8-002 et seq., 24-001 et seq.; *Saint-Alary-Houin*, Droit des enterprises en difficulté, para. 1237 et seq.; *Tabb*, Law of Bankruptcy, §5.1 et seq.; *van Zwieten*, Principles of Corporate Insolvency Law, Chapter 6. 4.21

43 The leading case is BVerwG, Urt. v. 23.9.2004 – 7 C 22/03 = NZI 2005, 51.
44 *Midland National Bank v. New Jersey Departement of Environmental Protection*, 474 U.S. 494 (1986).
45 Cf. above at para. 4.2 et seq.
46 See above at para. 2.10.
47 Details below at para. 10.9 et seq.

CHAPTER 5

EFFECTS OF THE OPENING OF INSOLVENCY PROCEEDINGS

In the fifth chapter we will learn how the opening of insolvency proceedings affects the estate and the current legal relationships between the debtor and its counterparty. This includes the decision as to whether executory contracts and pending lawsuits shall be terminated or continued and whether mutual rights to set-off can be enforced. However, not only the debtor's estate, but also the debtor itself can be affected, e.g. by dissolution and eventually liquidation of debtor companies. Furthermore, the legal position of creditors is also influenced, since they are now parties to collective enforcement proceedings and are no longer entitled to pursue their claims individually. 5.1

I. EFFECTS ON THE ESTATE

The fundamental idea of insolvency proceedings is to realise the debtor's assets (i.e. the insolvency estate) in collective enforcement proceedings to the benefit of the debtor's creditors.[1] Consequently, the **main effects** of the opening of insolvency proceedings are on the estate. At least in liquidation proceedings,[2] the debtor's assets are seized, the right of administration (below at para. 5.19) as well as the right of disposal (below at para. 5.4) are transferred from the debtor to the Insolvency Practitioner, and individual enforcement proceedings are displaced by the insolvency proceedings 5.2

1 Cf. above at para. 1.3.
2 For restructuring proceedings, particularly where they are debtor-in-possession proceedings, cf. below at para. 8.27.

(collective enforcement proceedings; below at para. 5.16).[3] The relevant rules aim at preserving the value of the estate, thus enforcing the principle of optimal realisation of the debtor's assets and ensuring the best possible satisfaction of creditors.

A. SEIZURE OF THE ESTATE

5.3 Implementing the basic idea of insolvency proceedings means to **confiscate the debtor's assets** in the first place. The estate, as described above in Chapter 4, is no longer managed for the benefit of the debtor but for the benefit of the creditors.[4] It is therefore withdrawn from the debtor and assigned to an Insolvency Practitioner who is tasked to realise the assets and distribute the proceeds among the creditors. Regularly, this effect is not expressly stated in the statutes. Unlike rules of individual enforcement law, insolvency law does not frequently mention the seizure or confiscation but is content instead with formulating the legal consequences of this impact for the debtor or even only for the Insolvency Practitioner. For many legislators, seizure of the insolvency estate is self-evident and does not need special reference.[5]

5.4 Instead, insolvency laws typically deal with the **transfer of the right of disposal** from the debtor to the Insolvency Practitioner.[6] At least in liquidation proceedings,[7] to liquidate the estate is the task of the Insolvency Practitioner who needs the right of disposal in order to be able to sell the assets at fair market value and pay the proceeds to the creditors on a *pro rata* basis. Complementarily, the right of disposal – if not the legal title[8] – must be withdrawn from the debtor who could otherwise transfer single

3 See the National Reports in *Faber/Vermunt/Kilborn/Richter*, Commencement of Insolvency Proceedings, each at para. 17 et seq.; further UNCITRAL Legislative Guide, p. 83 et seq., 161 et seq. and §3.2 PEIL: "Upon the opening of the proceedings the powers to manage and dispose of the assets are transferred to the administrator."

4 See the decision of the House of Lords in *Ayerst (Inspector of Taxes) v. C. & K. (Construction) Ltd.* [1976] AC 167.

5 Cf. below at para. 5.5.

6 See for §3.2 PEIL above in fn. 3.

7 In restructuring proceedings, leaving the debtor in their legal position – albeit under the supervision of the court and/or an Insolvency Practitioner – might be an option. For details of such debtor-in-possession proceedings, see below at para. 8.21 et seq.

8 In some jurisdictions, the legal title (for the meaning of this word see above at para. 4.4, fn. 10) over the estate is transferred to the Insolvency Practitioner. However, most national laws are content with shifting the right of disposal and administration from the debtor to the Insolvency Practitioner.

assets – particularly money – to single creditors thereby advantaging the recipient and violating the principle of equal treatment of creditors. Hence, it is basically a necessary consequence of the commencement of insolvency proceedings that the debtor is unable to transfer assets – be it movables or immovables –, to collect receivables, to terminate contracts, or to interfere in any other way with the estate.[9] However, the effect of the seizure is regularly restricted to the right to dispose of the estate in the sense that the debtor remains the owner of the assets (until they are sold by the Insolvency Practitioner),[10] keeps the right to dispose of assets which are not part of the estate,[11] and is still able to create new obligations (yet without binding the Insolvency Practitioner and without any effects for the estate and the insolvency proceedings[12]).

National laws put this in different words. For example, the French Code de Commerce does not refer to the seizure, yet simply transfers the right of management and disposal from the debtor to the Insolvency Practitioner (Art. L. 641-9(1) Code de Commerce). German law does not mention the seizure effect either, yet immediately and expressly transfers the right of disposal, with §80(1) Insolvenzordnung stating that upon the opening of the insolvency proceedings the debtor's right to manage and transfer the insolvency estate shall be vested in the Insolvency Practitioner. In England and Wales, sec. 143(1) Insolvency Act 1986 does not mention the debtor's rights[13] but describes the functions of the liquidator as "to secure that the assets of the company are got in, realised and distributed to the company's creditors" which is fostered by sec. 144(1), 167, para. 6 Sch. 4 Insolvency Act 1986 and which implies the transfer of the disposition right. US law goes a slightly different way. It mentions neither the seizure nor the debtor's disposition right but 5.5

9 For the administration of the estate, see below at para. 5.19.

10 Some national laws decide differently. For exceptions under English law, see sec. 306(1) Insolvency Act 1986 (the bankrupt's estate vests automatically in the trustee by force of law) and sec. 145(1) Insolvency Act 1986, according to which the court on application of the liquidator may order that property of the debtor vests in the liquidator. Cf. also *Re Stanford International Bank Ltd.* [2010] EWCA Civ 137 at para. 1 (for the law of Antigua).

11 Cf. above at para. 4.12 et seq.

12 Cf. above at para. 2.17.

13 In voluntary liquidation, the directors' powers cease according to sec. 103 Insolvency Act 1986. There is no similar rule for compulsory winding up, but it is recognised in case law that here the same applies, see *Re Farrow's Bank Ltd* [1921] 2 Ch 164 (CA) 173.

according to §363(b)(1) Bankruptcy Code,[14] the trustee "may use, sell, or lease (…) property of the estate",[15] which includes the disposal of cash. This rule is supported by §704(a)(1) Bankruptcy Code. However, the sale of assets belonging to the estate is hardly possible without the trustee's right of disposal. Interestingly, this does not coincide with the withdrawal of the debtor's disposition power, since it follows from the trustee's avoidance power in §549 Bankruptcy Code that post-commencement dispositions of the debtor are prohibited but not invalid.[16]

5.6 In most jurisdictions, the Insolvency Practitioner is granted an **unrestricted** right of disposal which means that Insolvency Practitioners have the legal power to dispose of the assets in any possible way. However, it goes without saying that this power is bound to the purposes of insolvency proceedings. Where these purposes are neglected, two kinds of legal sanctions are possible. One option would be to hold Insolvency Practitioners liable for damages if they did something they were legally able to do but not permitted to do. Another option would be to delimitate the Insolvency Practitioner's powers to acts in accordance with the purposes of insolvency proceedings, so that Insolvency Practitioners are legally not able to do what they are not permitted to do (*ultra vires* doctrine).[17]

5.7 **Example:** Where an Insolvency Practitioner gives an item belonging to the estate as a birthday gift to his or her spouse, this can either be invalid, because it is not covered by the Insolvency Practitioner's right of disposal. Or it can be valid but at the same time oblige the Insolvency Practitioner to pay damages to the estate, because the gift is covered by the power of disposal but not by the purposes of insolvency proceedings.

---

14 This rule requires notice and a hearing, which is not necessary if the Insolvency Practitioner continues to operate the debtor's business and acts in the ordinary course of business, §363(c)(1) Bankruptcy Code. For details, see rule 2002 Bankruptcy Rules, for establishing the ordinary course of business by either the horizontal dimension or the vertical dimension/creditor expectation test, see *Braunstein v. McCabe*, 571 F.3d 108 (1st Cir. 2009).

15 It is for this reason that §§521(a)(4), 542 Bankruptcy Code oblige the debtor and third parties to hand over all property of the estate in his or her possession to the trustee; cf. *In re Bentivegna*, No. 17-2727, 2017 BL 377254 (E.D. Pa. Oct. 20, 2017).

16 See para. 5.8 below. – However, doctrine in the US is unclear in this respect. Cf. *In re Chambers*, 575 B.R. 881 (Bankr. N.D. Iowa 2017): "legal title to assets of the estate vests in the trustee immediately by operation of law".

17 In England and Wales, an abuse of the powers of the Insolvency Practitioner is subject to control of the court (sec. 167(3), 168(5) Insolvency Act 1986). In Germany, abusive

Where debtors are deprived of their disposition right, **performances of the debtor** are invalid. This raises the question of acquisition in good faith. In many constellations, third parties who are not informed about the debtor's insolvency proceedings have no grounds to doubt the debtor's legal ability to dispose of their assets. Legislators therefore have to decide whether the third party's good faith should be protected, meaning that performances of the debtor to the benefit of parties acting in good faith are valid in spite of the debtor's lacking power of disposition, or whether the principle of equal treatment of creditors enjoys priority. For example, in Germany the invalidity of the debtor's performances is expressly stated in §81(1) Insolvenzordnung, permitting acquisition in good faith for titles to real estate only. US law goes the same way, since §549(c) Bankruptcy Code only protects "a transfer of an interest in (...) real property to a good faith purchaser without knowledge of the commencement of the case and for present fair value"; however, other transfers are not automatically void but may be voided by the trustee. In England and Wales, all dispositions made after the commencement of the winding up are void (sec. 127(1) Insolvency Act 1986). There is no protection of good faith but the court may order otherwise.[18] In French law it is deduced from Art. L. 641-9 Code de Commerce that transactions performed by the debtor after the opening of liquidation proceedings are void (or at least cannot be brought up as an objection to the claims of the estate[19]) and can be rescinded by the Insolvency Practitioner, even if the opponent had no knowledge of the debtor's insolvency. 5.8

Closely linked to the above-mentioned problem of performances *of* the debtor after the commencement of insolvency proceedings is the question of **performances *to* the debtor**: Can a third party who owes money to the debtor be exonerated from their obligation if the money is paid to the debtor instead of the Insolvency Practitioner? Since the debtor is no longer able to dispose of their assets, which includes the lack of legal competence to collect receivables, payments must be made to the Insolvency Practitioner. Where the third party knows of the debtor's insolvency proceedings, payments to the debtor are not satisfactory. The Insolvency Practitioner 5.9

transactions are only invalid if they are evidently incompatible with the purposes of insolvency proceedings (BGH, Urt. v. 14.6.2018 – IX ZR 232/17 = NJW 2018, 2494).

18 Cf. *Express Electrical Contractors Ltd v. Beavis* [2016] EWCA Civ. 765; *Re MKG Convenience Ltd. (in Liquidation) v. NISA Retail Ltd* [2019] EWHC 1383 (Ch).

19 See Cour de Cassation (chambre commerciale) – 3.11.2010 – 09-15546 = Bull. civ. 2010, IV, n° 163.

is still entitled to claim payment to the estate and the third party is referred to recollect the payment from the debtor, bearing the risk that the money is spent and no longer available. However, in some jurisdictions *bona fide* transactions are protected, so that the trustee cannot claim a second payment from the third party but can only claw-back the money from the debtor. For example, the German §82 Insolvenzordnung declares: "If the debtor received performance to settle an obligation after the opening of the insolvency proceedings although such obligation had to be performed to the credit of the insolvency estate, the performing party shall be discharged of his obligation if he was unaware of the opening of the proceedings at the time of his performance. If such party performed his obligation prior to publication of the order opening the proceedings, he shall be presumed to have been unaware of the opening of the proceedings." The same is true for US law. Here, collecting the property of the estate is the task of the trustee (§704(a)(1) Bankruptcy Code) and §542(b) Bankruptcy Code demands payment to the trustee. Payments to the debtor or other entities are only protected if the third party acted in good faith (without knowledge of the commencement of the case, §542(c) Bankruptcy Code).[20] Under French law, it is derived from Art. L. 641-9 Code de Commerce that payments to the debtor are invalid against the estate and that the Insolvency Practitioner can claim a second payment, even if the third party had no knowledge of the debtor's insolvency. In England and Wales, to call in receivables in liquidation proceedings is the duty of the court but normally transferred to the Insolvency Practitioner (sec. 160(1)(d) Insolvency Act 1986). However, there are no authorities, neither in statute nor in case law, dealing with the third party's payment to the debtor. Given that, under English law, the debtor holds the estate on trust for the creditors, payment to the debtor instead of the Insolvency Practitioner would most likely exonerate the third party.

5.10 **Examples:** Debtor D collects a life insurance sum of 2m from insurance company I which is unaware of the debtor's insolvency proceedings. Of this money, D pays 50,000 to creditor C and escapes with the rest to Uruguay. The Insolvency Practitioner cannot claim

20 §542(c) Bankruptcy Code implements the rule of the judgment of the US Supreme Court in *Bank of Marin v. England* (385 U.S. 99 [1966]) into the statute.

that I paid the wrong recipient if the applicable law protects the good faith of I.[21] However, the money is part of the estate[22] and D was not able to dispose of the money by paying C. Hence, the Insolvency Practitioner can claw-back the payment from C (unless C acted in good faith and the applicable law protects such good faith[23]) and must try to collect the rest from D.[24]

Debtor D gives creditor C a cheque drawn to D's bank B before the application for insolvency proceedings. After the application, C presents the check to B, which pays C. Where B is unaware of the application for insolvency proceedings, it enjoys *bona fide* protection. However, the payment can be challengeable against C under transactions avoidance law.[25] 5.11

A more complicated constellation is a performance of the debtor which has been commenced before, but finished after, the opening of the insolvency proceedings, e.g. by debtor D putting goods into a parcel and sending it to creditor C before the opening of proceedings who receives the goods after the opening of proceedings. Referred to the point in time where insolvency proceedings have been opened, this is a **pending acquisition** which is not easy to handle. The first question regards the point in time in which the debtor must be entitled to dispose of their assets. The answer depends on the applicable national law. If this law provides that the debtor's disposition right must be on hand until the completion of the performance (here: C receiving the parcel) the acquisition gets interrupted by the opening of the insolvency proceedings and the creditor's claim is not satisfied unless the applicable law protects good faith. If the national law is content with the debtor being entitled to dispose when conducting the performance (here: D dispatching the parcel) the debtor's subsequent loss 5.12

---

21 This was the result in a case decided by the German *Bundesgerichtshof*, see BGH, Urt. v. 15.4.2010 – IX ZR 62/09 = NJW 2010, 1806.

22 Cf. above at para. 4.5.

23 See above at para. 5.8.

24 This might be difficult if D is hiding abroad. Where large sums are at stake, Insolvency Practitioners involve so-called "asset tracers", tasking them with finding the money, and then try to freeze the debtor's assets abroad which can fail if D's host country does not cooperate.

25 Cf. for §§549, 550 Bankruptcy Code below at para. 6.14 and *Buckeye Check Cashing, Inc. v. Meadows (In re Meadows)*, 396 B.R. 485 (B.A.P. 6th Cir. 2008).

of the disposition right is innoxious unless the applicable insolvency law steps in and interrupts the acquisition process (possibly with an exception for good faith).

5.13 The latter solution can be found in many **jurisdictions**, either in statute or in case law, based on the conviction that no creditor should be able to improve their position after the opening of insolvency proceedings.[26] For example, according to the German §91 Insolvenzordnung, rights in objects forming part of the insolvency estate cannot be acquired with legal effect after the opening of the insolvency proceedings even if such acquisition of rights is not based on the debtor's transfer or effected by way of execution. Acquisition in good faith is only protected where titles to real estate are at stake. In England, similar effects are reached with the anti-deprivation rule,[27] according to which contractual provisions designed to remove assets held at the commencement of insolvency proceedings from the estate are void as being contrary to public policy unless it is a *bona fide* commercial transaction which does not have as its predominant purpose, or one of its main purposes, the deprivation of the estate. This rule is to some extent narrower than its German equivalent (the commencement of insolvency proceedings is required to be a trigger for the deprivation and only agreements are covered, not acquisition by force of law, or in any other way) and to some extent broader (proper commercial bargains executed in good faith are exempt), but it serves the same purpose, capturing transactions which have been commenced before and completed after the opening of insolvency proceedings. French law seems not to address this problem and under US law it is no problem, since (1) all perfection of creditors' rights is stayed by the commencement of insolvency proceedings (§362 (a) Bankruptcy Code) and (2) transactions of the debtor are subject to avoidance law no matter whether they were performed before or after the commencement of insolvency proceedings.[28] However, where precise allocation is necessary, it follows from §547(e) Bankruptcy Code that the time of perfection is decisive.

---

26 Cf. §3.4 PEIL: "Upon the opening of the proceedings a creditor with an insolvency claim cannot improve that creditor's position to the detriment of other creditors."

27 Extensively *Bork/Voelker*, The Anti-Deprivation Rule, Insolv. Int. 29 (2016), 65 et seq.; *Bork/Voelker*, §91 InsO und die Anti-Deprivation Rule, KTS 2013, 235 et seq.; *van Zwieten*, Principles of Corporate Insolvency Law, para. 7-01 et seq. The leading case is *Belmont Park Investments Pty Ltd v. BNY Corporate Trustee Services Ltd and Lehman Brothers Special Financing Inc* [2011] UKSC 38.

28 See above at para. 5.8 and below at para. 6.14.

Examples: In 2018, debtor D assigned all the company's current and future receivables to bank B as a security for a loan granted by B. After the opening of insolvency proceedings on 1 June 2020, the Insolvency Practitioner continues D's business and sells products manufactured in the debtor's factory to P on 15 September 2020. B claims the right to collect the purchase price from P. The receivables stemming from the contract between the Insolvency Practitioner and P are covered by the blanket assignment which D was able to stipulate, since in 2018 D was still entitled to dispose of their assets. However, the assignment had no effect on the claim against P before 15 September 2020, since receivables cannot be moved from one creditor to another before they come into existence. Hence, the assignment (or pledge or seizure) of future receivables leads to a pending acquisition and gets cut-off by the opening of insolvency proceedings where national (insolvency) laws provide for such interruption.[29] 5.14

S issues notes to noteholders which pay the consideration to B. B operates as a trustee holding the money paid by the noteholders on trust for the noteholders in case S goes insolvent. L, a London based company under English law, has agreed to pay S the amount necessary to satisfy the bondholders in exchange for rights to the trust, ranking prior to the rights of the noteholders. Only in case of L's insolvency, does the contract between S and L grant claims of the noteholders against B priority to the claims of L. Upon L's insolvency, the Insolvency Practitioner challenges this subordination clause as incompatible with the anti-deprivation rule. The UK Supreme Court decided to the contrary, finding that it was a commercially sensible transaction entered into in good faith.[30] 5.15

B. ENFORCEMENT BAN

A second – also necessary – effect of the opening of insolvency proceedings is a general enforcement ban.[31] Since insolvency proceedings 5.16

29 See for the USA §552(a) Bankruptcy Code and on this rule *Far East Natl. Bank v. U.S. Tr. (In re Premier Golf Props., LP)*, 477 B.R. 767 (B.A.P. 9th Cir. 2012); for Germany BGH, Urt. v. 18.4.2013 – IX ZR 165/12 = NZI 2013, 641.

30 Cf. above fn. 8.

31 Extensively UNCITRAL Legislative Guide, p. 83 et seq. and Recommendations 39–51.

are – at least for ordinary creditors – **collective enforcement proceedings**, parallel individual enforcement proceedings cannot be tolerated. They would favour the enforcing creditor who would receive full satisfaction to the detriment of all other creditors which is irreconcilable with the principle of equal treatment of creditors. Hence, such individual enforcement proceedings by ordinary creditors are not acceptable. They are also not necessary, since, firstly, the debtor's assets are already seized by the opening of the insolvency proceedings and can therefore not be seized a second time by individual enforcement proceedings, and, secondly, the claim of the creditor already gets enforced by the insolvency proceedings and does not need a second enforcement. As a result, ongoing enforcement proceedings commenced prior to the opening of insolvency proceedings must be stayed and new enforcement actions after the opening of insolvency proceedings are invalid or at least impermissible. Hence, official enforcement bodies (such as courts or bailiffs) must refrain from executing creditors' claims. However, this is only true for ordinary (unsecured) creditors whereas individual enforcement by secured or privileged creditors can be allowed.[32] In liquidation proceedings, the enforcement ban is typically an automatic legal consequence of the opening of the proceedings. However, in restructuring proceedings, enforcement bans are frequently at the discretion of the court which enables the court to tailor the ban to measure.

5.17 The enforcement ban described here must be distinguished from the **moratorium** as described above.[33] The former is a necessary effect of the opening of insolvency proceedings and continues until the end of the insolvency proceedings. The latter is a preliminary measure to protect the estate for a confined period of time, e.g. for the time necessary to decide on an application to open insolvency proceedings or necessary to prepare and implement a restructuring plan. It follows from these application areas that upon the opening of insolvency proceedings a moratorium (understood as a preliminary measure) is superseded by the enforcement ban (understood as a final measure).[34] Further, where the filing for insolvency proceedings commences such proceedings without any opening decision of the court (which is particularly the case for voluntary proceedings in the USA[35]), the moratorium cannot be distinguished from

32 For details, see below at para. 5.60 et seq., 7.13 et seq., 7.23 et seq.
33 At para. 3.7 et seq.
34 See also above at para. 3.10.
35 See §301(b) Bankruptcy Code and above at para. 3.2.

the enforcement ban because there is no preliminary phase during which a special protection of the estate is necessary.

Rules on enforcement ban can be found in many **national laws**. Examples are in England sec. 128(1) Insolvency Act 1986 ("any attachment, sequestration, distress or execution put in force against the estate or effects of the company after the commencement of the winding up is void"[36]), in France Art. L. 641-3, 622-21(2) Code de Commerce ("The issue of the commencement order shall also stay or prohibit any proceedings for enforcement on the part of these creditors on both movable and immovable properties in addition to any distribution procedure that did not result in a distribution prior to the commencement order") and in Germany §89(1) Insolvenzordnung ("individual insolvency creditors may not execute into the insolvency estate or into the debtor's other property during the insolvency proceedings"). All these rules tie the banning effect automatically to the opening decision. The same holds true for US law, where an automatic[37] enforcement stay is triggered by the filing for insolvency proceedings, §362(a)(2) Bankruptcy Code.[38] 5.18

C. ADMINISTRATION BY THE INSOLVENCY PRACTITIONER

It is the very own task of the Insolvency Practitioner to realise the debtor's assets, be it through sale of every single asset, or be it through asset deal or restructuring of the debtor company.[39] To fulfil this task, the Insolvency Practitioner does not only need the right of disposal (which is more of a technical relevance) but also the **right to manage the estate**. Principally, the Insolvency Practitioner must be entitled to all transactions – acts of disposition as well as contracts, but also mere factual measures – which are necessary to ensure the optimal realisation of the debtor's assets and 5.19

36 See also sec. 130(2) Insolvency Act 1986 and for not completed enforcement proceedings sec. 183(1) Insolvency Act 1986.

37 *McCarthy, Johnson & Miller v. N. Bay Plumbing, Inc. (In re Pettit)*, 217 F.3d 1072, 24 EBC 2695 (9th Cir. 2000).

38 In involuntary cases, the filing for insolvency proceedings also triggers the automatic stay (§362 (a) Bankruptcy Code) which continues after the opening decision of the court (order for relief).

39 Cf. above at para. 2.40.

the best possible satisfaction of the creditors' claims. This includes taking the assets in possession, administering the estate (e.g. by collecting debts from third parties, selling perishable goods, insuring valuable assets, or – more generally – by continuing the debtor's business), valorising the estate, and finally paying the proceeds proportionally to the creditors.[40] In accomplishing their duties, Insolvency Practitioners act as private persons which are commissioned by the court, the company, or the creditors[41] to administer the proceedings and the debtor's estate-related affairs as a "representative of the estate" (§323(a) Bankruptcy Code) or "agent of the company" (para. 69 Sch. B1 Insolvency Act 1986).

5.20 It depends on national law as well as on the nature of the proceedings in question whether and to what extent the right to manage the estate is – similar to the right of disposal – **shifted from the debtor to the Insolvency Practitioner**. This would mean that the debtor is no longer entitled to decide and act for the estate which, in the case of insolvent entrepreneurs, includes the debarment from running the business. Typically, this is the case in regular liquidation proceedings.[42] Alternatively, the debtor can be left in charge, be it in full or restrictively, be it uncontrolled or under the supervision of the court and/or an Insolvency Practitioner.[43]

5.21 Where the right of management is shifted to the Insolvency Practitioner, he or she is typically entitled to **all actions necessary** to fulfil his or her tasks when liquidating or restructuring the estate. However, national laws frequently implement elements of control, either by requiring leave of the court or consent of a creditors' committee or a creditors' meeting.[44] In the USA, for example, the trustee is entitled to all actions which are in the ordinary course of business whilst other transactions need "notice and

---

40 More details are listed in UNCITRAL Legislative Guide, p. 178 et seq.; see also the list of powers in Sch. 4 Insolvency Act 1986, §§363, 704 Bankruptcy Code and §4.1 PEIL: "The administrator collects and manages the debtor's assets."

41 See above at para. 2.42.

42 See for England and Wales sec. 167 Insolvency Act 1986, Sch. 4 Insolvency Act 1986; for France Art. L. 641-9(1) Code de Commerce; for Germany §80(1) Insolvenzordnung; for the USA §§363, 704 Bankruptcy Code; cf. above at para. 5.5.

43 Such debtor-in-possession proceedings are essential elements of national restructuring laws with which we will deal in more detail below at para 8.21 et seq.

44 Cf. §4.2 PEIL: "Management actions of major importance may be subject to the consent of the court or the creditors."

a hearing" (§363(b)/(c) Bankruptcy Code). In Germany, the Insolvency Practitioner shall obtain the consent of the creditors' committee if he or she intends to engage in transactions which are of particular importance to the insolvency proceedings.[45]

Example: Insolvency Practitioner P intends to terminate the contracts of some employees who are no longer needed for the further course of liquidation of the debtor company's business. He has the power to do so (without any participation of the debtor or its directors respectively), since he has now the right to manage the debtor company's affairs. This includes termination of contracts. However, insolvency law prerequisites and such of labour law must be met,[46] since the Insolvency Practitioner is not exempt from the applicable contract law unless insolvency law provides otherwise. 5.22

Where Insolvency Practitioners continue the business of the debtor they need the **right to use and to consume** assets belonging to the estate. For example, continuing the production of goods requires the use of the production machines and the consumption of commodities. Some national laws, when describing the powers of the Insolvency Practitioner, mention the right of usage and consumption expressly (e.g. §363(b)(1) Bankruptcy Code) while in others this right is included in the general administration right or the right to continue the debtor's business. Such empowering is quite natural where the usage and consumption of the debtor's assets belonging to the estate is at stake. However, such assets can be encumbered with security rights for third parties (e.g. a lien for a landlord) or can belong to third parties (e.g. delivery under retention of title or transfer of title by way of security). In these cases, third parties have a right of separate satisfaction or even of separation and it is highly questionable whether the Insolvency Practitioner is entitled to use and consume third parties' property. We will deal with this problem later on in this book.[47] 5.23

45 Cf. above at para. 2.35.

46 See below at para. 5.40 et seq.

47 See for now UNCITRAL Legislative Guide, p. 104 et seq.; more below at para. 7.15 et seq.

5.24 ***For further reading***: *Bork*, Einführung, §§14, 15; *Bork*, Rescuing Companies, para. 10.01 et seq.; *Fletcher*, Law of Insolvency, 22.006 et seq., 22-076 et seq.; *Saint-Alary-Houin*, Droit des enterprises en difficulté, para. 692 et seq., 1223, 1237 et seq.; *Tabb*, Law of Bankruptcy, §5.12 et seq., 5.16 et seq.; *van Zwieten*, Principles of Corporate Insolvency Law, para. 5-24, 13-21 et seq.

II. EFFECTS ON CONTRACTS

5.25 Every debtor who is subject to insolvency proceedings is party to **ongoing contracts**. Typically, natural persons have executory contracts with landlords, energy suppliers, telecommunication enterprises, banks, employers, or sport clubs, legal entities have contracts with employees, suppliers, customers, etc. Such contracts can be obsolete where the debtor is no longer able to perform; the continued performance of them can be detrimental to the estate and the general body of creditors; yet it can conversely also be advantageous or even essential for preserving the value of the estate or continuing the debtor's business. Hence, in every insolvency, the fate of these contracts has to be examined: are they automatically terminated by the opening of the insolvency proceedings or are they binding on the estate, do Insolvency Practitioners have an extraordinary right to terminate the contract or can they even chose whether they wish to continue the contractual relationship with the counterparty or not? Answers vary, depending on the national law, the kind of insolvency proceedings, and the nature of the contract.[48]

A. GENERAL

5.26 Restricting the reflection for now to liquidation proceedings, in many jurisdictions, contracts remain untouched where the **contract has been fulfilled by one party**. If either the debtor or the counterparty has already delivered the owed performance and is now waiting for the other side to

[48] See the National Reports in *Faber/Vermunt/Kilborn/Richter*, Commencement of Insolvency Proceedings, each at para. 23 et seq., and also in *Faber/Vermunt/Kilborn/van der Linde*, Treatment of Contracts, passim; further UNCITRAL Legislative Guide, p. 119 et seq.; *Chuah/Vaccari*, Executory Contracts in Insolvency Law.

pay, no reason exists to question the continuance of the contract. If it is the counterparty who has already delivered, such a counterparty is the typical ordinary creditor who, as an effect of the advance performance, has to file the claim for the counter-performance owed by the debtor with the court or the Insolvency Practitioner and can expect nothing more than satisfaction on a *pro rata* basis.[49] If it is the debtor who has already performed, the debtor's claim to payment is part of the estate. It is the task of the Insolvency Practitioner to collect the outstanding debt,[50] if necessary, by suing the counterparty for payment. In all these cases, the contract survives the opening of insolvency proceedings and is the legal cause for the mutual performances and obligations.

This is different where contracts are **not performed by either party.** 5.27
In such cases the law must decide whether the executory contract[51] subsists for the future and if and how the ongoing contract can be terminated. Various options are available and all can be found in current insolvency laws.[52] One option is to terminate the contract by force of law with immediate effect upon the opening of the insolvency proceedings. Examples are agency agreements, which in some jurisdictions are immediately terminated because it is now the task of the Insolvency Practitioner to act as an agent of the estate (and not the task of third parties who derive their competence from the debtor who has lost the right of administration and disposal[53]). Another option for legislators is to order the continuance of the contract with binding effect for the Insolvency Practitioner, which leaves the office holder with the same regular contractual termination rights as the debtor had before the opening of insolvency proceedings, unless the law provides for extraordinary termination rights. Laws contain such regulations mostly in order to protect the debtor (particularly insolvent natural persons) against being deprived of all contractual relationships as

49 Cf. *Bailey and another v. Angove's PTY Limited* [2016] UKSC 47 at para. 26.

50 See above at para. 5.9.

51 For the purposes of insolvency law, the term "executory contracts" is defined as a contract under which the obligations of both the debtor and the counterparty are so far unperformed; see for US law *Countryman*, Executory Contracts in Bankruptcy, 57 (1973) Minn. L. Rev. 439, 460 and *Tabb*, Law of Bankruptcy, §8.2. *Countryman's* definition has also coined English law, cf. *van Zwieten*, Principles of Corporate Insolvency Law, para. 6-22. German §103 Insolvenzordnung is construed accordingly, cf. BGH, Urt. v. 21.10.2015 – I ZR 173/14 = NZI 2016, 97; BGH, Urt. v. 15.11.1999 – II ZR 98/98 = NZI 2000, 126.

52 For details, see below at para. 5.32 et seq.

53 Cf. above at para. 5.4, 5.19 and below at para. 5.32.

soon as insolvency proceedings are opened. Examples in many – but by no means all – jurisdictions are lease agreements and particularly employment contracts which then survive the opening of insolvency proceedings (so that the employees do not lose their jobs immediately) but can possibly be terminated by the Insolvency Practitioner under facilitated conditions. A third option would be to leave it to the discretion of the Insolvency Practitioner whether he or she wishes to continue the contractual relationship or not.[54] In the first case, mutual obligations must be fulfilled by both the Insolvency Practitioner and the counterparty. In the second case, the contract can lapse or at least not be binding for the estate.

5.28 **National laws** approach the problem on different routes. For example, German insolvency law does, in §§103 et seq. Insolvenzordnung, not interfere where one party has already performed. Where both parties have not (or only partly) performed, some kinds of contracts are declared terminated by force of law upon the opening of proceedings, and some are declared to continue, and for all others termination is at the discretion of the Insolvency Practitioner. The latter solution is predominant in the US, since §365 Bankruptcy Code assigns to the trustee – albeit with a vast number of exceptions and subject to the court's approval – the right to "assume or reject any executory contract or unexpired lease of the debtor". The same holds true for England and Wales. Here, the opening of insolvency proceedings as such has no direct effect on the debtor's contracts. Instead, sec. 178(2)/(3)(a) Insolvency Act 1986 enables the Insolvency Practitioner to disclaim of "onerous" contracts which are not profitable for the estate. Alternatively, the Insolvency Practitioner can simply decline to perform, leaving the counterparty with the choice to

54 This solution is supported by the PEIL:

§6.1: "The opening of the proceedings does not automatically terminate a contract to which the debtor is a party."

§6.2: "The other party cannot enforce performance by the administrator."

§6.3: "(1) If the administrator demands performance of a contract which at the time of the opening of the proceedings neither party has fully performed, the debtor's obligations arising out of the contract must be satisfied as they fall due and in priority to insolvency claims. (2) If the administrator has decided not to perform such a contract, any claim of the other party based on non-performance of the contract is an insolvency claim. (3) The other party can demand that the administrator decides within a reasonable time whether to adopt the contract or not."

either claim for damages for breach of contract as an unsecured ordinary creditor (sec. 178(6) Insolvency Act 1986) or apply to the court for rescission of the contract under sec. 186 Insolvency Act 1986. However, this only applies to liquidation proceedings, whereas in administration and other rescuing proceedings no special rules on contracts are available; hence, they can only be terminated in accordance with their terms or general contract law. Similar results can be found in France. Under French law, all contracts survive the opening of insolvency proceedings but the Insolvency Practitioner is entitled to require the debtor's contracting party to perform executory contracts in exchange for the performance of the debtor's obligations (Art. L. 622-13(2), 641-11-1(2) Code de Commerce).

Interestingly, there are many **similarities between German and US law.** 5.29
In both jurisdictions, a contract is deemed to be performed by one side (and therefore not executory) if this party has substantially performed its main obligations, even if secondary obligations are still open;[55] in both jurisdictions the Insolvency Practitioner's right to choose is protected against "*ipso facto* clauses", i.e. contract clauses which provide for the termination or modification of the contract upon the debtor's insolvency (§119 Insolvenzordnung, §365(e) Bankruptcy Code);[56] in both jurisdictions, the Insolvency Practitioner's decision to assume the contract entails the application of general contract law;[57] in both jurisdictions, the contract is deemed to be rejected on the Insolvency Practitioner's inactivity within a certain period of time (triggered either by law or by request of the counterparty, §103(2)(2)/(3) Insolvenzordnung, §365(d) Bankruptcy Code);[58] and, in both jurisdictions, the counterparty has

---

55 See for Germany BGH, Urt. v. 16.5.2019 – IX ZR 44/18 = NJW 2019, 2166; Urt. v. 19.11.2015 – IX ZR 198/14 = NJW 2016, 711; for the USA *In re Exide Technologies*, 607 F.3d 957 (3rd Cir. 2012); *In re Interstate Bakeries*, 751 F.3d 955 (8th Cir. 2014).

56 For France, see Art. L. 622-13(1), 641-11-1(1) Code de Commerce accordingly. Whether this holds also true under the law of England and Wales is under debate, since the decision of the UK Supreme Court in *Belmont Park Investments Pty Ltd v. BNY Corporate Trustee Services Ltd and Lehman Brothers Special Financing Inc* [2011] UKSC 38 suggests that *ipso facto* clauses are pit against the anti-deprivation rule (above at para. 5.13) but are regularly judged as being commercially sensible; cf. *van Zwieten*, Principles of Corporate Insolvency Law, para. 7-14.

57 This means that the counterparty can terminate the contract only if the law applicable to the kind of contract in question allows for such termination. – For the counter-claim of the other party, see below at para. 5.33.

58 Similarly in France, Art. L. 641-11-1(3)No. 1 Code de Commerce. As opposed to this, the contract cannot be disclaimed under English law if the Insolvency Practitioner failed to disclaim within 28 days after being required by an interested person to do decide on this matter, sec. 178(5) Insolvency Act 1986.

an unsecured pre-proceedings damages claim for breach of contract as an ordinary creditor if the Insolvency Practitioner chooses to reject the contract (§103(2)(1) Insolvenzordnung, §§365(g), 502(g)(1) Bankruptcy Code).[59]

5.30 **Example**: Debtor D has ordered a truck from V. Where V has already delivered the truck, he has to file his claim for the purchase price with the Insolvency Practitioner or court and will be treated as an ordinary creditor. Where D has already paid the purchase price, the Insolvency Practitioner can claim the delivery of the truck. Where neither party has performed, the Insolvency Practitioner can chose between accepting (which will happen if the truck is necessary for the insolvency proceedings, e.g. for continuing the business or for delivering goods already manufactured and sold, or if it was simply a very good deal and he or she can sell the truck at a higher price) and rejecting the contract (which will be advisable if the company will be liquidated and the truck is no longer needed for the conduct of the proceedings).[60]

B. EXECUTORY CONTRACTS

5.31 National laws vary significantly as regards the treatment of executory contracts which shall be illustrated taking some **typical kinds of contracts** as examples.

1. *Agency Agreements*

5.32 As indicated above,[61] agency agreements deserve closer consideration. Agents who have been commissioned by the debtor derive their competence to act for the estate from the debtor's power to manage the estate and dispose of the assets. If, upon the opening of insolvency proceedings, these powers and rights are transferred to the Insolvency Practitioner, the debtor is no longer legitimised to act for the estate and neither are their agents. On the contrary, this is now the **exclusive**

---

59 Similarly sec. 178(6) Insolvency Act 1986 in England and Wales and Art. L. 641-11-1(5) Code de Commerce in France.

60 See also below at para. 5.33 et seq.

61 At para. 5.27.

competence of the Insolvency Practitioner. It is for this reason, that, in many jurisdictions, the opening of insolvency proceedings entails the termination of all agency agreements, frequently including the termination of representative authority. However, in jurisdictions where account agreements with banks are classified as agency agreements, the result of such rules would be that the debtor is no longer holder of a bank account. Examples for the automatic termination of agency contracts are the German §§115–116 Insolvenzordnung. Similarly, in England and Wales, all agency contracts – as are employment contracts[62] – are terminated as an effect of the winding-up order of the court.[63] No special regime exists in the USA so that agency agreements are subject to the general rule in §365(a) Bankruptcy Code which gives the trustee the choice between assumption and rejection.[64] The same holds true for France where agency contracts are not automatically terminated by the opening of insolvency proceedings.[65] Hence, it is for the Insolvency Practitioner to decide under Art. L. 641-11-1(2) Code de Commerce whether the contract shall be assumed or rejected.

2. *Sales Agreements*

The fate of sales agreements depends on the factual circumstances. Where the **buyer is insolvent**, the counterparty who has already delivered is referred to filing the claim for payment with the court or the Insolvency Practitioner as an ordinary creditor.[66] However, vendors can secure themselves by retention of title which entitles them to terminate the contract and to rescind the goods delivered to the debtor, thereby enforcing a right to separation.[67] If the counterparty has not yet delivered, the contract is not yet executed by both parties. In many jurisdictions the law entitles the Insolvency Practitioner to decide whether the contract shall bind the estate or not. Examples are in English law sec. 178 Insolvency Act 1986, in France Art. L. 641-11-1(2) Code de Commerce, in German law §103 Insolvenzordnung and in the USA §365(a) Bankruptcy Code. 5.33

62 Cf. below at para. 5.43.

63 *Gosling v. Gaskell and Grocott* [1897] AC 575 (HL); the power of attorney can be void under sec. 284(1) Insolvency Act 1986, *Sanders v. Donovan* [2012] BPIR 219.

64 See above at para. 5.28.

65 Cour de Cassation (chambre commerciale) – 28.06.2017 – 15-17394 = ECLI:FR:CCASS:2017:CO00987. An exception can be found in Art. L. 641-12-1 Code de Commerce for trust agreements where the debtor is the beneficiary.

66 See above at para. 5.26.

67 More on this above at para. 2.23 and below at para. 7.22.

If the decision is in favour of continuation the contract is binding on the estate and the Insolvency Practitioner may demand delivery from the counterparty in exchange for paying the agreed price as expenses of the proceedings.[68] If the Insolvency Practitioner declines continuance of the agreement it depends on national law whether the contract is terminated by this decision[69] or still in force but only binding on the debtor (and to be transacted by the debtor and the counterparty after the termination of insolvency proceedings).[70]

5.34 Where the **vendor is insolvent**, the same rules generally apply. If neither party has performed the sales agreement is either terminated by law or the Insolvency Practitioner is entitled to choose. This is sometimes restricted if the debtor has delivered under retention of title. In this case national laws try to protect the buyer by excluding the extraordinary termination right of the Insolvency Practitioner and guaranteeing the buyer's right to acquire title by paying the agreed price.[71] If the buyer has made an advance payment, filing the claim for the counter-performances (or for damages) with the court or the Insolvency Practitioner is due. If the debtor has already delivered the Insolvency Practitioner can claim the agreed price to be paid to the estate by the buyer. Another exception can be found for real estate purchase agreements. As opposed to France and Germany, special rules are available under English law (where the buyer is deemed to have equitable ownership which he or she should not be deprived of[72]) and particularly in the USA under §365(i) Bankruptcy Code. If the vendor of real estate property is subject to insolvency proceedings and the Insolvency Practitioner choses to reject the contract according to §365(a) Bankruptcy Code, the buyer may treat the contract as terminated

---

68 See on that above at para. 2.25 and for England and Wales *Re Lundy Granite Co Ex p. Heavan* [1871] 6. Ch. App. 462; for Germany §55(1)No. 2 Insolvenzordnung. For the USA, it is derived from §365(g)(2) Bankruptcy Code, cf. *In re Norwegian Health Spa, Inc.*, 79 B.R. 507 (Bankr. N.D. Ga. 1987). In France, such debts shall be paid as soon as they fall due (Art. L. 641-11-1(2)(2), 641-13(1) Code de Commerce), otherwise the creditor's claim enjoys priority according to Art. L. 641-13(2) Code de Commerce.

69 This is the effect of the Insolvency Practitioners disclaimer under sec. 178 Insolvency Act 1986 in England and Wales.

70 This is the case in Germany unless the counterparty terminates the contract with the debtor, cf. BGH, Urt. v. 25.4.2002 – IX ZR 313/99 = BGHZ 155, 353. The same holds true in the USA where "rejection" of the contract does not equal "termination", cf. §365(i) Bankruptcy Code and extensively *Tabb*, Law of Bankruptcy, §8.7.

71 See for Germany §107(1) Insolvenzordnung.

72 *Pearce v. Bastable's Tristee in Bankruptcy* [1901] 2 Ch. 122; *Re Bastable Ex. P. trustee* [1901] 2 K. B. 518.

or may remain in possession, provided the vendee was in possession at the time of the commencement of the proceedings. If the buyer remains in possession he or she has to continue all payments due under the purchase agreement. If the buyer treats the contract as terminated, he or she has a claim for damages (§§365(g)(1), 502(g)(1) Bankruptcy Code) but is protected through a statutory lien securing the recovery of the already paid portion of the purchase price (§365(j) Bankruptcy Code).

3. *Lease Contracts*

Of significant importance are lease contracts. Frequently, natural persons are living in leased premises and have a huge interest in not being immediately homeless upon the opening of insolvency proceedings. Similarly, companies which operate their business from leased premises can only continue business and be restructured if the lease agreement is not terminated by the opening of insolvency proceedings. Many national laws **protect the debtor** and their interests by providing for the continuance of the contract with the landlord, sometimes combined with extraordinary termination rights for the Insolvency Practitioner but not for the landlord. This gives the Insolvency Practitioner the choice to either continue the tenancy (which entails the obligation to pay the rent as expenses of the proceedings[73]) or to terminate the tenancy if the premises are either not needed or not affordable, whereas the landlord can only terminate the agreement according to general contract law. 5.35

When it comes to national laws, such rules can be found in **German law** where §108 Insolvenzordnung provides for the continuance of lease agreements (albeit for immovables only[74]). This leads to the application of general contract law if the landlord is insolvent. If the debtor is the tenant, the landlord is not allowed to terminate the contract for behindhand rents due before the opening of insolvency proceedings (§112 Insolvenzordnung) and the Insolvency Practitioner is enabled not only to terminate the contract deviant from general contract law at a term of three months but also to release the lease contract from the estate,[75] so that the debtor can keep their home and pay the rent from unseizable income (§109 Insolvenzordnung). 5.36

---

73 See again above at para. 2.25, 5.33.

74 Hence, lease agreements concerning (e.g.) computers or cars are subject to the Insolvency Practitioner's choice not to continue the contract, §103 Insolvenzordnung (above at para. 5.33).

75 On this, see above at para. 4.18.

5.37 Under **French law**, it follows from Art. L. 641-12(1)No.1 Code de Commerce that in principle the general rule in Art. L. 641-11-1(2) Code de Commerce applies also to lease contracts. Hence, such contracts are not terminated automatically upon the opening of liquidation proceedings but are subject to the Insolvency Practitioner's choice to assume or reject the agreement. However, there are some modifications for the lease of real estate used by the debtor for business activities in Art. L. 641-12 Code de Commerce. This norm gives the debtor's landlord permission to apply to the court for termination of the tenancy agreement, even if the Insolvency Practitioner decided not to reject the contract, if the reason for the termination of the agreement occurred prior to the opening of the proceedings (Art. L. 641-12(1)Nr.2 Code de Commerce) or the rent related to the time after the opening of the proceedings has not been paid for at least three months (Art. L. 641-12(1)No.3 Code de Commerce).

5.38 In the **USA**, in principle the general rule of §365(a) Bankruptcy Code applies which gives the trustee the choice between assumption and rejection.[76] However, where the lease concerns personal property and the debtor is an individual in liquidation (Chapter 7) proceedings, the debtor may notify the creditor in writing that her or she desires to assume the lease (§365(p)(2) Bankruptcy Code). The lessor may, at its option, accept this "assumption" or not. If it is accepted, the debtor is entitled to possession but also has to pay the rent personally from unseizable income (not from the estate). Another special regime exists where the debtor is a landlord and the counter-party is the lessee under a (not expired) real estate lease. If the trustee decides to reject the tenancy agreement, §365(h) Bankruptcy Code gives the tenant – similar to a buyer[77] – the choice between treating the contract as terminated or to retain the right under the lease. In the former case, the tenant has to relinquish the premises and can file a claim for damages as an unsecured creditor[78] with the court or the Insolvency Practitioner (§§365(g)(1), 502(g)(1) Bankruptcy Code). In the latter case, the lessee has to pay the rent and may remain in possession, both as agreed in the contract, but cannot claim any performance of the debtor or the estate (e.g. regarding maintenance, etc.). This may cause damages which

76 See above at para. 5.28.

77 Cf. above at para. 5.34. For license agreements, see §365(n) Bankruptcy Code.

78 *Doral Commerce Park, Ltd. v. Teleglobe Communications Corp. (In re Teleglobe Communications Corp.)*, 304 B.R. 79 (D. Del. 2004).

can be off-set against the future rent (§365(h)(1)(B) Bankruptcy Code), not against the estate.[79]

In **England and Wales**, the general rule in sec. 178 Insolvency Act 1986 applies. Hence, the Insolvency Practitioner can disclaim of "onerous" lease contracts, bringing them to an end for the period in time starting with the disclaimer (sec. 178(4)(a) Insolvency Act 1986). However, this is only true as far as the purpose is pursued to hold the estate free from further liabilities.[80] For example, if the premises have been subleased to a third party, the sublease will continue between the landlord and the subtenant as if leased by the latter directly from the former. 5.39

4. *Employment Contracts*

Of similar importance is the destiny of employment contracts. Many national laws attempt to **protect the employees** of an insolvent employer by providing for the continuance of the employment contract. If so, employees do not lose their jobs upon the opening of the employer's insolvency proceedings, can claim wages for the time after the opening of proceedings as expenses of the proceedings,[81] and can only be made redundant according to general labour law, albeit with certain aggravations, e.g. regarding the period of notice or the necessary involvement of work councils, etc.[82] 5.40

For example, under **German law,** the debtor's employment contracts with employees are neither terminated by force of law nor are they subject to the Insolvency Practitioner's right to assume or reject the contract. Instead, employment contracts survive the opening of insolvency proceedings according to §108(1) Insolvenzordnung and are assigned to general labour law. Consequently, the Insolvency Practitioner who wants to reduce the number of employees (or even make all of them redundant) has to observe the legal prerequisites and limits of dismissal. Insolvency law offers little support in this regard, except for §113 Insolvenzordnung (which delimits notice periods to a maximum of three months) and §§120 et seq. (which 5.41

---

79 *McDonald's Corp. v. Stratosphere Corp. (In re Stratosphere Corp.)*, 23 Fed. Appx. 749 (9th Cir. 2001).

80 *Hindcastle Ltd v. Barbara Attenborough Associates Ltd* [1997] AC 70.

81 Cf. *In re Spectrum Info. Techs., Inc.*, 193 B.R. 400 (Bankr. E.D.N.Y. 1996).

82 See §7.1 PEIL: "The administrator or the employee may terminate a contract of employment following special rules."

facilitate necessary negotiations with the works council). For the time period between the opening of insolvency proceedings and the dismissal coming into effect employees are preferential creditors with their wage claims which have to be paid as expenses of the proceedings out of the estate, whereas employees with claims dated back to the time prior to the opening of the proceedings are unsecured ordinary creditors.

5.42 **US law** does not contain special rules on employment contracts. Hence, §365(a) Bankruptcy Code applies here as well which gives the trustee the choice between assumption and rejection.[83] Special protection exists only in debtor-in-possession proceedings where §1113 Bankruptcy Code confirms the right to choose between assumption and rejection for collective bargaining agreements (but denies a unilateral right to change such agreements) and §1114 hinders the debtor to modify retiree benefit unless the court orders so. However, individual employees are not protected at all.

5.43 In **England and Wales**, employment contracts are treated differently. Here, the general disclaimer rule of sec. 178 Insolvency Act 1986 does not apply in liquidation. Instead, the publication of the winding-up order of the court operates as a notice of dismissal to all employees,[84] but the liquidator is entitled to waive this effect and to continue employing those who are needed for carrying on the debtor's business or properly liquidating the estate.[85] In administration proceedings, employment contracts are not automatically terminated. Instead, the administrator may decide whether he or she wishes to continue employing the debtor's employees or not, and has 14 days to reach this decision under para. 99(5) Sch. B1 Insolvency Act 1986.[86] After this deadline passes, the administrator is considered to have affirmed the employment contracts, and they continue to apply as usual. The primary consequence of this affirmation is that claims for salaries and wages gain super priority under para. 99(5)/(6) Sch. B1 Insolvency Act 1986, so that they are paid even before the expenses of the administration. In affirmed employment contracts, general labour law applies as usual and such contracts may only be terminated by either side in accordance with its terms.

---

83 See above at para. 5.28 and *In re Spectrum Info. Techs., Inc.*, 193 B.R. 400 (Bankr. E.D.N.Y. 1996).

84 *Re General Rolling Stock Co v. Chapman's Case* [1865–66] L.R. 1 Eq. 346; *In re Oriental Bank Corp (MacDowall's Case)* [1886] 32 Ch. D. 366.

85 *Ex parte Harding* [1867] 3 Eq. 341.

86 The short time is criticised in *Powdrill v. Watson* [1995] 2 AC 394.

In **France**, Art. L. 641-11-1(6) Code de Commerce exempts employment contracts from the Insolvency Practitioner's general right to choose between assumption and rejection. Hence, employment agreements are not affected automatically by the opening of the insolvency proceedings. This entails principally the application of general labour law. However, Art. L. 641-10(3), 631-17 Code de Commerce modify the right of dismissal on both a substantive and a procedural level. Substantively, the law requires the dismissal to be urgent, inevitable, and indispensable for economic reasons. As regards proceedings, the Insolvency Practitioner shall implement a dismissal plan in accordance with Art. L. 1233-57-4, 1233-58 Code du travail and ask the court for permission to give notice. 5.44

For further reading: *Bork*, Einführung, §16; *Bork*, Rescuing Companies, para. 12.01 et seq.; *Fletcher*, Law of Insolvency, para. 8.017 et seq., 16.119 et seq., 22.005, 26.017; *Saint-Alary-Houin*, Droit des enterprises en difficulté,. 613 et seq., 1258 et seq.; *Tabb*, Law of Bankruptcy, §8.1 et seq.; *van Zwieten*, Principles of Corporate Insolvency Law, para. 6-21 et seq. 5.45

III. EFFECTS ON TRIALS

Similar questions as to the effects of the opening of the insolvency proceedings on contracts are raised as to the effects on current trials. It is a **consequence of the shift of the right of administration and disposal**[87] that the procedural enforcement of claims which are property of the estate is no longer within the power of the debtor. Instead, it is the Insolvency Practitioner who is tasked with litigation. This typically condenses in three rules: first, trials are halted as an effect of the opening of insolvency proceedings; second, where the debtor is the claimant, the Insolvency Practitioner has a choice between continuing the trial with effect for the estate (so that the proceeds fall into the estate if the case is won and the costs are borne by the estate if the case is lost) or releasing[88] the trial (so that the debtor may continue and keep the proceeds if the case is won 5.46

87 Above at para. 5.19.

88 For the concept of release from the estate, see above at para. 4.18.

against the expectations of the Insolvency Practitioner); third, where the debtor is the defendant, the claimant creditor is bound to file the claim with the court and/or the Insolvency Practitioner.[89]

5.47 These rules can be found in various **national laws**. For example, in Germany, trials are suspended upon the opening of insolvency proceedings (§240 Zivilprozessordnung). Where the debtor was the claimant, it is for the Insolvency Practitioner to decide whether the trial shall be continued with effect for the estate or be released to the benefit of the debtor (§85 Insolvenzordnung). Where the debtor was the defendant, continuation of the trial is impermissible, since the claimant has to file the claim with the Insolvency Practitioner and can only continue litigation if the filing is objected by the Insolvency Practitioner or another creditor (§§87, 180(2) Insolvenzordnung). Under US law, all actions against the debtor are stayed as an effect of the commencement of insolvency proceedings (§362(a)(1) Bankruptcy Code).[90] This includes trial proceedings and arbitration.[91] It follows from rule 6009 Bankruptcy Rules, that it is for the trustee to decide whether the trial shall be continued or not, no matter whether the debtor was the claimant (plaintiff) or the defendant. Creditors have to file their claims under §501 Bankruptcy Code, Rules 3002(b), 5005(a)(1) Bankruptcy Rules with the clerk of the court where the case is pending. Similar rules apply under English law, since all actions and proceedings against the debtor are automatically stayed and may not be continued by the Insolvency Practitioner or the creditor without leave of the court (sec. 130(2) Insolvency Act 1986). As a result, the creditor is referred to file for proof of claims with the Insolvency Practitioner under rules 14.2. et seq. Insolvency Rules 2016.[92] In France, it follows from Art. L. 641-3(1), 622-21(1)No.1 Code de Commerce, Art. 360 Code de procedure civile that legal proceedings against the debtor are also affected by the stay. Instead, creditors shall submit their claims to the liquidator (Art. L. 641-3(4) Code de Commerce). This is confirmed by Art. L. 641-3(1), 622-22, R. 622-20 Code de Commerce which orders the stay to be continued until it is necessary to resume the proceedings in order to verify the

89 For details, see below at para. 7.7 et seq. – The trial will typically stay halted and will be closed if the creditor's claim is not objected by other creditors or the Insolvency Practitioner. If the claims gets objected, the trial can be continued with the objecting party.

90 See, however, the exceptions in §362(b) Bankruptcy Code.

91 *In re Johnson*, 548 B.R. 770 (Bankr. S.D. Ohio 2016).

92 Cf. *Cook v. Mortgage Debenture Ltd* [2016] EWCA Civ. 103 at para. 12.

claim and determine its amount. Beyond that, it is for the Insolvency Practitioner to decide whether legal actions shall be initiated or pursued (Art. L. 641-4(1)(2) Code de Commerce).

For further reading: *Bork*, Einführung, §17; *Fletcher*, Law of Insolvency, para. 22-006 et seq., 26-005; *Saint-Alary-Houin*, Droit des enterprises en difficulté, para. 693 et seq., 1241; *Tabb*, Law of Bankruptcy, §3.3 et seq.; *van Zwieten*, Principles of Corporate Insolvency Law, para. 5-24. 5.48

IV. SET-OFF

Creditors who are enabled to set their claims off[93] against counterclaims 5.49 of the debtor (respectively the estate) enjoy a special **security** for their claims, since they can satisfy these claims against the debtor by utilising the debtor's counterclaims, similar to a pledge or lien on the debtor's claims.[94] There is no need for such creditors to worry about their satisfaction, since they are sufficiently secured by the right to set-off, provided the counterclaim of the estate is at least as high as the creditor's claim. However, the first prerequisite for this security is that the creditor is entitled to set-off according to substantive law, i.e. that the preconditions for set-off are met regardless of the insolvency proceedings. The second prerequisite is that the relevant insolvency law accepts such a substantive right to set-off. Most national insolvency laws pay particular attention to this subject and react in different ways.[95] For example, some accept set-off rights unconditionally or – just the opposite – ignore or at least modify them in insolvency proceedings. Others apply transactions avoidance law to the creation of the set-off right and most laws do not recognise such rights if they have been established after the commencement of insolvency proceedings. Rules that

93 The techniques of set-off vary from country to country. For example, whilst in England and Wales this regularly requires a court order or a specific contractual provision, in Germany only one party must declare the set-off towards the other party (§388 BGB), and in the USA any act of one side accounting the mutual claims suffices.

94 *Stein v. Blake (No 1)* 2 WLR 710.

95 See the National Reports in *Johnston/Werlen/Link*, Set-off Law and Practice; also UNCITRAL Legislative Guide, p. 155 et seq. and §9.3 PEIL: "The opening of the proceedings does not prevent set-off."

prevent creditors from setting the claims of the debtor off against their own claims are of immense importance for the creditor. When they bite, the creditor must pay their own obligations in full to the estate, while still being treated as an unsecured ordinary pre-insolvency creditor in respect of their own claims against the debtor.

5.50 In **England and Wales**, the Insolvency Act 1986 itself contains rules on set-off for individuals only. According to sec. 323 Insolvency Act 1986, mutual debts are accounted by force of law, provided that the creditor had no notice of the bankruptcy petition at the time the claim became due. The Act is silent on set-off in corporate insolvencies. There are, however, similar provisions (not subject to alteration by party agreement[96] or the discretion of the court[97]) in the Insolvency Rules (rules 14.25, 14.26 Insolvency Rules 2016). These statutory rules can be summarised as follows.[98] Claims susceptible to be set off against one another are, with retroactive effect from the point at which proceedings were opened, collected in a single account and automatically balanced against one another without the need for offsetting declarations or any other action from the parties, provided that the creditor had no notice of the bankruptcy petition at the time the claim became due. The requirements are that the claims were mutual at the start of insolvency proceedings and concern the payment of money or are able to be converted into claims which concern the payment of money. The creditor must also be entitled to a *pro rata* dividend without offsetting, meaning that if the limitation period has run on his claim[99] or if the office-holder has successfully contested it,[100] he is left in the cold. Under this legal system, the claims need not be due at the opening of proceedings, nor need conditions or time-limits have been met, as long as the offsetting right itself comes to fruition during the proceedings.[101] As far as offsetting

---

96 *National Westminster Bank Ltd v. Halesowen Presswork & Assemblies Ltd* [1972] 2 WLR 455.

97 *Klempka v. Miller* [2008] EWHC 3554 (Ch); *Re Bank of Credit and Commerce International SA (No 10)* [1997] Ch 213.

98 Cf. the key decisions of the House of Lords and the Supreme Court in *Inveresk plc v. Tullis Russell Papermakers Ltd* [2010] UKSC 19; *Re Bank of Credit and Commerce International SA (In Liquidation) (No 8)* [1997] BCC 965; *Secretary of State for Trade and Industry v. Frid* [2004] 2 AC 506; *Stein v. Blake (No 1)* [1995] 2 WLR 710.

99 Cf. *Pott v. Clegg* [1847] 153 ER 1212.

100 Cf. *Bank of Credit and Commerce International (Overseas) Ltd (In Liquidation) v. Habib Bank Ltd* [1999] 1 WLR 42.

101 *Re Kauphting Singer & Friedlander Ltd* [2010] EWCA Civ. 518; *Secretary of State for Trade and Industrie v. Frid* [2004] 2 AC 506.

positions are based on grounds subject to challenge,[102] the situation is thus: if the offsetting is based on the assignment of a claim against the insolvency debtor to one of their debtors, it is not subject to challenge for lack of involvement by the debtor. But if the offsetting is grounded in the conduct of the debtor themselves, it is subject to challenge under sec. 238, 239, 423 Insolvency Act 1986. The same applies if the substantive law set-off right has already led to offsetting, although even this regularly requires a court order or specific contractual provision.

In **France**, the topic of set-off is dealt with in Art. L. 622-7(1) Code de Commerce which is applicable not only in safeguard (restructuring) proceedings but also in liquidation proceedings (Art. L. 641-3(1) Code de Commerce). Set-off is mentioned in the context of the prohibition to pay ordinary creditors outside the regular dividend distribution. Art. L. 622-7(1) Code de Commerce holds that the court decision commencing the proceedings shall automatically prohibit payment of claims arising prior to the issue of the commencement order, except set-off payments of connected claims. However, two different situations have to be distinguished. If both claims were certain, due, and enforceable before the opening of insolvency proceedings they are cleared by force of law and Art. L. 622-7 Code de Commerce is not applicable. Only if these conditions are not met at the point in time when proceedings were opened can Art. L. 622-7 Code de Commerce be applied. Hence, if the conditions for the set-off are met after the opening of the insolvency proceedings the right to set-off depends on the prerequisites that both the debtor's and the creditor's claims are mutual and "connected" and the claim against the insolvent debtor has been registered. The required connection is to be construed narrowly and can normally only be affirmed where both claims stem from the same contractual relationship (e.g. vendor's claim to receive the price against debtor's claim to be paid damages for flawed delivery[103]). The connection is preserved even in case of an assignment of the claim. However, in both cases, set-off is not possible if the conditions for the set-off are created by an assignment of the debt with the only purpose to establish the necessary requirements for a set-off.[104] Generally, the connection must not have 5.51

102 Extensively on transactions avoidance law below in at para. 6.12.

103 Cf. Cour de Cassation (chambre commerciale) – 26.1.2015 – 13-18656 = Bull. civ. 2015, IV, no. 10.

104 Cour de Cassation (chambre commerciale) – 22.10.2013 – 12-27044 = ECLI:FR:CCASS:2013:CO01003.

been deliberately provoked,[105] which brings transactions avoidance law in through the back door.[106]

5.52 **German** law deals with this subject in §§94 et seq. Insolvenzordnung. §94 Insolvenzordnung makes it clear that offsetting positions gained before the opening of insolvency proceedings are not affected. The only exception is under §96(1)No.3 Insolvenzordnung, when the offsetting position is itself based on grounds subject to challenge.[107] The particularity of §96(1)No.3 Insolvenzordnung is, on the one hand, that it hinders offsetting by force of law, making challenge by the Insolvency Practitioner unnecessary, but also that it automatically and retroactively reverses previously declared offsetting, reactivating the former claims at the opening of proceedings. If the offsetting position is anchored in mutual obligation at the start of proceedings but the offsetting itself is not yet possible because the obligations are of different types or a claim is conditional or not yet due, the potential offsetting position is also protected in principle, but only if the debtor's claim is not enforceable earlier than that of the creditor (§95(1)(3) Insolvenzordnung). If the offsetting position is only accrued after the opening of proceedings, offsetting is prevented by §96(1)No.1 and 2 Insolvenzordnung. This is true when the claim of the insolvency debtor only arises after the opening of proceedings (§96(1)No.1 Insolvenzordnung), perhaps because the office-holder has transferred assets to the previously unsecured creditor (like the alienation of inventory in the course of the operation of the business[108]) or because a bank has offset a negative balance with payments received after the opening of proceedings.[109] And it is also true when an insolvency debtor of the debtor is assigned a claim of a third party against the insolvency debtor in order to be able to offset (§96(1)No.2 Insolvenzordnung).[110]

---

105 Cour de Cassation (chambre commerciale) – 13.02.2007 – 05-13526 = Bull. civ. 2007, IV, No. 36.

106 See also below at para. 6.12.

107 The primary ground of avoidance is §131 Insolvenzordnung (cf. below at para. 6.24), and the necessary incongruent coverage can be shown, for example, where a creditor assigns his claim to a debtor of the debtor or where assets are sold to a creditor with the result that the creditor can be repaid by offsetting the sale price against the claim.

108 BGH, Urt. v. 22.4.2010 – IX ZR 8/07 = NZI 2010, 682.

109 BGH, Urt. v. 26.6.2008 – IX ZR 47/05 = NZI 2008, 551.

110 Cf. BGH, Urt. v. 10.12.2009 – IX ZR 1/09 = NZI 2010, 138.

Offsetting positions gained after the opening of proceedings are therefore only protected in one circumstance: when the creditor accrues an ex post claim against the estate,[111] either by performance rendered to the office-holder or through the retroactive accrual of statutory claims. In these cases, the creditor has to be paid in full, and therefore there is no reason to maintain a ban on offsetting.

In the **USA**, a right to set-off is principally not affected by the commencement of insolvency proceedings (§553(a) Bankruptcy Code).[112] Moreover, the creditor's claim is deemed to be a secured claim to the extent of the amount subject to set-off, and as an unsecured claim only to the extent the amount subject to set-off is less than the amount of the claim (§506(a)(1) Bankruptcy Code). The creditor may use the right to set-off as a defence if the Insolvency Practitioner demands payment on the debtor's[113] claim (§542(b) Bankruptcy Code). However, there are some important prerequisites and restrictions (with numerous counter-exceptions which will be neglected here).[114] First, the right to set-off – as are other secured claims – is covered by the stay (§362(a)(7) Bankruptcy Code). Hence, the creditor must obtain relief from the stay if set-off shall be exercised (§362(d) Bankruptcy Code). Second, set-off is only possible for allowed claims[115] (§§553(a)(1), 502 Bankruptcy Code). Third, set-off is excluded under certain conditions if the creditor obtained the set-off right within the time period of 90 days prior to the commencement of insolvency proceedings. This is related to transactions avoidance law and applies where the claim was assigned to the creditor from a third party within this time period or after the commencement of proceedings, if the debtor was already insolvent (§553(a)(2) Bankruptcy Code) which is 5.53

111 An example would be VAT claims from deliveries or services rendered after the opening of proceedings that can be offset by tax authorities against a taxation refund claim that arose before the opening of proceedings, cf. BGH, Urt. v. 22.10.2009 – IX ZR 147/06 = NZI 2010, 17.

112 However, this rule does not create but merely recognises set-off rights, *Citizens Bank of Maryland v. Strumpf*, 516 U.S. 16, 116 S. Ct. 286, 133 L. Ed. 2d 258 (1995).

113 Triangular set-off is not allowed in bankruptcy proceedings, *In re Elcona Homes Corp.*, 863 F.2d 483 (7th Cir. 1988); *In re Lehman Bros.*, 458 B.R. 134 (Bankr. S.D.N.Y. 2011); *In re Semcrude, L.P.*, 399 B.R. 388 (Bankr. D. Del. 2009).

114 Cf. *Mine Serv. Co. v. James River Coal Co. (In re James River Coal Co.)*, 534 B.R. 666 (Bankr. E.D. Va. 2015).

115 More on this below at para. 7.11.

rebuttably presumed (§553(c) Bankruptcy Code). It applies also where the debt owed to the debtor by the creditor was incurred by the creditor after 90 days before the commencement of the proceedings, if the debtor was insolvent and the creditor acted for the purpose of obtaining a right of set-off against the debtor (§553(a)(3) Bankruptcy Code). Finally, where the creditor has already declared set-off on or within 90 days before the commencement of proceedings, the Insolvency Practitioner may recover from the creditor the amount so offset to the extent that the creditor improved their position[116] during the 90-day-period until the time of set-off such claim (§553(b) Bankruptcy Code).

5.54 **Example:** D has a claim of 5,000 against A, C has a claim of 5,000 against D. Since D is in financial trouble, C is afraid of getting not more than 3% as her share of the proceeds, once insolvency proceedings are opened. Hence, A and C come to an agreement as follows: C assigns her claim to A, who must be apprehensive of being obliged to pay the full amount of his debt to the Insolvency Practitioner; in return, A shall declare set-off and pay 2,500 to C (which is advantageous for him, since he pays only 2,500 to C, not 5,000 to D, and also for C, since she receives 2,500 and not only 150). After the commencement of the proceedings (shortly after the agreement between A and C), the Insolvency Practitioner claims 5,000 from A and refers him to file the claim which A received from C by assignment to the insolvency schedule. This is the correct solution, since creating a set-off situation by assignment is declared either void or challengeable in national insolvency laws[117] (except for England and Wales[118]).

---

116 In the words of §553(b) Bankruptcy Code: "to the extent that any insufficiency on the date of such setoff is less than the insufficiency on the later of 90 days before the date of the filing of the petition; and the first date during the 90 days immediately preceding the date of the filing of the petition on which there is an insufficiency" (the latter expression being defined as the amount by which a claim against the debtor exceeds a mutual debt owing to the debtor by the holder of such claim).

117 See for Fance Cour de Cassation (chambre commerciale) – 22.10.2013 – 12-27044 = ECLI:FR:CCASS:2013:CO01003; for Germany §96(1)No. 3 Insolvenzordnung and above in fn. 107; for the USA §553(a)(2) Bankruptcy Code.

118 Cf. above at para. 5.50.

For further reading: *Bork*, Einführung, §23; *Bork*, Rescuing Companies, para. 11.01 et seq.; *Fletcher*, Law of Insolvency, para. 9.051 et seq., 23.018 et seq.; *Saint-Alary-Houin*, Droit des enterprises en difficulté, para. 718 et seq.; *Tabb*, Law of Bankruptcy, §6.27 et seq.; *van Zwieten*, Principles of Corporate Insolvency Law, para. 9-01 et seq. 5.55

V. EFFECTS ON THE DEBTOR

Besides the transfer of the right of disposal and the right to manage the estate to the Insolvency Practitioner,[119] the opening of insolvency proceedings has further effects on the debtor's legal position. Typically, **all debtors** are obliged by national insolvency laws to cooperate with the Insolvency Practitioner.[120] Typical examples are the duties to hand over the assets belonging to the estate[121] and to give all information the Insolvency Practitioner needs for proper execution of their tasks.[122] 5.56

A quite far-reaching consequence is the dissolution of **companies**. In most jurisdictions, the opening of insolvency proceedings (at least of proceedings aiming at liquidation) has the effect that companies are dissolved, wound up, and eventually erased.[123] Hence, the result of liquidation proceedings is not only the valorisation of the company's assets and the distribution of the proceeds on a *pro rata* basis but also that the debtor company no longer exists and that the unsatisfied part of the creditor's claim extinguishes. However, where the debtor is a natural person, such extinguishing is not possible which is why many jurisdictions provide for a discharge. We will deal with this subject later on in this book.[124] 5.57

---

119 Above at para. 5.4, 5.20.

120 See §521(a)(3) Bankruptcy Code.

121 Cf. above at para. 5.4a. E.g. §521(a)(4) Bankruptcy Code.

122 E.g. §97 et seq. Insolvenzordnung, §521 Bankruptcy Code.

123 See for for England and Wales sec. 73 et seq., 205 Insolvency Act 1986, sec. 1000 et seq. CA 2006; France Art. 1844-7No.7 Code Civil; Germany §§42(1)(1), 728 (1)(1) BGB, 131(1)No.3 HGB, 262(1)No.3 AktG, §60(1)No.4 GmbHG.

124 Below at para. 9.2 et seq.

5.58 ***For further reading***: *Bork*, Einführung, §14 C/D; *Fletcher*, Law of Insolvency, para. 9.051 et seq., 25.001 et seq.; *Saint-Alary-Houin*, Droit des enterprises en difficulté, para. 571 et seq., 1247; *Tabb*, Law of Bankruptcy, §§2.5c, 10.4; *van Zwieten*, Principles of Corporate Insolvency Law, para. 1-40.

VI. EFFECTS ON CREDITORS

5.59 The opening of insolvency proceedings has also severe effects for the creditors. This is certainly true for unsecured **ordinary creditors**.[125] They are now parties of collective enforcement proceedings which hinders them from acquiring rights from the estate[126] and bans them from pursuing and enforcing their claims individually.[127] Instead, they are bound to the rules of insolvency proceedings. The main consequence is that ordinary creditors are obliged to file their claims with the court and/or the Insolvency Practitioner[128] and are referred to the distribution of the dividend.[129] This typically leads to an only partial satisfaction of the claim with the rest being enforceable against the debtor's assets after the termination of the insolvency proceedings unless the debtor is dissolved or a discharge is granted.[130]

5.60 However, this is only true for unsecured ordinary creditors, not for **preferential creditors**.[131] They have priority claims which rank ahead of the ordinary creditors and are paid in full. Preferential creditors are typically not banned from enforcing their claims and are not referred to the rules for lodging the claims and receiving the dividend.

---

125 More on them above at para. 2.13 et seq. What is said in the text holds also true for subordinated creditors, cf. above at para. 2.28 et seq.

126 See above at para. 5.8 et seq.

127 Cf. above at para. 5.16 et seq. See also §3.3 PEIL: "A claim against the debtor existing at the time of the opening of the proceedings ('insolvency claim') can be pursued only through submission and admission under the conditions of the proceeding, without prejudice to security rights and rights of set-off."

128 Details below at para. 7.5 et seq.

129 More on this below at para. 7.39 et seq.

130 Cf. above at para. 5.57.

131 See for them above at para. 2.24 et seq.

The above-mentioned rules do also not – or at least not unrestrictedly – apply to **secured creditors.**[132] In principle, creditors who have a right *in rem* (security right) in respect of assets belonging to the estate may enforce their security, realise the collateral, and keep the proceeds to the amount necessary to satisfy their claim. They are bound to the rules applicable to ordinary creditors only insofar as the proceeds are not sufficient to cover the whole claim. Only with this unsecured part of the claim they are ordinary creditors and entitled to the dividend. However, national laws provide for many detailed regulations binding on secured creditors. We will pay them more attention below.[133] 5.61

Finally, creditors with a **right to separation**[134] are typically not affected by the opening of the insolvency proceedings. Since they claim that certain assets are not part of the estate, they are entitled to surrender of the objects in question and can enforce their claims against the Insolvency Practitioner. Whether this holds true unconditionally or whether some – at least procedural – restrictions must be observed will be explained in more detail below.[135] 5.62

For further reading: *Bork*, Einführung, §14 B; *Fletcher*, Law of Insolvency, para. 26-001 et seq.; *Saint-Alary-Houin*, Droit des enterprises en difficulté, para. 693 et seq., 1223; *Tabb*, Law of Bankruptcy, §3.1 et seq.; *van Zwieten*, Principles of Corporate Insolvency Law, para. 5-24. 5.63

132 For them, see above at para. 2.21 et seq.

133 At para 7.13 et seq.

134 More on them above at para. 2.23.

135 At para. 7.22.

CHAPTER 6

TRANSACTIONS AVOIDANCE

In the sixth chapter we will learn that certain transactions performed prior to the commencement of insolvency proceedings can be set aside after the opening of insolvency proceedings when certain conditions are met. Although they are valid under general civil law, national laws permit avoidance where transactions are detrimental to the general body of creditors and contrary to certain principles of insolvency law. The following text will evolve the policies behind transactions avoidance law, the general prerequisites and the special requirements (avoidance grounds) and it will also explain the legal consequences. 6.1

I. BASICS

We have seen in the previous chapter that the **effect of the opening of insolvency proceedings** is typically the shift of the power of disposal from the debtor to the Insolvency Practitioner. Hence, transactions made *after* this point in time are not valid, since the debtor no longer has power of disposal and individual enforcement acts by single creditors are prohibited and invalidated by insolvency law. As opposed to this, transactions performed *prior* to the commencement of insolvency proceedings are normally not affected, since the estate is not seized retroactively. This leaves performances of the debtor, e.g. gifts to the spouse or payments to creditors, unviolated. However, almost all national laws share the opinion that, under certain conditions, this might be contrary to foundational principles of insolvency law. They therefore mitigate the harsh consequences of the clear cut-off date (opening of the proceedings)[1] and allow for the challenging of 6.2

1 Cf. *Angove's Pty Ltd v. Bailey* [2016] UKSC 47; cf. for the underlying fixation principle above at para. 1.11, 2.17, 4.4.

certain transactions in order to tackle fraudulent displacement of assets to the benefit of a third party.[2] This is to ensure the equal treatment of creditors. Relevant rules are suggested in the UNCITRAL Legislative Guide[3] and in the PEIL[4] and can be found in nearly all jurisdictions,[5] e.g. in England and Wales (sec. 238–245, 339–348, 423–425 Insolvency Act 1986), France (Art. L. 632-1–632-4 Code de Commerce), Germany (§§129–147 Insolvenzordnung) and the USA (§§544–553 Bankruptcy Code). Since most of these rules are typically only applicable in opened insolvency proceedings, such opening is a prerequisite for transactions avoidance and the nullity or voidability of such transactions is a further effect of the opening of insolvency proceedings.

6.3 The idea of such transactions avoidance goes back to Roman law where the *praetor* was enabled to grant the so-called ***actio Pauliana***, i.e. to order the claw-back of transactions which were fraudulent in respect of creditors.[6] The Latin expression "*actio Pauliana*" can be found in many languages, e.g. *Pauline (or Paulian) action* in English or *action paulienne* in French, and is still used in modern laws. However, in some jurisdictions it is not (or not exclusively) part of insolvency law but rather located in general civil law[7] and it is not always restricted to insolvency proceedings but also applicable outside such proceedings, e.g. in private enforcement proceedings.[8]

6.4 The **effect** of transactions avoidance cannot be summarised in one word. It depends on the case at hand and varies from country to country.[9] Sometimes, the legal result is that the respective transaction is declared null and void by force of law; sometimes the legal consequence is a claim of rescission, regularly to be enforced by the Insolvency Practitioner; sometimes it suffices to simply ignore the transaction (e.g. when a creditor

---

2 In the following text, the beneficiary of a vulnerable transaction will also be labelled as "counterparty", "opponent" or "defendant".

3 UNCITRAL Legislative Guide, p. 135 para. 148 et seq. with Recommendations 93 et seq.

4 §8.1(1) PEIL: "A juridical act unfairly detrimental to the creditors performed by the debtor within a certain period of time before the opening of the proceeding, is subject to reversal."

5 See the National Reports in *Faber/Vermunt/Kilborn/Richter*, Commencement of Insolvency Proceedings, each at para. 24.1.

6 The Digest 22, 1, 38, 4.

7 Examples are Croatia, France, Italy, Portugal, and Spain.

8 Examples are Czech Republic, Germany, the Netherlands, Slovakia, and Slovenia.

9 See also §8.1(2) PEIL: "The administrator can recover or seek annulment of any benefit which has been obtained from the debtor."

tries to enforce a lien which was created in a voidable way); and sometimes the legal effects are left to the discretion of the court. We will deal with this variety of legal consequences in more detail below.[10]

It goes without saying that not all transactions performed prior to the opening of insolvency proceedings are subject to avoidance rules. Principally, persons dealing with the subsequent debtor can **trust in the stability of performances** and have no need to take a future insolvency of their counterparty into account. Hence, insolvency triggered transactions avoidance needs to be restricted to the necessary measure and legislators have to find the right balance between the interest of the general body of creditors in "swelling the assets" and improving their return from the estate on the one hand and the legitimate interests of the persons who have benefitted from the transaction to keep what they have received on the other hand. Insolvency laws do that by binding transactions avoidance to objective and subjective requirements which narrows the scope of voidable transactions from "all" to "some". 6.5

II. GENERAL PREREQUISITES

It is for this purpose that many jurisdictions distinguish between general requirements which must be met in **all transactions avoidance cases** and specific avoidance grounds which stand abreast so that only one of them must be realised.[11] Not all of the general prerequisites dealt with in this paragraph can be found in all jurisdictions. Some national insolvency laws can do without such requirements and in others they cannot be found in the wording of the statute but in case law only. However, there is an overlap which proves the common idea of transactions avoidance law. 6.6

A. TRANSACTION

Typically, insolvency laws do not define the term "transaction".[12] Although it should be clear that this comprises all **human acts which have legal** 6.7

10 At para. 6.47 et seq.

11 More on them below at para. 6.18 et seq.

12 For an exception, see §101(54) Bankruptcy Code: "The term 'transfer' means (A) the creation of a lien; (B) the retention of title as a security interest; (C) the foreclosure

consequences, further clarification is necessary. First, voidable transactions are in many jurisdictions not only acts of disposition (e.g. payment or transfer of title) but also real acts which have legal consequences. Second, forbearance can also be a challengeable transaction.

6.8 **Examples:** (1) D[13] processes raw materials belonging to G. This results in a final product which by anticipated transfer of title belongs to G. Where this is challengeable, G has to return the legal advantage acquired by this course of events.[14] (2) D feeds a pig belonging to E. Where this happens in a challengeable way, E has to return the increase in value resulting from the feeding. (3) D has a claim against X and omits to interrupt the limitation period by suing in due time. Where this is challengeable, the Insolvency Practitioner can enforce the claim and X's objection of limitation is disregarded.

6.9 Third, a distinction can be made according to the **person performing the transaction**. In many jurisdictions, only transactions of the debtor are subject to avoidance law whereas others include performances of a creditor or a third party.

6.10 **Examples:** (1) G gets satisfaction by individual enforcement: this is voidable where all types of actions are challengeable but is not voidable where only performances of the debtor are challengeable. (2) Debtor D has a claim against A and a debt to C. A pays D's debt to C. This is a transaction of the debtor only if A acted at the instruction of D. Whether it is challengeable depends on the detriment to the general body of creditors.[15] (3) D has a claim against A but fails to sue A within the limitation period. Forbearance can be a voidable transaction where it has detrimental effects to the estate.

---

of a debtor's equity of redemption; or (D) each mode, direct or indirect, absolute or conditional, voluntary or involuntary, of disposing of or parting with (i) property; or (ii) an interest in property."

13 This character is used for the insolvent debtor throughout this chapter.

14 Cf. the decision of the German BGH (Urt. v. 9.7.2009 – IX ZR 86/08 = NZI 2009, 644): Brewing beer is a voidable transaction where it leads to a lien encumbering the brewed beer as a security for beer tax claims. As a result, the tax authorities may not enforce the lien.

15 For that, see below at para. 6.17.

National laws proceed quite differently in this respect. In Germany, all human acts with legal consequences are covered, which includes not only acts of disposition but of all kinds, including forbearance (§129(2) Insolvenzordnung) and transactions of creditors and third parties. The same holds true for France (Art. L. 632-1, 632-2 Code de Commerce[16]) and the USA where §§547(b), 548(a)(1) Bankruptcy Code require a "transfer" and §101(54) Bankruptcy Code defines this term very broadly,[17] including non-debtor performances such as foreclosure[18] (provided they result in a diminution of the debtor's assets), but excluding acts which extinguish the debtor's rights as this is not seen as a transfer.[19] As opposed to this, in England and Wales, where the term "transaction" is defined in sec. 436(1) Insolvency Act 1986 as including "a gift, agreement or arrangement", only performances of the debtor are challengeable (sec. 238(2), 239(2), 423(1) Insolvency Act 1986).[20] 6.11

The definition of relevant transactions has consequences for the avoidance of **set-off**.[21] In many jurisdictions, granting a right of set-off or operating such a right can be challenged as a preference. Subject to some modifications, this holds true for France (under the conditions of Art. L. 632-2 Code de Commerce[22]), Germany (§§94–96, 130, 131 Insolvenzordnung[23]) and the USA (§553 Bankruptcy Code), and also for England and Wales, provided the debtor participated in the transaction (sec. 239 Insolvency Act 1986).[24] 6.12

16 Individual enforcement is voidable according to Art. L. 632-2(2) Code de Commerce; cf. Cour de Cassation (chambre commerciale) – 12.10.1999 – 96-13133 = Bull. Civ. 1999 IV no 166. Where French law requires "payments", these can only be made by the debtor, not by a third party.

17 Cf. above fn. 9.

18 *BFP v. Resolution Trust Corp.*, 511 U.S. 531, 114 S. Ct. 1757, 128 L. Ed. 2d 556 (1994); *Boberschmidt v. Society Nat'l Bank (In re Jones)*, 226 F.3d 917 (7th Cir. 2000).

19 See *In re Wey*, 854 F.2d 196 (7th Cir. 1988).

20 As for individual enforcement, it follows from sec. 346 Insolvency Act 1986 that avoidance is not possible if the enforcement was completed before the commencement of bankruptcy proceedings.

21 For details on set-off in insolvency proceedings, see above at para. 5.49 et seq.

22 See below at para. 6.26.

23 More below at para. 6.24.

24 Cf. below at para. 6.23.

B. PRIOR TO THE OPENING OF INSOLVENCY PROCEEDINGS

6.13 It follows from the restricting effects of the opening of insolvency proceedings that transactions avoidance is not necessary for transactions performed after the opening since they are invalid anyway.[25] It is for this reason that some laws draw a clear line and **restrict the scope** of transactions avoidance law to acts performed before the opening of proceedings.[26] Examples are Germany where §129(1) Insolvenzordnung expressly states that "transactions made prior to the opening of insolvency proceedings and disadvantaging the insolvency creditors may be contested by the insolvency administrator under §§130–146." In other jurisdictions, it is decided by the requirement that the transaction must be made during a certain suspect period which runs backwards from the commencement of the insolvency proceedings.[27] However, this raises two questions.

6.14 The first question is whether **post-petition transactions**, i.e. transactions performed between the application for and the opening of insolvency proceedings, are covered by the relevant transactions avoidance law. It follows from the wording of §129(1) Insolvenzordnung[28] that the answer is "yes" in Germany unless a preliminary Insolvency Practitioner pays debts created by themselves.[29] The answer is also "yes" in France[30] and in the US where §549 Bankruptcy Code enables the trustee generally (subject to some exceptions) to avoid a transfer of property of the estate that occurs after the commencement of the case.[31] In England and Wales,

---

25 Cf. above at para. 6.2.

26 For §8.1. PEIL see above at fn. 4. – Against this background, transactions avoidance law can also be connected to the fixation principle (cf. above at para. 1.11). The debtor and the counterparty of the transaction try to evade the moment of fixation by diminishing the estate just before official insolvency proceedings are opened. For example, in the Netherlands, transaction avoidance law is therefore seen as a means of "reconstructing" the estate to the size that it should have had at the moment of fixation. Cf. *Franken*, Het insolventiepassief, para. 3.2.

27 Cf. §547(b)(4)(A) Bankruptcy Code (90 days before the date of the filing of the petition) and sec. 240 (1)(a) Insolvency Act 1986 (period of 2 years ending with the onset of insolvency). The same holds true for France where the "période suspecte" is defined from the day the debtor ceased payments (Art. L. 632-1 Code de Commerce) until the opening decision of the court. General remarks in the UNCITRAL Legislative Guide, p. 147 para. 188 et seq. and Recommendation 89.

28 Cited above at para. 6.13.

29 Details above at para. 3.13.

30 Cf. above fn. 27.

31 See also §552 Bankruptcy Code.

transactions avoidance law also covers the time between the application for and the opening of administration and winding-up proceedings[32] (sec. 240(3)(d)/(e), 127, 284(3) Insolvency Act 1986).

The second question regards timing: at which **point in time** is a transaction deemed to be performed?[33] For example, where a debtor dispatches an envelope with cash before the opening of proceedings and the creditor receives the money after the opening of proceedings, is this payment subject to transactions avoidance (because the debtor acted before the opening) or is it invalid anyway (because the satisfying effect of the payment occurred after the opening of proceedings and is therefore subject to the rules on shift of disposition powers[34])? German law answers this question expressly in §140 Insolvenzordnung (which in principle refers to the effect and not to the performance of the transaction), and US law in §§547(e), 548(d)(1) Bankruptcy Code (which principally refer to the perfection of the transaction).[35] The French Code de Commerce is silent on this matter but it is generally agreed that the point in time when the transaction was effected is relevant.[36] Differently, in England and Wales, statute refers to the point in time when the debtor "enters into" the transaction (sec. 240(1), 341(1) Insolvency Act 1986) which presumably – the definition of "transaction" in sec. 436(1) Insolvency Act 1986 is not very helpful in this respect and authorities are silent on this matter – refers to the (irrevocable) depart of the asset rather than to its arrival. 6.15

C. DETRIMENT TO THE GENERAL BODY OF CREDITORS

The idea of transactions avoidance law is to enable the Insolvency Practitioner to rescind the advantages from the benefitted person in 6.16

32 For bankruptcy proceedings, sec. 284(3) Insolvency Act 1986 prepones the effects of the bankruptcy order. Hence, transaction avoidance is not necessary, since transactions after the application for bankruptcy proceedings are void anyway; cf. also above at para. 6.2, 6.13. For a validation order by the court under sec. 284 Insolvency Act 1986 see *Hood v. HRMC and JD Classics Limited* [2019] EWHC 2236 (Ch).

33 The same question arises regarding the question as to whether the transaction lies outside or within the suspect period, cf. below at para. 6.21.

34 As explained above in Chapter 5; cf. at para. 5.12.

35 Cf. *Mottaz v. Oswald (In re Frierdich)*, 294 F.3d 864 (7th Cir. 2002).

36 See for an assignment of claims Cour de Cassation (chambre commerciale) – 6.6.2001 – 98-14355.

order to **enhance the estate** and to improve the *pro rata* satisfaction of the creditors' claims. This is not possible if the transaction in question did not diminish the (future) estate, because if the estate was not diminished the claw-back cannot enhance it. It is for this reason, that some jurisdictions expressly require that the transaction was detrimental to the general body of unsecured creditors.[37] In Germany, for example, §129(1) Insolvenzordnung[38] postulates the transaction to be disadvantageous to the creditors. Similarly, §547(b)(5) Bankruptcy Code requires the transaction to enable the creditor to receive more than such creditor would receive without the transaction in insolvency proceedings. This wording indicates that transactions to the benefit of another person put this person in a better position and at the same time deprive the estate of assets which in opened insolvency proceedings are missing for the satisfaction of the creditors' claims.[39] Vice versa, if the recipient is not put in a better position, the transaction is normally not detrimental to the general body of creditors.[40] In England and Wales, the Insolvency Act 1986 is silent on this matter. However, it is generally agreed that transactions avoidance law is drafted in order to tackle acts detrimental to the general body of creditors.[41] Only in France it is not necessary to establish a disadvantage to the creditors, although Art. L. 632-4(2) Code de Commerce prescribes that the avoidance action shall result in reforming the debtor's assets.

6.17 **Examples:** (1) Regarding the examples discussed at para. 6.8: in the first example, G requires title on property which did not exist before the transaction and the estate loses the raw materials belonging to D; in the second example, E's pig is now more valuable than before the transaction and the estate is diminished in value due to the feeding expenses; in the third example, the estate loses a claim and X loses an obligation. (2) Regarding the examples discussed at para. 6.10: in

37 For §8.1. PEIL see above at fn. 4.

38 Cited above at para. 6.13.

39 Cf. *Abramson v. St. Regis Paper Co.*, 715 F.2d 934 (5th Cir. 1983); *Natl. Bank of Newport v. Natl. Herkimer County Bank of Little Falls*, 225 U.S. 178, 32 S. Ct. 633, 56 L. Ed. 1042 (1912).

40 See also §550(a) Bankruptcy Code: The recovery must benefit for the estate; cf. *Mellon Bank, N.A. v. Dick Corp.*, 351 F.3d 290 (7th Cir. 2003).

41 Cf. *Doyle v. Saville* [2002] BPIR 947; *Rubin v. Eurofinance SA* [2012] UKSC 46; *Parry/Shivji* in: Parry/Ayliffe/Shivji (eds.), Transactions Avoidance in Insolvencies, para. 5.51 et seq.

the first example, G gets satisfaction and the estate loses the seized assets; in the second example, C receives satisfaction and D loses a claim against A (either directly, if A acted on D's instruction, or indirectly, if A's payment resulted in a recourse action which could be set-off against D's claim). However, there might be no detriment to the general body of creditors if D had no claim against A. In this case, the debtor's assets are not touched and the result of A's payment to C is either advantageous for the creditors (because there is one creditor less participating in the distribution of the proceeds) or neutral (if A is entitled to reimbursement for the payment to C, leading to an exchange of creditors only: A instead of C; differently, however, if A is secured and C was not). (3) D pays creditor C whose claim is sufficiently secured. This is not detrimental to the general body of creditors unless the security right is voidable itself. (4) D is owner of real estate already encumbered with four mortgages the sum of which exceeds the value of the real estate. D grants a fifth mortgage to bank B. The granting of this fifth ranking mortgage is not detrimental to the general body of creditors, since the value of the real estate was already exhausted by the four higher-ranking mortgages and the real estate was of no economic interest for the unsecured creditors anyway. (5) M gives D money to enable D to pay one of their creditors. Under German law, this is detrimental to the general body of creditors unless D held the money on trust for M. Under US law, it is not a transfer of the debtor's property if an insolvent debtor pays one of their creditors with funds from a third party which were clearly "earmarked" to pay a specific antecedent debt; it is more a substitution of creditors (M instead of C) than a transfer of the debtor's property.[42]

III. AVOIDANCE GROUNDS

The above-mentioned general prerequisites are not sufficient to narrow the scope of transactions avoidance law in an adequate manner; they alone cannot protect the legitimate expectations of persons dealing with the (future) debtor that they can keep what they have received.[43] The task is 6.18

42 *Buckley v. Jeld-Wen, Inc.*, 986 F.2d 228 (8th Cir. 1993).

43 Cf. above at para. 6.5.

therefore to define which expectations are legitimate and need protection against claw-back and which are not. National laws typically do this by establishing certain avoidance grounds, i.e. rules which put transactions avoidance under **additional prerequisites** in order to balance the principles of optimal satisfaction of the debtors claims and of protection of trust. Typical avoidance grounds, available in most jurisdictions, tie on the granting of preferences (A.), transactions at an undervalue (B.), and intentionally fraudulent transactions (C.).[44]

6.19 Most jurisdictions alleviate the conditions for transactions avoidance where the opponent is a **closely related party**.[45] If persons who benefitted from the transaction are closely connected with the debtor it can be presumed that they knew of the debtor's financial difficulties and used this insider-knowledge to feather their own nest. Insolvency laws are therefore sceptical about closely related parties and react by prolonging suspect periods or by shifting the burden of proof regarding the debtor's insolvency or required mental elements to the defendant. Typical addressees of such rules are (where the debtor is a natural person) spouses, partners, relatives, or housemates and (where the debtor is a legal entity) directors, shareholders (at least shareholders with a significant influence), and contractual partners with special insight into the debtor company's financial affairs. Details are regulated in England and Wales in sec. 249, 435 Insolvency Act 1986, in Germany in §138 Insolvenzordnung, and in the USA in §101(31) Bankruptcy Code. In France, no insider rules are available in transactions avoidance law.

A. PREFERENCES

6.20 Preferences can be defined as "**performances to the benefit of a creditor who would be worse off without this performance**". Preferences are by

---

44 See also UNCITRAL Legislative Guide, p. 141 para. 170 et seq. (with Recommendation 87) and §8.2 PEIL: "Juridical acts subject to reversal include:

a) A transaction with the intent of defrauding creditors;
b) A transaction for inadequate countervalue;
c) A transaction with a creditor for which no enforceable obligation existed;
d) A transaction with a creditor after the filing of the insolvency application or in a situation of imminent insolvency;
e) The creation of a security right to secure a pre-existing obligation."

45 Cf. UNCITRAL Legislative Guide, p. 145 para. 182 et seq. with Recommendation 90 et seq.

definition transactions to the benefit of creditors only; transactions to third parties (e.g. a gift to a spouse) are not included. Transactions in favour of creditors are preferences if these creditors receive a better treatment than they would have received in insolvency proceedings without the performance. A typical example is a payment to a creditor in the vicinity of insolvency proceedings. By this payment, the creditor's claim is fully satisfied whereas in insolvency proceedings the creditor, would he or she not have received the payment, would only be entitled to a *pro rata* distribution. Hence, by receiving the payment, the recipient is preferred to other creditors who were in the same position before the payment and who do not get full satisfaction of their claims. It follows from this that the underlying tenet of the avoidance of preferences is the principle of equal treatment of creditors. Without the payment, all creditors – including the recipient – would be paid the same share of their claims, would be satisfied on a *pro rata* basis according to the *pari passu* principle. Where insolvency laws allow explicitly for the avoidance of preferences,[46] they undertake to enforce this principle of equal treatment of creditors by preponing its application to a certain time period prior to the opening of insolvency proceedings.[47]

However, recognising the adverse need for protection of legitimate expectations, avoidance of preferences is typically bound to **additional prerequisites**. Such protection of trust can be granted in various ways. First means are *suspect periods*, requiring the preference to be performed within a certain time span (e.g. three months or one year) prior to the commencement of insolvency proceedings, leaving all transactions outside this time span unchallengeable. A second typical requirement is the *substantive insolvency* of the debtor at the point in time when the transaction was performed, which is reasonable, since the principle of equal treatment of creditors is a principle of insolvency law[48] and is only applicable where the debtor is insolvent. Protection of trust can further be granted by the requirement of *mental elements* (subjective prerequisites, such as knowledge of the creditor of the debtor's substantive insolvency or 6.21

46 Preferences can also be subject to the more general rule of transactions defrauding creditors; cf. below at para. 6.43.

47 *Canright v. General Finance Corp.*, 35 F. Supp. 841 (E.D. Ill. 1940). For details, see the Report on Transactions Avoidance laws: "Clash of Principles: Equal Treatment of Creditors vs. Protection of Trust", available at www.ceril.eu/projects/kopie-avoidance-actions/.

48 See above at para. 1.11.

good faith as a defence). We will see below,[49] that nearly all transactions avoidance laws use these means singly or conjunctly.

6.22 Even if all these objective and subjective prerequisites are met, national laws provide for **exceptions** from the avoidance of certain preferences. Typical appearances of such exceptions are transactions which are part of a contemporaneous exchange for adequate new value, transactions in the ordinary course of business[50] and transactions in the context of a serious restructuring attempt.

6.23 Taking a closer look to the rules on preferences in national insolvency laws,[51] communalities and differences become visible. To begin with **England and Wales**, sec. 239 Insolvency Act 1986 allows for the avoidance of preferences under several conditions. First, the term "preference" is defined very broadly in sec. 239(4) Insolvency Act 1986, which states that "a company gives a preference to a person if (a) that person is one of the company's creditors or a surety or a guarantor for any of the company's debts or other liabilities, and (b) the company does anything or suffers anything to be done which (in either case) has the effect of putting that person into a position which, in the event of the company going into insolvent liquidation, will be better than the position he would have been in if that thing had not be done." Second, the transaction must be performed within a suspect period which is six months prior to the opening of insolvency proceedings (sec. 240(1)(b), 341(1)(c) Insolvency Act 1986). Third, sec. 240(2), 341(2) Insolvency Act 1986 require the debtor's inability to pay debts[52] at the point in time when the preference was given. The fourth prerequisite is a mental element: the debtor's decision to grant the preference must be influenced by a desire to put the creditor in a better position (sec. 239(5), 340(4) Insolvency Act 1986). If the recipient is closely connected to the debtor, the suspect period is two years (sec. 240(1)(a), 341(1)(b) Insolvency Act 1986) and the debtor's desire is presumed (sec. 239(6), 340(5) Insolvency Act 1986). The creditor's knowledge or intent is irrelevant. Although there is no general exception for transactions performed in the ordinary course of business, the exchange of assets against cash payments or other new value transactions

---

49 At para. 6.23 et seq.

50 For them, cf. UNCITRAL Legislative Guide, p. 140 para. 164 et seq.

51 Cf. also UNCITRAL Legislative Guide, p. 143 para. 177 et seq.

52 For definition, cf. above at para. 1.18. In bankruptcy proceedings, overindebtedness is sufficient (sec. 341(3)(b) Insolvency Act1986).

are not challengeable, if they can be judged as not being detrimental to the general body of creditors.[53] Transactions made as a means of saving the debtor's business are assumed to be performed without the required intent.[54] In such cases, the court may also refuse to make a repayment order (or make a validation order).[55]

German insolvency law addresses preferences in §§130, 131 Insolvenzordnung. These rules distinguish between "congruent" and "incongruent coverages". According to §131(1) Insolvenzordnung, a transaction granting or facilitating a security or satisfaction to a creditor is incongruent if the creditor had no entitlement to such security or satisfaction, or to the kind, or date of such security or satisfaction. In both cases, the suspect period is three months prior to the application for insolvency proceedings (or after such application but before the opening of proceedings). Congruent coverages are only voidable if the debtor company was substantively insolvent at the point in time when the transaction was made, and a further (subjective) prerequisite is the knowledge of the creditor of the debtor's inability to pay debts (§130(1) Insolvenzordnung). If the creditor is a closely related person, this knowledge is rebuttably presumed (§130(3) Insolvenzordnung). For incongruent coverages, there are no subjective requirements. The only additional prerequisite is the debtor's inability to pay debts; if the payment has been made during the last month before (or after) the application for insolvency proceedings even this is not necessary (§131(1) Insolvenzordnung); it then suffices that the transaction was incongruent. German law contains no exceptions for transactions in the context of restructuring attempts or performances in the ordinary course of business. However, §142 Insolvenzordnung exempts congruent coverages from the avoidance rule in §130 Insolvenzordnung[56] if the debtor instantaneously received an equitable consideration (so-called "*Bargeschäft*"). 6.24

53 *Re Fairway Magazines Ltd* [1992] BCC 924; *Re Ledingham-Smith* [1993] BCLC 635; *Parry/Shivji* in: Parry/Ayliffe/Shivji (eds.), Transactions Avoidance in Insolvencies, para. 5.67 et seq. See also *Express Electrical Contractors Ltd v Beavis* [2016] EWCA Civ. 765.

54 *Re Lewis of Leicester Ltd* [1995] BCC 514; *Parry/Shivji*, in: Parry/Ayliffe/Shivji (eds.), Transactions Avoidance in Insolvencies, para. 5.107 et seq.

55 See for the legal consequences below at para. 6.52.

56 However, avoidance as an intentionally fraudulent transaction (§133 InsO) remains possible.

6.25 In the **USA**, preferences are dealt with in §547 Bankruptcy Code. The rule defines preferences as any transfer of an interest of the debtor in property to or for the benefit of a creditor, for or on account of an antecedent debt owed by the debtor before such transfer was made, that enables such creditor to receive more (not: earlier) than such creditor would receive otherwise (§547(b)(1)/(2)/(5) Bankruptcy Code). It is required that the transaction was made while the debtor was insolvent – i.e. overindebted within the meaning of §101(32) Bankruptcy Code[57] –, which is rebuttably presumed (§547(b)(3)/(f) Bankruptcy Code).[58] The suspect period is 90 days before the filing of the petition, one year for insiders (§547(b)(4) Bankruptcy Code).[59] Mental elements are not required. However, US law provides for many exceptions in §547(c) Bankruptcy Code. Particularly transactions made against contemporaneous or subsequent exchange of new value (§§547(c)(1)/(4)/(a)(2), 549(b) Bankruptcy Code), made in the ordinary course of business (§547(c)(2) Bankruptcy Code), or of minor value ($600 in consumer and $6,425 in non-consumer cases, §547(c)(8)/(9) Bankruptcy Code) are not challengeable.

6.26 The system is different in **France**. French insolvency law has no special rule for preferences. Instead, Art. L. 632-1(1) Code de Commerce lists – quite straightforwardly – certain types of transactions and declares them generally void, provided the debtor had ceased payments. Generally speaking, the transactions listed in Art. L. 632-1(1) Code de Commerce appear to concern unusual legal acts. As far as preferences are concerned, particularly the numbers 3 (payments in non-mature debts), 4 (payments through unusual payment means) and 6, 9 (granting securities for as yet unsecured debts)[60] from this list are important.[61] The only additional prerequisite for these types of transactions is that they have occurred since the date of the cessation of payments[62] (which refers to Art. L. 631-8 Code de Commerce according to which the court shall state the day the debtor ceased payments, without going back more than eighteen months before the opening decision). Other payments – i.e. payments on mature

---

57 See above at para. 1.30.

58 Cf. *In re Imagine Fulfillment Services, LLC* 489 B. R. 136, 144 et seq. (Bankr. C. D. Cal. 2013).

59 This insider-rule is safeguarded by §550(c) Bankruptcy Code.

60 Numbers 1 and 2 concern transactions at an undervalue; cf. below at para. 6.29.

61 They all would be deemed "incongruent" under German law, cf. above at para. 6.24.

62 See for this term, above at para. 1.22.

debts and payments made in exchange for valuable consideration – appear to be made in a normal way of business are – at the discretion of the court – only voidable if the debtor's counterparty knew of the cessation of payments (Art. L. 632-2 Code de Commerce).

In **summary** it can be said, that the four jurisdictions evaluated here 6.27
have rules on preferences. All are sceptical for transactions benefitting creditors in the vicinity of insolvency proceedings, particularly unusual performances ("incongruent coverages"), all require the substantive insolvency of the debtor, and all provide for a suspect period, albeit with different length: three months in Germany and the USA, six months in England and Wales (but two years if the opponent is a closely related party) and up to eighteen months in France. Only with respect to mental elements does a colourful picture become apparent: German insolvency law requires the creditor's knowledge of the debtor's insolvency, albeit only for "congruent coverages". A similar rule can be found in France. The law of England and Wales requires the debtor's desire to put the creditor in a better position and US law on preferences has no subjective prerequisites at all. As regards exceptions, transactions for new value are protected in England and Wales, Germany and the USA, in France only if the creditor acted in good faith. A special exception for transactions made in the ordinary course of business (others than such for new value) is only available in the USA. Alleviations as it concerns proving the applicability of the transaction avoidance provisions with respect to closely connected parties are contained in English, German, and US law but not in French law.

Example: C, a creditor of D, applies for the opening of insolvency 6.28
proceedings against D. Before the court's opening decision, D pays V, a supplier who refuses to deliver goods urgently needed for the continuation of D's business unless outstanding debts are paid. After the opening decision, the Insolvency Practitioner sues V for repayment. This would be successful in England and Wales under sec. 239, 240 Insolvency Act 1986 unless the court is convinced that D did not act with the necessary desire to put V in a better position, since D paid old debts in order to get new deliveries. Under French law, all depends on V's knowledge of D's cessation of payments (Art. L. 632-2 Code de Commerce). Also, in Germany, V has to pay the money back provided V knew of the debtor's inability to pay debts or

of the insolvency application (§130 InsO). The "*Bargeschäft*"-exception of §142 Insolvenzordnung cannot be applied, since D paid outstanding debts, not the compensation for new deliveries. The same results are likely in the USA, since it is not in the ordinary course of business (§547(c)(2) Bankruptcy Code) if an outstanding debt is paid after the application for insolvency proceedings.

B. TRANSACTIONS AT AN UNDERVALUE

6.29 Legislators are also sceptical of transactions at an undervalue[63] which can be defined as "**performances to the benefit of the opponent which result in a reduction of assets without (or with no compensating) counter-performance**". The policy behind this avoidance ground is not the principle of equal treatment of creditors, since the recipient of (e.g.) a gift is not necessarily a creditor. It also does not aim at preventing the debtor from being generous to the detriment of their creditors,[64] since gifts are not suspicious as such and are not an appearance of fraudulent behaviour.[65] Rules on transactions at an undervalue are rather based on the conviction that someone who has received a performance without consideration is not – or not in the same way as a person who granted a compensating counter-performance – worthy of protection of trust. Hence, the limitations for the avoidance of gratuitous transactions are less strict compared to the avoidance of preferences. Typically, suspect periods are longer and neither insolvency of the debtor nor mental elements are required.

6.30 A decisive point is the definition of "**undervalue**". There is no dissent that gifts are captured by these avoidance rules, albeit typically with an exception for conventional gifts of minor value, such as birthday gifts or donations to charities, churches, or political parties. However, (partly) gratuitous are also mutual transactions if the value of the debtor's performance

---

63 Cf. also UNCITRAL Legislative Guide, p. 143 para. 174 et seq.

64 However, it is frequently stated that the requirement for debtors is to "be just before you are generous", i.e. "pay your creditors from the assets with which you are liable for your debts before you make gifts"; cf. *Clark*, The duties of the corporate debtor to its creditors, Harvard Law Review 90 (1976/1977), 505, 510. See also for Germany BGH, 19.7.2018 – IX ZR 307/16 = NZI 2018, 800 at para. 31.

65 Differently US law and partly the law of England and Wales; cf. below at para. 6.31, 6.34.

significantly exceeds the counter-performance of the opponent, i.e. more than a reasonable assessment of market value would judge as exchange for fair value. Notwithstanding a margin of discretion, a transaction against an unusually low compensation should be deemed gratuitous.

In **England and Wales,**[66] sec. 238(4), 339(3) Insolvency Act 1986 define transactions at an undervalue as such without any consideration or with a consideration the value of which is significantly less than the value of the transaction provided by the debtor company. Transactions at an undervalue are voidable if they were entered into by the debtor within a suspect period of two years prior to the commencement of insolvency proceedings (sec. 238(2), 240(1)(a) Insolvency Act 1986), in bankruptcies five years prior to the commencement of the proceedings (sec. 341 (1) Insolvency Act 1986). Surprisingly, there is not only the requirement of substantive insolvency of the debtor (sec. 240(2) Insolvency Act 1986)[67] but also the opponent's defence that the debtor acted in good faith and for the purpose of carrying on business, provided there were reasonable grounds for believing that the transaction would benefit the company (sec. 238(5) Insolvency Act 1986).[68] Note, however, that transactions at an undervalue can also be challenged as intentionally fraudulent transactions under sec. 423 Insolvency Act 1986.[69] In all cases, an exception for conventional gifts is not available. 6.31

France enables the avoidance of transactions at an undervalue under the same conditions as for the avoidance of preferences.[70] According to Art. L. 632-1(1) No. 1 and 2 Code de Commerce, transactions of the debtor are void if they are performed against no consideration (No. 1) or if the debtor's obligations significantly exceed those of the other party (No. 2), provided that they were performed during the cessation of payments period fixed by the court. Hence, insolvency of the debtor is necessary. However, it is at the discretion of the court to prolong this suspect period for a maximum of six months if there was no consideration at all 6.32

66 A comparison between English and German law is given by *Bork*, Transactions at an undervalue, JCLS 2014, 453–477.

67 Substantive insolvency is rebuttably presumed if the opponent is a party closely connected to the debtor; see for this above at para. 6.19. In bankruptcies, substantive insolvency is only required if the transaction was performed not less than two years prior to the commencement of the proceedings (sec. 341 (2) Insolvency Act1986).

68 In bankruptcies, no such defence is possible, which means that mental elements are of no importance.

69 See below at para. 6.38.

70 Cf. above at para. 6.26.

(Art. L. 632-1(2)). In all cases, mental elements are not required and exceptions for conventional gifts are not available.

6.33 In **Germany**, transactions at an undervalue are challengeable under §134 Insolvenzordnung. This norm is quite straightforward. Nothing more is required than a gratuitous performance (which is not specified in the statute but construed in the sense explained above at para. 6.30) by the debtor in the suspect period of four years prior to the application for insolvency proceedings. It is not relevant whether the debtor was substantively insolvent when the transaction was performed and neither intent of the debtor nor knowledge of the beneficiary is necessary. "Usual casual gifts of minor value"[71] are exempted from transactions avoidance by §134(2) Insolvenzordnung.

6.34 Quite differently, **US** law classifies transaction at an undervalue under certain prerequisites as fraudulent transactions (§548(a)(1)(B) Bankruptcy Code). Since there are no subjective requirements, these cases are labelled "constructive fraud".[72] Fraudulent in this sense are transactions of the debtor performed within two years prior to the commencement of insolvency proceedings (§548(a)(1) Bankruptcy Code), provided that the debtor received no reasonable consideration (§548(a)(1)(B)(i) Bankruptcy Code)[73] and (a) was substantively insolvent,[74] or (b) was left with unreasonably small capital,[75] or (c) intended to incur debts beyond the debtor's ability to pay when due,[76] or (d) made the transaction with an insider under an employment contract and not in the ordinary course of business (§548(a)(1)(B)(ii) Bankruptcy Code). Charitable contributions – yet not conventional gifts – are exempted by §548(a)(2) Bankruptcy Code. Note, however, that fraudulent conveyances are also voidable under state laws.[77]

---

71 According to case law, the limit is 200 € per gift and 500 € per year, cf. BGH, 4.2.2016 – IX ZR 77/15 = NJW 2016, 2412.

72 As opposed to "actual fraud", cf. below at para. 6.41.

73 This is sometimes seen very harshly; cf. *DeGiacomo v. Sacred Heart Univ., Inc. (In re Palladino)*, 942 F.3d 55 (1st Cir. 2019), where the court held that payment of college tuition for an adult child was a constructive fraudulent transfer because the payment "depleted the estate and furnished nothing of direct value to the creditors who are the central concern of the code provisions at issue."

74 Which, in the USA, means overindebtedness, cf. above at para. 1.30.

75 Cf. above at para. 1.27.

76 This is seen as an appearance of inability to pay debts, *Burtch v. Opus LLC (In re Opus East LLC)*, 698 Fed. Appx. 711 (3rd Cir. 2017).

77 See for details below at para. 6.41.

In **sum**, all national insolvency laws enable the tackling of transactions at an undervalue by the debtor and all include in this term not only gifts but also transactions against no adequate consideration. Suspect periods are quite long, two years in the USA, in England and Wales for insolvencies, and (at the utmost) in France, four years in Germany and five years in England and Wales for bankruptcies. Substantive insolvency is required in England and Wales as well as in France, to some extent in the USA and not in Germany. Most jurisdictions refrain from subjective prerequisites, England and Wales being the only exception where the defence of the debtor's good faith is granted. Conventional gifts are exempted in Germany, charitable contributions in the US. 6.35

Example: D, a leading employee of a worldwide operating broker house, presents a precious locket to his wife W as a birthday gift. 30 months later, D becomes bankrupt. After the opening of bankruptcy proceedings, the Insolvency Practitioner challenges the gift and requires restitution from W. This is only successful in Germany where the mere transaction at an undervalue suffices and the exception for usual casual gifts does not apply, since the gift is not of minor value. In France and the USA, the transaction was outside the relevant suspect period. Further, D was not substantively insolvent when presenting the gift, which is necessary in England and Wales, France and the USA. Subjective prerequisites are not applicable, since they are only relevant in England and Wales and in corporate insolvencies only (sec. 238(5) Insolvency Act 1986), not in personal bankruptcies (cf. sec. 338, 341 Insolvency Act 1986). 6.36

C. INTENTIONALLY FRAUDULENT TRANSACTIONS

A third group of voidable performances are intentionally fraudulent transactions,[78] roughly defined as "any act performed with the (as the case may be: implied) **intent to disadvantage the general body of creditors** or similar mental elements (such as knowledge)". This type is the modern form of the *actio Pauliana*[79] the appearance of which can be established 6.37

78 See also UNCITRAL Legislative Guide, p. 142 para. 172 et seq.
79 Cf. above at para. 6.3.

in nearly all jurisdictions. However, rules on defrauding creditors are not or not exclusively included in insolvency law in many national laws, but rather in general civil law which raises the question as to whether they can be enforced by the Insolvency Practitioner. *Actio Pauliana*-type rules are typically marked by intensive mental elements, long suspect periods, and little objective criteria. However, wording and location of the relevant rules vary from country to country.

6.38 For example, in **England and Wales**, sec. 423 Insolvency Act 1986, which applies to insolvencies as well as bankruptcies, allows for the avoidance of transactions defrauding creditors, albeit with significant restrictions. First, it is only applicable to transactions at an undervalue (sec. 432(1) Insolvency Act 1986) which narrows the scope of the rule considerably.[80] Second, although there is no suspect period[81] and the debtor needs not to be substantively insolvent, there must be a "victim" of the transaction under sec. 423 Insolvency Act 1986, and creditors will not be victims if the debtor company can nevertheless pay all creditors in full at the point in time when the transaction was performed. Further, the debtor is required to act for the purpose of putting assets beyond the reach of – or otherwise prejudicing – current or future creditors (sec. 423(3) Insolvency Act 1986). As regards standing, the avoidance can be enforced by the Insolvency Practitioner or a creditor disadvantaged by the transaction (sec. 424(1)(a) Insolvency Act 1986).[82] In the latter case, the creditor acts on behalf of all prejudiced creditors (sec. 424(2) Insolvency Act 1986), which is no incentive to pursue this. The burden of proof for all prerequisites is with the claimant, even where closely related parties are involved.

6.39 **France** has no rule on transactions defrauding creditors in its insolvency law. As reported above,[83] purpose or intent on the debtor's side is generally irrelevant. Only knowledge of the opponent authorises the court to set aside transactions not voidable by force of law (Art. L. 632(1) Code de Commerce). However, Art. 1167 of the French Code de Civil enables a creditor to challenge fraudulent actions entailing personal damage for this creditor. There is no hardening period and special knowledge of the counterparty is not required. In insolvency proceedings, this claim can be enforced by the Insolvency Practitioner.

---

80 For example, payments on existing claims can never be tackled as a transaction defrauding creditors.

81 Only general limitation periods apply.

82 For an example, see *BTI 2014 LLC v. Sequana SA and ors* [2019] EWCA Civ. 112.

83 At para. 6.26, 6.32.

Under **German** law, fraudulent transactions can be challenged under §133 Insolvenzordnung. All acts of the debtor detrimental to the general body of creditors and granted within ten years prior to (or after) the application for insolvency can be avoided if the debtor company acted in bad faith (i.e. with the intent to disadvantage the general body of creditors) and the opponent knew of this intention. Substantive insolvency of the debtor is not required. However, since this rule is dominantly characterised by mental elements which are difficult to prove, the BGH has found a wide range of circumstantial evidence. Especially if the parties knew that the debtor company was (at least imminent) insolvent, the subjective requirements are indicated and it is for the opponent to prove that the debtor acted in good faith or that the debtor's intent was unknown to him.[84] In addition, §133(4) Insolvenzordnung presumes the mental elements for closely related parties if an exchange contract causes an immediate disadvantage to the general body of creditors, a rule which covers not only disadvantageous contracts but also payments. 6.40

In the **USA**, fraudulent transfers and obligations are covered by §548 Bankruptcy Code, provided they are made by the debtor within two years prior to the commencement of insolvency proceedings. This rule, which covers all transactions,[85] distinguishes between actual fraud and constructive fraud. "Actual fraud" is given where the debtor acted with the actual, subjective intent to hinder, delay, or defraud current or future creditors (§538(a)(1)(A) Bankruptcy Code). Although statute is silent on this matter, such intent can be indicated by the opponents close relationship to the debtor.[86] "Constructive fraud" means that this intent is irrebuttably presumed for transactions at an undervalue where certain additional prerequisites, particularly substantive insolvency of the debtor, are met (§548(a)(1)(B) Bankruptcy Code).[87] For actual fraud, substantive insolvency of the debtor is not required yet grants circumstantial evidence 6.41

---

84 BGH, 14.6.2018 – IX ZR 22/15 = ZIP 2018, 1794; 18.1.2018 – IX ZR 144/16 = NZI 2018, 264; 14.9.2017 – IX ZR 3/16 = NZI 2018, 114; 6.7.2017 – IX ZR 178/16 = NZI 2017, 850; 5.3.2009 – IX ZR 85/07 = BGHZ 180, 98 = NJW 2009, 1601 Rdnr. 10; 29.11.2007 – IX ZR 121/06 = BGHZ 174, 314 = NJW 2008, 1067; 13.4.2006 – IX ZR 158/05 = BGHZ 167, 190 = NJW 2006, 2701.

85 For some important exceptions, see §548(a)(2)/(c) Bankruptcy Code.

86 *Reade v. Livingston*, 8 Am. Dec. 520 (N. Y. Ch. 1818).

87 For details, see above at para. 6.34.

for the debtor's intent.[88] In addition, fraudulent conveyances can also be tackled by the Insolvency Practitioner if an unsecured creditor is entitled to do so under state law[89] (§544(b) Bankruptcy Code).

6.42 **Summing up**, all jurisdictions explored here have rules on transactions defrauding creditors. They can mostly be found in insolvency law, but in some countries they are additionally (USA) or exclusively (France) implemented in general civil law. With the exception of England and Wales (transactions at an undervalue only), all transactions are covered and substantive insolvency of the debtor is not required. Suspect periods are either rather long (ten years in Germany, two years in the USA) or not provided for at all (England and Wales, France, in the US according to state law). The decisive prerequisite is the debtor's purpose or intent to prejudice creditors (England and Wales, Germany, USA, not explicitly in France), the proof of such mental elements being sometimes alleviated where closely connected parties are involved (Germany, the US). Entitled to enforce the avoidance rules is the Insolvency Practitioner (all jurisdictions), in some countries with a concurrent standing of every disadvantaged creditor (England and Wales, France, USA).

6.43 **Example**: D is heavily insolvent. She pays creditor C who knows of D's insolvency and puts significant pressure on D to receive performance. One year later, insolvency proceedings are opened against D. The Insolvency Practitioner sues C for repayment. This will be fruitless in England and Wales, since the payment was not a transaction at an undervalue (as required in sec. 423 Insolvency Act 1986) and cannot be challenged as a preference because it was performed outside the suspect period.[90] In France, the payment can be tackled as a preference (Art. L. 632-2 Code de Commerce).[91] The Insolvency Practitioner will also succeed in Germany where the mutual knowledge of the debtor's

88 See for the "badges of fraud" sec. 4(b)(9) Uniform Voidable Transactions Act and *Liquidation Trust of Hechinger Inv. Co. of Delaware v. Fleet Retail Finance Group (In re Hechinger Inv. Co. of Delaware)*, 327 B.R. 537 (D. Del. 2005); *United States v. Theall*, 609 Fed. Appx. 807 (5th Cir. 2015).

89 States laws cannot be explained in detail here. However, it should be mentioned that no suspect periods but only general limitation periods apply.

90 Cf. above at para. 6.23.

91 See above at para. 6.26.

substantive insolvency is assessed as an indication for the subjective prerequisites[92] as required in §133 Insolvenzordnung. Under US law, the payment can be challenged as "actual fraud" under §548(a)(1)(A) Bankruptcy Code.

D. OTHERS

The typical avoidance grounds described here are frequently accompanied by further rules which either **modify or supplement the basic norms** for special situations. For example, the law on preferences is sometimes altered for payments on cheques,[93] the law on intentionally fraudulent transactions for extortionate credit transactions.[94] 6.44

Most jurisdictions class the creation of **security rights** as voidable transactions[95] and some even have special norms for avoiding such rights.[96] For example, in England and Wales, sec. 245 Insolvency Act 1986, which does not confer challenge rights onto the office-holder, intervenes into the law of credit securities and directly voids (and thereby spares the office-holder the trouble of challenging) "late floating charges" in so far as they exceed the value of a simultaneously or subsequently rendered counter-performance (a line of credit, delivery of goods, performance of services) over which the debtor had free disposal (sec. 245(2)/(6) Insolvency 6.45

---

92 Most recently BGH, Urt. v. 19.9.2019 – IX ZR 148/18 = NZG 2020, 25; Urt. v. 12.9.2019 – IX ZR 264/18 = NZI 2019, 851; Urt. v. 18.7.2019 – IX ZR 258/18 = NJW-RR 2019, 1263.

93 See for France Art. L. 632-3 Code de Commerce, for Germany §137 InsO.

94 An example is sec. 244 Insolvency Act1986. According to this norm, the Insolvency Practitioner may apply to the court to adjust or set aside the terms of an extortionate credit arrangement which was concluded within the three years leading up to the insolvency proceedings. Sec. 244(3) Insolvency Act1986 defines credit as extortionate if it demands vastly exorbitant payments from the debtor relative to the amount of risk taken on by the creditor or in some other way represents a gross violation of the principles of fair dealing.

95 See also UNCITRAL Legislative Guide, p. 145 para. 180 et seq. with Recommendation 88; further *McCormack/Bork* (eds.), Security Rights and the European Insolvency Regulation, Chapter 4 p. 121 para. 367 et seq.

96 Cf. §545(3)/(4) Bankruptcy Code which enable the Insolvency Practitioner to challenge statutory landlords' liens.

Act 1986).[97] The charge must have been issued in the year leading up to the opening of insolvency proceedings (sec 245(3)(b)/(5) Insolvency Act 1986), and the company must have been unable to pay its debts or rendered so by the issuance of the security (sec. 245(4) Insolvency Act 1986). If the security-holder is a closely connected person, the relevant time is two years (sec. 245(3)(a)/(5) Insolvency Act 1986) and there is no requirement that the company must be unable to pay its debts (arguably sec. 245(4) Insolvency Act 1986). In addition, sec. 874 Companies Act 2006 declares certain securities, such as floating charges, void against the estate if the registration requirements of sec. 859A Companies Act 2006 are not met. Similar rules can be found in §§544(a), 545(2), 547(e), 548(d) Bankruptcy Code. The reason for such rules is that unregistered security rights can be set aside by a *bona fide* purchaser and that creditors who were not aware of the "secret charge" might have given credit which they would not have given if they knew of the charge.

6.46 A special case are **shareholder loans**. Payments to shareholders (e.g. distribution of profits) can be void if they lack the necessary basis in company law (e.g. a resolution of the shareholders' meeting).[98] In these cases, they can be rescinded as unjust enrichment as well as transactions at an undervalue.[99] Shareholder loans are a different matter. Shareholders tend to finance their company with loans instead of equity capital, expecting a return of the loan in full (in good times) or at least on a *pro rata* basis (if the company is insolvent). It can frequently be observed that such loans are – suspiciously[100] – paid back in the vicinity of insolvency. Reacting to this phenomenon, transactions of the debtor company made with regard to shareholder loans can be challenged in Germany under §135 Insolvenzordnung without further requirements if (1) the debtor is a company which does not have a natural person as a general partner, nor has a general partner which is a company that has a natural person as its own general partner, and (2) performance was rendered no more than one year (for the granting of security rights over collateral ten years) prior to

97 See *Crumpler & Anr (Liquidators of Peak Hotels and Resorts Ltd) v. Candey Ltd* [2019] EWCA Civ. 345.

98 For an example, see *Burnden Holdings (UK) Ltd v. Fielding* [2019] EWHC 1566 (Ch).

99 *BTI 2014 LLC v. Sequana SA and ors* [2019] EWCA Civ. 112.

100 It is presumed that the shareholder took advantage of their insider knowledge of the company's financial crisis; cf. *Berisford, Inc. v. Stroock & Stroock & Lavan (In re 1634 Assocs.)*, 157 B.R. 231 (Bankr. S.D.N.Y. 1993).

the insolvency application. Compared to the regular rule on "congruent coverages",[101] neither substantive insolvency of the debtor nor mental elements of the parties are required and the suspect period is significantly longer (one respectively ten years instead of three months). Similar rules can be found in the laws of Croatia, Italy (albeit in Company Law), and Portugal. In Slovakia, all payments of dividends to shareholders can be contested unless the company has fully satisfied all registered unsecured claims. US law provides for the avoidance of transactions benefitting the general partner of an insolvent partnership[102] (§548(b) Bankruptcy Code). However, such rules are rare. Most jurisdictions are satisfied with treating (influential) shareholders as closely related parties.[103]

IV. LEGAL CONSEQUENCES

Although there are many similarities regarding the avoidance grounds, national laws[104] diverge substantially as regards the legal consequences. This is also a matter of the principle of efficiency: the best transactions avoidance law is useless if it cannot be enforced efficiently. A first important aspect in this respect is whether the legal consequences are **determined by statute or are left at the discretion of the court**. In the latter case, it is difficult to predict what the outcome of the avoidance action might be. Hence, legal certainty and efficiency plead in favour of statutory regulation. However, while the legal consequences are comprisingly determined by statute in Germany (§§143 et seq. Insolvenzordnung) and the USA (§§546, 550 Bankruptcy Code), they are at the court's discretion in England and Wales (sec. 238(3), 239(3), 339(2), 340(2) Insolvency Act 1986) and partly in France (Art. L. 632-1(2), 632-2 Code de Commerce). 6.47

A second relevant aspect is whether transactions subject to avoidance law are – upon opening of insolvency proceedings, as the case may be – automatically **void by force of law or voidable by court decision**. Most national laws require a decision of the court. This is certainly true for jurisdictions where the legal consequences are at the discretion of the court 6.48

101 Cf. above at para. 6.24.

102 As opposed to corporations, *Jacobs v. Altorelli (In re Dewey & LeBoeuf LLP)*, 518 B.R. 766 (Bankr. S.D.N.Y. 2014).

103 More on this above at para. 6.19.

104 For §8.1(2) PEIL see above at fn. 9. See further UNCITRAL Legislative Guide, p. 148 para. 192 et seq., p. 151 para. 202 et seq. and Recommendations 93 et seq.

(England and Wales), but also for countries where the legal consequences result in a claim of the estate (to be enforced by the Insolvency Practitioner) against the defendant for returning the received (Germany, USA). In France, the wording of the statute is ambiguous. On the one hand, Art. L. 632-1(1) Code de Commerce declares that certain transactions "shall be considered null and void" which indicates nullity by force of law. On the other hand, Art. L. 632-4 Code de Commerce mentions an "action for annulment" which speaks in favour of voidability. It is prevailing opinion that the wording of the statute does address the discretion of the court to set voidable transactions aside (given under Art. L. 632-1(2), 632-2 Code de Commerce, not under Art. 632-1(1) Code de Commerce) rather than the distinction between "void" and "voidable".

6.49 The next question is whether defendants may allege **lapse of enrichment**, i.e. that they have consumed or spent the object received. Generally, it is an important aspect of transaction avoidance law that the opponent is not worse off than he or she would be without the voidable act. The expectation of the defendants not to be put in a worse position than they would be in without the vulnerable transaction is legitimate and deserves protection which means that recipients should not be obliged to return more than they have received. However, this must not be confused with the defence of lapse of enrichment. For example, where the debtor has made a gratuitous contribution of 10,000 to a church in a challengeable way and the church has used the money to pay the salaries of its priests, the church can repay 10,000. When it does so, it is not worse off than without the gift. A different question is whether the church can claim lapse of enrichment because it spent the money received. To answer this question, one needs, first, to decide whether the prerequisites of lapse of enrichment are met (which is highly debatable in the previous example because the church had to pay its priests anyway[105]) and, second, whether the national insolvency law permits the defence of lapse of enrichment. For example, Germany allows it, albeit only for transactions at an undervalue (§143(2) Insolvenzordnung). US law is very restrictive in this respect: if the defendant is unable to return the received the court may order to pay the value of the received (§550(a) Bankruptcy Code), and the same holds true for England and Wales, and France.

6.50 Finally, legal consequences for **third parties** must be discussed. It is of particular importance whether Insolvency Practitioners can challenge

---

105 See for Germany BGH, 27.10.2016 – IX ZR 160/14 = NZI 2017, 31.

voidable transactions against persons other than the recipient[106] where they have profited from the transactions. In Germany, a transaction may be contested not only against the heir or another comprehensive legal successor of the recipient but also against other legal successors if they were aware of the circumstances giving rise to the enrichment of the recipient (which is rebuttably presumed for closely related persons) or received the enrichment by way of a gratuitous transfer (§145 Insolvenzordnung). A similar rule can be found in the USA where §550(a)(2)/(b) Bankruptcy Code entitles the Insolvency Practitioner to recover the property transferred from immediate or mediate successor of the transferee unless this person acted for value, in good faith, and without knowledge of the voidability of the predecessor's transaction.[107] The same holds true in England and Wales where the court can proceed against third parties unless they acted in good faith and for value (sec. 241(2), 342(2) Insolvency Act 1986). In France, the nullity of the challengeable transaction can also be held out towards third parties such as successors, even if they acted in good faith.[108]

Example: D gifts R a box of exquisite wine, R gives the box as a gift to her friend F. Under the law of England and Wales, the court may order that R pays a sum to the estate representing the value of the wine; instead it may order F to return the wine to the estate, since F did not act for value. The same holds true under US law. In Germany, R can claim lapse of enrichment and F is obliged to return the wine to the estate. 6.51

Taking a closer look to national laws, **England and Wales** is a special case. Here, statute does not give the Insolvency Practitioner a substantive-law claim against the opponent for the reversal of the transaction. Instead, they merely accrue the right to ask the court (sec. 238(2), 239(2), 339(1), 340(1) Insolvency Act 1986) which then uses its discretion to decide 6.52

106 It should be noted that a "third party" can in actual fact be the "recipient", e.g. where the debtor gives money to someone who is an agent for the recipient only; cf. *Skandinaviska Enskilda Banken AB (Publ) v. Conway* [2019] UKPC 36. The determination of the recipient has priority to the question of transactions avoidance against third parties.

107 See below at para. 6.55.

108 Cour de Cassation (chambre commerciale) – 3.2.1998 – 95-20389 = Bull. civ. 1998, IV, n° 53. See also below at fn. 112.

what remedies are best suited to restoring the parties to the position they would be in if the transaction had never taken place (sec. 238(3), 239(3), 339(2), 340(2) Insolvency Act 1986). The discretion of the court is wide and includes the power to make no order at all. Although sec. 241, 342 Insolvency Act 1986 contain a number of examples by way of guidance, the list is not exhaustive. The court can order the reversal of the transaction or the renunciation of securities, but it can also order counter-performance or relieve the obligation to render agreed counter-performance, adjust the amount of performance due, and order the payment of additional compensation. The decision is made based on the interests of the creditors who benefit from the reversal, not of the parties to the transaction. Hence, lapse of enrichment can be taken into account.[109] It is at the discretion of the court whether it orders compensation, makes no order at all or makes an order against a successor, i.e. a third party to whom the recipient has transferred the received. However, the latter is not possible if the third party acted in good faith and for value (sec. 241(2), 342(2) Insolvency Act 1986), the absence of good faith being presumed where the third party had notice of the relevant surrounding circumstances and of the relevant proceedings, or was connected with, or was an associate of, either the company in question or the person with whom that company entered into the transaction (sec. 241(2A), 342(2A) Insolvency Act 1986).

6.53 **French** law declares transactions void by force of law if they meet the prerequisites of Art. L. 632-1(1) Code de Commerce. Although Art. L. 632-4 Code de Commerce mentions an "action for annulment", this is merely declarative as far as Art. L. 632-1(1) Code de Commerce is concerned. As opposed to Art. L. 632-1(2), 632 Code de Commerce, the court has no discretion. It is bound to treat the transaction as null and void (retroactively and with *erga omnes* effect) and has to decree the legal consequences resulting from this nullity (e.g. obliging the recipient to return the received or obliging a surety to indemnify the creditor who has to return the payment which has been received in a challengeable way). According to Art. L. 632-4 Code de Commerce, the action for annulment shall result in reforming the debtor's assets.

6.54 In **Germany**, the legal consequence of the challengeable transaction is a claim against the recipient (or – under the conditions of §145 Insolvenzordnung – against a successor of the recipient) to return the

[109] Under the – restrictively applied – principle of "change of position"; see for details *Skandinaviska Enskilda Banken AB (Publ) v. Conway* [2019] UKPC 36.

received to the estate (§143(1) Insolvenzordnung). This claim emerges with the opening of insolvency proceedings, no matter whether the Insolvency Practitioner has knowledge of the voidable transaction or not. As a consequence, any property of the debtor sold, transferred or relinquished under the contestable transaction must be restituted to the insolvency estate. Lapse of enrichment is only relevant where a transaction at an undervalue shall be reversed (§143(2) Insolvenzordnung).

In the **USA**, challengeable transactions are not void by force of law 6.55
but voidable by court order. Hence, avoidance needs litigation, which follows from the rule on the limitation period in §546(a) Bankruptcy Code.[110] However, by avoidance the transaction is set aside which does not automatically lead to a claim for recovery. It is for this reason that §550 Bankruptcy Code enables the Insolvency Practitioner to recover, for the benefit of the estate, the property transferred from the initial transferee of such transfer or the entity for whose benefit such transfer was made or any immediate or mediate transferee of such initial transferee. Once recovered from the opponent, the property becomes property of the estate (§541(a)(3) Bankruptcy Code). The value of such property can only be recovered if the court so orders. However, such an order prevents the defendant from claiming lapse of enrichment. Third parties can also be obliged, since §550(a)(2)/(b) Bankruptcy Code entitles the Insolvency Practitioner to recover the property transferred from immediate or mediate successor of the transferee unless this person acted for value, in good faith and without knowledge of the voidability of the predecessor's transaction.[111]

Example: D assigns a claim against T to C in a challengeable way. T pays 6.56
to C. After the opening of Insolvency proceedings, I, the Insolvency Practitioner of D, demands a second payment from T. This will be successful under French law where the assignment is null and void under Art. L. 632-1(1) Code de Commerce and third parties affected by this nullity are not protected even if they acted in good faith.[112] Under German law, T would be protected under §407 Bürgerliches Gesetzbuch

110 On this time bar, see *Kelley v. Stone & Baxter, LLP (In re Brownlee)*, 606 B.R. 109 (Bankr. M.D. Ga. 2019).

111 Cf. *Matter of Bernard L. Madoff Inv. Sec. LLC*, 548 B.R. 13 (Bankr. S.D.N.Y. 2016).

112 Cour de Cassation (chambre commerciale) – 11.10.2011 – 10-11938 = Bull. civ. 2011, IV, n° 155.

provided good faith can be established; as a result, C is obliged to pay the amount received from T to I. In the USA, third parties are only liable if they are successors and they are protected if they acted in good faith (§550(a)(2)/(b) Bankruptcy Code); hence, C would be ordered to hand over the amount received from T to I. In England and Wales, the same result seems most likely, albeit at the discretion of the court only (sec. 241(2A), 342(2A) Insolvency Act 1986).

6.57 ***For further reading***: *Bork*, Einführung, §20; *Bork*, Rescuing Companies, para. 11.18 et seq.; *Fletcher*, Law of Insolvency, para. 8-087 et seq., 16-112 et seq.; *Saint-Alary-Houin*, Droit des enterprises en difficulté, para. 1151 et seq.; *Tabb*, Law of Bankruptcy, §6.1 et seq.; *van Zwieten*, Principles of Corporate Insolvency Law, para. 13-01 et seq.

CHAPTER 7

RIGHTS AND RANKING OF CREDITORS

In the seventh chapter we will deal with several classes of creditors. We will distinguish between ordinary, secured, preferential, and subordinated creditors and will learn which rights are assigned to these classes and what they are expected to do in order to exercise such rights. We will further explain the order of satisfaction these several classes of creditors can expect. 7.1

I. BASICS

It has been explained in various passages of this book that the situation of **insolvency** is characterised by the debtor's inability to pay their debts[1] and that insolvency proceedings are therefore first and foremost collective enforcement proceedings.[2] These proceedings aim at an optimal satisfaction of the creditors' claims and, in consequence, it is important to determine who is a creditor, which claims must be considered when it comes to the distribution of the proceeds of the debtor's estate, and in which order the relevant claims shall be satisfied. 7.2

We have already seen in Chapter 2 of this book that **creditors** can be grouped into four typical groups: ordinary creditors, secured creditors, preferential creditors, and subordinated creditors.[3] For all these groups, it must be elaborated which rights the respective group members have in insolvency proceedings directed against their debtor, how these rights are 7.3

1 Extensively above at para. 1.18 et seq.
2 Above at para. 1.3 et seq.
3 See above at para. 2.12 et seq. and the National Reports in *Faber/Vermunt/Kilborn/Richter*, Commencement of Insolvency Proceedings, each at para. 15.1.

enforced, and which procedural contribution the Insolvency Practitioners on the one hand and the creditors one the other hand are expected to perform. In the end, it all boils down to the question which grade of satisfaction of their claims the group members can expect and how this satisfaction can be ensured.

7.4 As regards the **ranking** of creditors, secured creditors must be named first. In many jurisdictions, they do not need to wait for the distribution of the proceeds of the debtor's estate. Instead, their claims are satisfied by realising the collateral. As opposed to this, all other (unsecured) creditors[4] receive satisfaction from (the proceeds of) the estate in a certain order: preferential creditors are supposed to be satisfied in full before any distribution to other creditors can be made. Ordinary creditors come second: their claims are satisfied from what is left of the proceeds which is normally not enough to grant full satisfaction; hence, satisfaction on a *pro rata* basis is due.[5] In consequence, third ranking subordinated creditors come away empty-handed, since they are only entitled to any payments if all ordinary creditors are fully satisfied which only happens in rare cases. However, national laws vary when it comes to the details.[6]

II. ORDINARY CREDITORS

7.5 Therefore, a closer look is appropriate. The first, most important, and most sizable group is the group of ordinary creditors. We have already elaborated that ordinary creditors are natural or legal persons that have an **unsecured claim** against the debtor which arose on or before the commencement of the insolvency proceedings.[7] Such unsecured creditors are – next to the debtor – the main participants in insolvency proceedings, since these collective enforcement proceedings are primarily carried out for the benefit of ordinary creditors. These creditors could enforce their

---

4 This includes secured creditors where the proceeds from the collateral are not sufficient to satisfy the secured claim in full.

5 Cf. §12.2 PEIL: "Creditors with insolvency claims have an equal right to be paid in proportion to and in accordance with the ranking of claims. They are entitled to a distribution only if higher ranking insolvency claims can be satisfied to their full amount admitted."

6 See the National Reports in *Faber/Vermunt/Kilborn/Richter/Tirado* (eds.), Ranking and Priority of Creditors, passim.

7 See above at para. 2.12 et seq.

claims in individual enforcement proceedings against the debtor, were it not for the insolvency of the debtor.[8] Hence, the interests of unsecured ordinary creditors, bundled in collective insolvency proceedings, are at the forefront. Typically, insolvency law respects ordinary creditors as principle parties to the proceedings and assigns them various rights.

First, ordinary creditors have various **procedural rights**,[9] starting with the legal power to file an application for the opening of insolvency proceedings,[10] encompassing the right to proper information about the course of the proceedings under the principle of transparency,[11] and finishing with the right to participate and vote in creditors' meetings.[12] These procedural rights aim at enabling creditors to protect their substantive rights against improper infringement and at ensuring the optimal satisfaction of the creditors' claims. Ordinary creditors are subject to the decisions of the court and the Insolvency Practitioner and they are not "masters of the proceedings". But they are usually entitled to influence and challenge the major decisions of the procedural bodies, albeit only under certain conditions.[13] Procedural rights can be assigned to every single creditor or to a quorum of creditors. For example, in most jurisdictions, every creditor is entitled to apply for the opening of insolvency proceedings[14] whereas a quorum is typically necessary for the summoning of a creditors' meeting.[15] 7.6

Second, the creditors' claims as **substantive rights** are important. Insolvency proceedings are all about satisfying these claims and they are therefore the main features of the proceedings. An imposing question 7.7

8 Cf. above at para. 5.59.
9 General remarks in the UNCITRAL Legislative Guide, p. 190 para. 75 et seq. with Recommendation 126.
10 For this, see above at para. 3.2 et seq.
11 Cf. UNCITRAL Legislative Guide, p. 193 para. 86 and §10.1 PEIL: "Creditors must be informed of the time and place for submission of claims, the authority where claims must be submitted and whether secured claims must be submitted."
12 Details above at para. 2.31 et seq.
13 Cf. above at para. 2.44.
14 But see for the USA above at para. 3.2 fn. 6.
15 E.g. England and Wales sec. 379ZA Insolvency Act 1986 (10% in value or number or ten creditors in bankruptcies); Germany §75(1)No. 3 Insolvenzordnung (five creditors whose claims together represent one fifth of the sum resulting from the value of all claims). Differently, in the USA, the Insolvency Practitioner may summon a creditors' meeting on the request of any single party in interest (§2003(f) Bankruptcy Rules). French law does not provide for creditors' meetings. See also above at para. 2.41.

is how these claims are established. Since insolvency proceedings are collective proceedings, this is typically treated as a matter of creditors' autonomy.[16] It is not the task of the Insolvency Practitioner or the court to validate the debtor's debts but it is the task of the creditors to file their claims with the court or the Insolvency Practitioner[17] which leads to the creditors' participation in the distribution of the proceeds unless the filing is challenged.[18] National laws follow this path in comparable ways.[19]

7.8 In **England and Wales**, nothing can be found on establishing the creditors' claims in the Insolvency Act. This subject is completely assigned to the Insolvency Rules 2016 where chapter 14 deals with "Claims by and Distribution to Creditors in Administration, Winding up and Bankruptcy". According to para. 14.3(1) Insolvency Rules 2016, a creditor wishing to recover a claim must submit a proof to the office-holder. The office-holder may admit or reject a proof for dividend in whole or in part (para. 14.7(1) Insolvency Rules 2016). The decision of the Insolvency Practitioner may be challenged in court by the creditor but also by the debtor, any shareholder, or any other creditor (para. 14.8 Insolvency Rules 2016). It is then for the court to decide whether the creditor participates in the distribution of the proceeds with the asserted claim.

7.9 **France** requires all ordinary creditors (except employees) to submit their claims to the Insolvency Practitioner (Art. L. 641-3(4), 622-24 et seq. Code de Commerce). The office-holder, after having received the debtor's views, is tasked to ascertain the submitted claims and to draw up a list with his or her proposals for their admission, rejection, or referral to the court (Art. L. 641-14(1), 624-1 Code de Commerce). It is then for

16 Cf. above at para. 2.30. General remarks in the UNCITRAL Legislative Guide, p. 190 para. 77 et seq.

17 See also UNCITRAL Legislative Guide, p. 252 para. 13 et seq. with Recommendations 169 et seq. and §10.2 PEIL: "A claim is submitted by a notification indicating the amount and nature of the claim and stating whether a preference or security right is invoked." However, some jurisdictions exclude certain types of creditors – e.g. those with foreign tax claims or claims arising from legal activity – entirely from participation in the proceedings; cf. UNCITRAL Legislative Guide, p. 250 para. 6 et seq. This will be disregarded in this book.

18 Cf. UNCITRAL Legislative Guide, p. 256 para. 28 et seq. with Recommendations 177 et seq. and §10.3 PEIL: "An insolvency claim can be disputed by the administrator. A disputed insolvency claim is admitted if and to the extent that the dispute is decided in favour of the creditor. Pending the dispute, a disputed insolvency claim can be admitted conditionally."

19 See also UNCITRAL Legislative Guide, p. 249 para. 1 et seq.

the court to decide on the admission or rejection of the submitted claims (Art. L. 641-14(1), 624-2 Code de Commerce) which can be appealed by the creditor, the debtor, and the Insolvency Practitioner (Art. L. 641-14(1), 624-3 Code de Commerce).

Under **German** law, creditors are excluded from pursuing their claims individually (§87 Insolvenzordnung) and instead have to file their claims with the Insolvency Practitioner (§174 Insolvenzordnung) who registers all filings in a schedule (§175 Insolvenzordnung) which is the basis of the verification meeting (§176 Insolvenzordnung). In this meeting, all filed claims are called individually and can be objected to. If no one objects the claim is verified, gets registered in a schedule kept by the court, and participates in the distribution of the proceeds (§178 Insolvenzordnung). If either the Insolvency Practitioner or a fellow creditor objects, the filing creditor has to sue the objecting party in order to reach a judgement on the justification of the filing. Objection of the debtor is also possible but does not hinder the verification; it is only relevant for the creditor's entitlement to enforce the claims (to the amount not satisfied in the insolvency proceedings) after the termination of the proceedings (§201(2) Insolvenzordnung).[20] 7.10

In the **USA**, the allowance of claims[21] is necessary. This requires a proof of claim (§501(a) Bankruptcy Code) which is defined as a "written statement setting forth a creditor's claim" (Rule 3001(a) Bankruptcy Rules) and has to be filed by the creditor[22] with the clerk of the court (Rules 3002(b), 5005(a) Bankruptcy Rules). The claim is deemed to be allowed[23] unless a "party in interest" objects (§502(a) Bankruptcy Code). Statute does not define the term "party in interest".[24] However, it is common ground that all persons whose pecuniary interests are directly affected by the bankruptcy proceedings are parties in interest.[25] This includes the Insolvency 7.11

20 More below at para. 7.41.

21 Cf. the definition in §101(5) Bankruptcy Code.

22 As an exception, the debtor may file a proof of claim under §501(c) Bankruptcy Code if the creditor fails to do so in a timely manner. The policy of this norm is to protect the debtor against full post-bankruptcy liability (without being reduced by the distribution of the proceeds).

23 Even if it is obviously not enforceable, *Midland Funding, LLC v. Johnson*, 137 S. Ct. 1407, 197 L. Ed. 2d 790, 85 U.S.L.W. 4239 (2017).

24 But see §1109(2) Bankruptcy Code.

25 *Lavenhar v. First Am. Title Ins. Co. (In re Lavenhar)*, 808 F.3d 794 (10th Cir. 2015).

Practitioner.[26] Other ordinary creditors only have standing to object if a trustee is not appointed[27] or refuses to object.[28] The debtor, secured creditors,[29] and third parties (e.g. sureties) may also object if they have an interest in clearing up the legitimacy of the filing. If such objection is made, the bankruptcy court will determine the validity and the amount of the claim as well as the absence of statutory grounds for disallowance (§502(b) Bankruptcy Code).

7.12 **Example**: C has sold a car to D. After the opening of insolvency proceedings against D, C sues D for payment. This is impermissible in all jurisdictions, since creditors are no longer entitled to enforce their claims individually. Instead, verification under insolvency law is necessary. C has to file the claim with the Insolvency Practitioner (England and Wales, France, Germany) or the court (USA) and seek court assistance only where the claim is disputed.

III. SECURED CREDITORS

7.13 Insolvency laws are to recognise security rights,[30] since they are designed to stand the test in the debtor's insolvency and the credit system relies entirely on this recognition. As already mentioned above,[31] in most – albeit not all – jurisdictions, secured creditors are **privileged**. They are not bound to the rules applicable on ordinary creditors.[32] They are satisfied from the collateral, i.e. from (the proceeds of) assets belonging to the debtor and encumbered with rights *in rem*. Realisation of the collateral and distribution of the proceeds are executed separately from the realisation of the residual estate and from the distribution of its proceeds to ordinary creditors which is why the position of a secured creditor is described as a

---

26 Cf. §704(a)(5) Bankruptcy Code.

27 This is the case in chapter 11 proceedings, cf. below at para. 8.16.

28 *In re Ulz*, 401 B.R. 321 (Bankr. N.D. Ill. 2009).

29 See *In re Savidge*, 57 B.R. 389 (D. Del. 1986).

30 Cf. §9.1 PEIL: "A security right continues to exist after the opening of the proceedings. Enforcement may be subject to special rules."

31 At para. 2.21 et seq., 5.61.

32 See also UNCITRAL Legislative Guide, p. 269 para. 62 et seq. with Annex I.

right to separate satisfaction.[33] However, there is intensive debate about the ranking (certain unsecured claims having super-priority over secured claims) and financial contributions (i.e. duty to hand in a part of the proceeds to the Insolvency Practitioner) of secured creditors.[34] We will encounter examples of restrictions very soon.

Typical **security rights** are – depending on the applicable law and provided they are validly created and not voidable under transactions avoidance law – for immovables mortgages, for movables (including receivables) liens, transfer of title or assignment by way of security and certain appearances of retention of title, finally floating charges for the estate as a whole.[35] However, in some jurisdictions, not only rights *in rem* but also other protected legal positions grant a right to separate satisfaction. Examples are certain appearances of rights of retention, at least if they entitle the creditor possessing an asset belonging to the debtor not only to hold the asset back but also to realise this asset and to satisfy a claim against the debtor from the proceeds.[36] Further, rights to set-off can also be assessed as security rights which allow for separate satisfaction.[37] 7.14

Having a **right to separate satisfaction** means that secured creditors, different from ordinary creditors,[38] typically do not need to file their secured claims with the Insolvency Practitioner or the court, unless the value of the collateral does not cover the entire amount of the claim.[39] The respective rules do apply to ordinary creditors only and are not applicable to secured creditors.[40] Instead, the collateral is realised separately, be it by single disposition, be it together with the entire estate, the business, or other assets of the same kind (e.g. disposition of the debtor company's car 7.15

33 To be distinguished from the right to separation, see above at para. 2.23 and below at para. 7.22.

34 Extensively *Finch/Milman*, Corporate Insolvency Law, p. 70 et seq. Further, among others, on the one hand *Finch*, Security, Insolvency and Risk, 62 (1999) The Modern Law Review, 633 et seq.; *Janger*, When The Uniform Law Process Will Fall, 83 (1988) Iowa Law Review, 569 et seq.; on the other hand *Mokal*, The Search for Someone to Save, 22 (2002) Oxford Journal of Legal Studies, 688 et seq.

35 Cf. the national reports in *McCormack/Bork*, Security Rights and the EIR.

36 Cf. for Germany §51 No.2/3 Insolvenzordnung; for France Cour de Cassation (chambre commerciale) – 30.1.2019 – 17-22223 = ECLI:FR:CCASS:2019:CO00075.

37 More above at para. 5.49.

38 See above at para. 7.7 et seq.

39 Cf. §10.5 PEIL: "A secured insolvency claim is admitted to the extent that it cannot be satisfied from the proceeds of the assets subject to the security right."

40 Exceptions are France (below at para. 7.18) and the USA (below at para. 7.20).

pool) and the secured claim is satisfied from the proceeds. Only a surplus which is not needed for satisfying the secured claim has to be handed over to the estate.

7.16 An important question regards the **entitlement for the realisation**. In most national laws on security rights, it is for the secured creditor to sell the encumbered asset. However, since separate realisation of single assets by each secured creditor would tear apart the business, national insolvency laws sometimes shift the entitlement from the creditor to the Insolvency Practitioner in order to ensure the chance to sell the business as a whole. This shift of entitlement can be accompanied by the Insolvency Practitioner's right to use or even consume the encumbered assets in the ordinary course of business, provided the creditor's satisfaction is guaranteed in a compensatory way. In any case, the creditor is entitled to the proceeds of the collateral, notwithstanding prescribed contributions to the estate. A look to national laws[41] presents a colourful picture.

7.17 Under the law of **England and Wales**, assets encumbered with security rights are not part of the insolvency estate. Hence, the secured creditor is entitled to realise the collateral outside the insolvency proceedings and the proceeds go – as far as they are needed for satisfying the secured claim – entirely to the security holder. However, the creditor may leave the realisation to the Insolvency Practitioner and if they do so the costs of realisation must be payed from the proceeds. An exception is made for floating charges. They rank after the expenses of the proceedings and after preferential claims (sec. 175(2)(b), 176ZA(1) Insolvency Act 1986) and sec. 176A Insolvency Act 1986 requires that before payments to floating charge-holders can be made, a so-called 'prescribed part' of the net assets of the debtor[42] be set aside for the unsecured creditors.[43] Secured creditors

41 See also §9.2 PEIL: "An asset subject to a security right is realised by the administrator or the secured creditor. The secured creditor is entitled to the proceeds of such asset, up to the amount of the secured claim and subject to the rights of creditors with higher ranking claims."

42 "Net" understood to include the assets remaining after the payoff of the other secured creditors (i. e. except for the holder of the floating charge), privileged creditors, and process costs.

43 The size of the prescribed part depends on the absolute amount of the net assets and is regulated in the Insolvency Act 1986 (Prescribed Part) Order 2020, SI 2020, 211. For net assets under £10,000 the prescribed part is 50%, above this threshold it is 50% of the first £10,000 plus 20% of the remaining net assets up to a maximum of £800,000.

are not entitled to be paid out of the prescribed part even where they can only be partially repaid by the remaining assets and an unsecured partial claim remains. Apart from that, intrusion into security rights is only possible on the basis of a moratorium, since moratoria apply also to secured creditors.[44] They can only dispose of the collateral with the consent of the Insolvency Practitioner or the permission of the court. Usage and disposition of the collateral by the Insolvency Practitioner is then possible under sec. 70, 71 Sch. B1 Insolvency Act 1986.

France treats security rights as follows: First, secured creditors[45] must also submit their claims to the Insolvency Practitioner and ask for admission.[46] If the collateral is in the possession of the debtor or Insolvency Practitioner respectively, the latter may use and dispose of it. The proceeds must be lodged in favour of the secured creditor who must be paid in full provided the proceeds of the collateral cover the secured claim (Art. L. 622-8, 626-22 Code de Commerce).[47] If the proceeds are not sufficient the creditor is treated as an ordinary creditor for the unsecured part of the claim (Art. L. 643-6, 643-7 Code de Commerce). If the Insolvency Practitioner does not realise the collateral within three months, the right of separate satisfaction by disposal shifts to the secured creditor (Art. L. 643-2 Code de Commerce). Where secured creditors have possession of the collateral, they are entitled to retain it (Art. L. 622-7, 631-14 Code de Commerce) and be paid in full (Art. 641-13(2) Code de Commerce). The court may permit the redemption of the right to retain by satisfying the secured claim to the amount that the asset is worth (Art. L. 622-7 Code de Commerce). 7.18

In **Germany**, secured creditors are satisfied from the proceeds of the collateral separately from the ordinary course of the proceedings (§§49 et seq. Insolvenzordnung). As regards the entitlement for the realisation of the collateral, the central provision is §166(1) Insolvenzordnung, which places the realisation of movable collateral in the hands of the Insolvency Practitioner, at least insofar as he or she has possession. The same holds true for receivables assigned to the creditor by way of security (§166(2) 7.19

44 See para. 43(2) Sch. B1 Insolvency Act 1986.
45 Note that secured creditors are outranked by employees; see for details below at para. 7.27.
46 Cf. above at para. 7.9.
47 One must bear in mind that certain creditors enjoy priority over secured creditors when it comes to distributing the proceeds of the estate; see below at para. 7.40 et seq.

Insolvenzordnung), whereas all other securities can be realised by their holders (§173 Insolvenzordnung) as long as they are permitted to do so under substantive law.[48] The creditor can also realise charges over land (§49 Insolvenzordnung). With respect to usage rights, an Insolvency Practitioner with realisation rights may also use the collateral (fixed assets) or consume it in production (circulating assets) under §172 Insolvenzordnung. On the other hand, the law respects the security interest of the creditor by providing restitution claims for use and to substitute securities if the collateral is compounded, intermixed, or manufactured. As regards distribution of the proceeds, the Insolvency Practitioner may retain a portion of the proceeds in favour of the estate as costs (usually 9%), and may take into account the fact that VAT on the realisation is to be paid to revenue authorities.

7.20 Under **US law**, secured claims are defined as allowed claims secured by a lien[49] on property in which the estate has an interest, to the extent that value in the collateral supports the creditor's claim (§506(a)(1) Bankruptcy Code). This means – similar to France but diverging from other jurisdictions – that a secured creditor has to lodge the claim with the clerk of the court[50] in order to receive allowance. Nevertheless, if the creditor fails to do so the security right does not lapse and the creditor may seek satisfaction from the collateral even after a discharge (§506(d)(2) Bankruptcy Code).[51] However, security rights are affected by the automatic stay (moratorium, §362(a)(4) Bankruptcy Code) and this transfers the right of usage and disposal to the Insolvency Practitioner (§363 Bankruptcy Code) unless relief is granted by the court (§362(d) Bankruptcy Code). Compensation for usage and the proceeds enjoy "super-priority" over all other preferential claims (§507(b) Bankruptcy Code) and are paid out to the secured creditor but the Insolvency Practitioner is entitled to subtract the costs and expenses connected to the realisation of the collateral (§506(c) Bankruptcy Code).

48 For example, a secured creditor may not enforce the security right under substantive law where the secured claim is directed against a third party and is not due; cf. BGH, Urt. v. 11.4.2013 – IX ZR 176/11 = NZI 2013, 596.

49 For definition, see §101(37) Bankruptcy Code and further §101(36)/(51)/(53) Bankruptcy Code. §506 Bankruptcy Code includes rights to set-off; see for this above at para. 5.53.

50 Cf. above at para. 7.11.

51 *Long v. Bullard* 117 U.S. 617 (1886).

Example: D owns a truck which is burdened with a security right (right *in rem*) to the benefit of C. After the opening of insolvency proceedings against D, the Insolvency Practitioner asks whether she may use the truck for delivery of goods produced in D's factory. The answer is certainly "yes" where C has given his consent, either on request of the Insolvency Practitioner or *ex ante* in the security agreement.[52] Without C's consent, the Insolvency Practitioner is entitled to use the truck under French, German, and US law. Under English law, permission of the court is necessary. 7.21

Security rights which entitle the security holder to a right to separate satisfaction must be distinguished from a **right to separation**. The latter is available where a person can claim that an asset does not belong to the debtor and is therefore not part of the estate.[53] Examples are the legal position of a vendor who has delivered under retention of title,[54] of a trust beneficiary for whom the debtor holds assets on trust,[55] or of a landlord who can – after termination of the tenancy agreement – claim for surrender of the leased asset.[56] Such rights to separation are mostly based on property law yet can also be originate from contract law. For example, where a landlord is not the owner of a leased item, he or she can claim for surrender of this asset based not on property law but on the tenancy agreement or statutes on lease contracts. In many jurisdictions, such separation from the estate is not subject to special rules in insolvency law. Instead, the right to separation can be enforced against the Insolvency Practitioner according to general civil (contract or property) law in the same way as it could be enforced against the debtor before the commencement of the insolvency proceedings.[57] 7.22

52 It has to be checked carefully whether permissions to use or dispose of collateral are still valid after the commencement of insolvency proceedings. Cf. for Germany BGH, Urt. 24.1.2019 – IX ZR 110/17 = BGHZ 221, 10 = NJW 2019, 1940.

53 This includes joint assets, e.g. items belonging jointly to the debtor and his or her spouse; cf. UNCITRAL Legislative Guide, p. 81 para. 20 et seq.

54 See above at para. 5.33 and the example at para. 4.4.

55 See §541(d) Bankruptcy Code. As a trustee, the debtor has legal title but neither legal nor equitable interest.

56 Cf. above at para. 2.23.

57 Expressly stated in §§47 et seq. Insolvenzordnung.

IV. PREFERENTIAL CREDITORS

7.23 Insolvency proceedings are designed to satisfy claims (on a *pro rata* basis and under the principle of equal treatment of creditors) which have been established before the commencement of insolvency proceedings.[58] However, nearly all jurisdictions privilege certain classes of creditors which rank ahead of ordinary creditors.[59] They receive **preferential treatment** by being entitled to full satisfaction of their claims before a single penny can be distributed to the ordinary creditors. Typically, two sorts of preferential creditors can be observed.[60] The first comprises all creditors who finance the proceedings or support them by rendering the counter-performances to the Insolvency Practitioner; this group covers the costs and expenses of the proceedings. Second, states tend to privilege certain classes of ordinary creditors by entitling them to full satisfaction (provided the estate is sufficient) although their claims have been established before the opening of the proceedings; typical examples are claims of employees or revenue authorities.[61]

7.24 Preferential creditors are not (treated as) ordinary creditors. Hence, the **rules for ordinary creditors** do not always apply. Preferential creditors are in most jurisdictions not obliged to lodge their claims with the court or the Insolvency Practitioner.[62] They are typically not banned from enforcing their claims and are not referred to the rules for receiving the dividend.[63] Instead, Insolvency Practitioners are bound to pay them in full as soon as their claims fall due.

7.25 A special situation may occur where it turns out during the insolvency proceedings that the **estate is not sufficient** to pay all preferential creditors, let alone ordinary creditors. National laws must take this deficiency into account and provide for rules which regulate the order in which the remaining means are to be distributed. They should also consider rules

58 See above at para 2.17.

59 See also UNCITRAL Legislative Guide, p. 270 para. 66 et seq.

60 Details above at para. 2.25 et seq.

61 Sometimes quite strange privileges can be found, e.g. for grain producers and fishermen in §507(a)(6) Bankruptcy Code.

62 However, in some jurisdictions (e. g. the Netherlands), "creditors of the estate" (regarding costs and expenses of the proceedings) are treated differently from privileged ordinary creditors.

63 Cf. above at para. 5.60.

on the liability of an Insolvency Practitioner who has created debts of the estate which cannot be paid from the insufficient estate.

In **England and Wales**, first priority is given to the expenses of the proceedings (sec. 176ZA Insolvency Act 1986).[64] Ranking after them, there are two groups of preferential debts: ordinary and secondary preferential debts.[65] Sec. 175(1A), 386(1A) with para. 8-15B Schedule 6 Insolvency Act 1986 privileges five groups of ordinary preferential debts. Generally speaking, priority is granted to certain employment-related pre-insolvency claims.[66] Interestingly, ordinary preferential debts are comprised in one class. They rank after the expenses of the proceedings but ahead of secondary preferential debts (sec. 175(1B) Insolvency Act 1986) and floating charge holders (sec. §175(2)(b) Insolvency Act 1986) and rank equally among themselves. They are to be paid in full unless the estate is insufficient in which case they are to be satisfied on a *pro rata* basis (sec. 175(1B) Insolvency Act 1986). As opposed to expenses of the proceedings which have to be paid in full when they fall due, all preferential debts must be proven according to the rules explained above at para. 7.8. 7.26

France has a strict order of privileged creditors. Highest ranking are employees with their wage claims for (up to) 60 days prior to the commencement of the proceedings. This *super privilège* is contained in labour law (Art. L. 3253-2 et seq. Code du travail, applicable in insolvency proceedings by reference of Art. L. 625-9 Code de Commerce) and even outranks secured creditors (Art. L. 626-22 Code de Commerce). The privileged claims are covered by a bad debt insurance provided by employers through *L'Association pour la gestion du régime de Garantie des créances des Salariés* (*AGS*) to which the claims are demised and which enjoys the super-priority in the distribution of the proceeds. *AGS's* claims to recourse are followed by the costs and expenses of the proceedings – provided they have not been paid as they fell due –, certain tax claims and claims of employees accrued between 60 days and 6 months prior 7.27

64 For priorities among the costs and expenses see rules 3.51(2), 7.108(4), 10.149 Insolvency Rules 2016. The internal order is subject to a decision of the court, sec. 112, 156 Insolvency Act 1986, rules 7.110(1), 3.51(3) Insolvency Rules 2016.

65 Secondary preferential debts are certain financial deposits (sec. 175((3), 386(1B) with para. 15BA, 15BB Schedule 6 Insolvency Act 1986) and only relevant in insolvencies of credit institutions; they can be neglected here.

66 Crown preferences for tax claims have been abolished in 1986 and 2002.

to the commencement of the proceedings (Art. 2331(4), 2375(2) Code Civil, Art. L. 622-17, 631-14, 641-13 Code de Commerce). Privileged pre-commencement claims (except those of employees) must also be filed with the Insolvency Practitioner for admission.[67]

7.28 **Germany** is very reluctant in acknowledging preferential creditors. Only the costs (fees for the court, the Insolvency Practitioner, and the members of a creditors' committee) and the expenses of the proceedings (debts created or upgraded by the Insolvency Practitioner) are entitled to preferential treatment as "creditors of the estate" (§§53 et seq. Insolvenzordnung) whereas not a single group of ordinary creditors is privileged. That holds particularly true for employees whose claims are protected by public unemployment insurance.[68] Preferential creditors are not bound to the rules of lodging the claims, are entitled to full satisfaction, and may enforce their claims against the Insolvency Practitioner during the proceedings (§90 Insolvenzordnung). Insufficiency of the estate has to be reported by the Insolvency Practitioner to the court and leads to either immediate termination of the proceedings (where the remaining means are not sufficient to cover the costs of the proceedings, §207 Insolvenzordnung) or to grouping the preferential creditors into classes (cost before expenses and expenses created after the report of insufficiency before expenses created prior to this report, §§208 et seq. Insolvenzordnung), meaning that the proceeds of the estate are primarily paid to the higher ranking class until they are all paid in full. The Insolvency Practitioner can be held liable for damages if a preferential debt created by a legal transaction of the Insolvency Practitioner cannot be paid in full unless he or she could not be aware of the probable insufficiency of the insolvency estate (§61 Insolvenzordnung).

7.29 A long list of priorities is available in the **USA**. §507 Bankruptcy Code lists ten – intricately shaped – groups of preferential creditors. It starts with the fee of the Insolvency Practitioner (§507(a)(1)(C)

---

67 See above at para. 7.9.

68 So called "*Insolvenzgeld*": employees are entitled to receive unpaid wages up to three months prior to the opening of insolvency proceedings. The funds are provided by the *Bundesagentur für Arbeit* (Federal Employment Agency) which is financed by mandatory contributions from all employers. For details see §§165 et seq. Sozialgesetzbuch III.

Bankruptcy Code). Domestic support obligations as defined in §101(14A) Bankruptcy Code (§507(a)(1) Bankruptcy Code, relevant in individual bankruptcies only) are given priority over administrative expenses as defined in §503 Bankruptcy Code (§507(a)(2) Bankruptcy Code). Finally, certain claims of employees and pensioners (§507(a)(4)/(5) Bankruptcy Code) as well as tax claims (§507(a)(8) Bankruptcy Code) are included. This "waterfall scheme" is mandatory.[69] Some creditors rank ahead of the groups listed in §507(a) Bankruptcy Code, i.e. they enjoy "super-priority". This holds true for post-petition lenders (§364(c)(1) Bankruptcy Code) and compensation claims of secured creditors (§507(b) Bankruptcy Code). Priorities do not entitle the privileged creditor to immediate satisfaction or enforcement but only to preferential treatment in the final distributions of the proceeds. Each group has to be paid in full before distributions to a lower ranking class can be made (§726(a) Bankruptcy Code). If the estate is not sufficient to pay a class in full, creditors belonging to this class will receive payments on a *pro rata* basis only (§726(b) Bankruptcy Code).

Example: D company has rented its premises from landlord C. After the commencement of insolvency proceedings, C requires payment of outstanding rent for the three months before and the time after the opening of proceedings. The latter will be successful in most jurisdictions, since debts stemming from tenancy agreements which are continued after the opening of proceedings are preferential debts.[70] As regards rent for the period before the opening of the proceedings, landlords are ordinary creditors. This is final in France, Germany, and the USA. In England and Wales, however, courts are inclined to treat certain rents as expenses of the proceedings.[71] 7.30

69 *Czyzewski v. Jevic Holding Corp.*, 137 S. Ct. 973, 197 L. Ed. 2d 398, 41 IER Cases 1613, 85 U.S.L.W. 4115 (2017).

70 Cf. above at para. 5.35.

71 The leading case is *In re Lundy Granite Co* [1870–71] LR 6 Ch App 462; see also *Kahn & Anr v. Commissioners of Inland Revenue* [2002] UKHL 6; *Pillar Denton Ltd & ors v. Jervis* [2014] EWCA Civ. 180; *Shinners & Anr v. London Trocadero* (2015) LLP [2019] EWHC 2932 (Ch).

V. SUBORDINATED CREDITORS

7.31 Most insolvency laws subordinate the claims of certain creditor groups which would otherwise be classified as ordinary or even new creditors.[72] Typical ordinary – i.e. pre-commencement[73] – creditors subordinated by statute are shareholders who have granted a loan to their company (instead of increasing the company's share capital) or donees who are entitled to a gratuitous performance of the debtor. The **policy** behind this subordination is that such creditors are not in the same way worthy of protection as other ordinary creditors, since they are closer to the insolvency risk (shareholders) or since they have not suffered a loss through delivering a compensating performance (donees). Interestingly, this policy is frequently mirrored in transactions avoidance law where gratuitous performances (all jurisdictions)[74] and payments to shareholders (some national laws)[75] are voidable under alleviated conditions. Furthermore, national laws tend to subordinate certain post-commencement claims which would otherwise be claims of new creditors.[76] Examples are claims for payment of post-petition interest on pre-petition claims or for reimbursement of the expenses arising from the participation in the proceedings. Finally, subordination can result from a subordination agreement between debtor and creditor or between creditors (§39(2) Insolvenzordnung, §510(a) Bankruptcy Code[77]).

7.32 Subordinated creditors build a group of their own. They are only entitled to participate in the proceeds from the estate if **all ordinary creditors are fully satisfied**. This means that the proceeds are distributed to the preferential and ordinary creditors and only what is left can be paid to the subordinated creditors.[78] Typically, the proceeds are not sufficient to pay ordinary creditors in full. Hence, nothing is left for distribution to the subordinated creditors. Where – by way of exception – a surplus is

72 See for details above at para. 2.28; further UNCITRAL Legislative Guide, p. 267 para. 55 et seq.

73 More at para. 2.17 above.

74 Cf. above at para. 6.29 et seq.

75 Details above at para. 6.46.

76 See above at para. 2.28.

77 In England and Wales, such agreements are not mentioned in the Insolvency Act 1986 but recognised in case law; cf. *Cheah Theam Swee v. Equiticorp Finance Group Ltd* [1991] UKPC 39.

78 More below at para. 7.40 et seq.

available, all subordinated creditors are satisfied on a *pro rata* basis unless national law (or a subordination agreement) provides for a ranking of various groups of subordinated creditors.

Since subordinated creditors are typically left empty-handed, they are frequently **excluded from the proceedings** (and also from any other enforcement against the debtor). They have no recoverable rights and therefore no legitimate interest in participating in the proceedings. Subject to national insolvency laws, subordinated creditors are not entitled to file their claims with the court or the Insolvency Practitioner unless a distribution to this lowest ranking class appears to be likely. However, in this latter case the same rules apply as for ordinary creditors. Insofar, reference can be made to para. 7.5 et seq. 7.33

Although rule 14.12(2) Insolvency Rules 2016 states that all debts other than preferential debts rank equally between themselves, **England and Wales** know various forms of subordinated debts. First, any surplus remaining after the payment to ordinary creditors shall be applied in paying post-commencement interest (sec. 189(2) Insolvency Act 1986, rule 14.23(7) Insolvency Rules 2016).[79] Second, there are two categories of "deferred debt" which cannot be proven and paid unless all other claims (including interest claims) have been satisfied (rule 14.2(4)(b) Insolvency Rules 2016): claims of shareholders which are held in their capacity as members[80] (sec. 74(2)(f) Insolvency Act 1986) and claims held by directors if ordered so by the court (sec. 215(4), 246ZA(4) Insolvency Act 1986).[81] Shareholders as such (i.e. without any claims for payment) are only entitled to participate in the distribution of the liquidation proceeds if all other ordinary or subordinated creditors are satisfied. 7.34

Insolvency law in **France** does not provide for any subordination of claims. This also holds true for shareholders whose claims (including loans) are treated as unsecured ordinary debts. Hence, shareholders are also obliged to file their claims with the Insolvency Practitioner for admission.[82] However, shareholders as such (i.e. without any claims for payment) are 7.35

79 See for details *Commissioners for Her Majesty's Revenue and Customs v Joint Administrators of Lehman Brothers International (Europe) (In Administration)* [2019] UKSC 12.

80 Not: as creditors. Hence, shareholder loans are not covered by this rule.

81 For the "prescribed part" of floating charges, cf. above at para. 7.17.

82 See above at para. 7.9.

only entitled to participate in the distribution of the liquidation proceeds if all other claims of unsecured ordinary creditors are satisfied.

7.36 The law is different in **Germany**. Here, statute provides for various groups of subordinated creditors which are satisfied in the order of groups and on a *pro rata* basis inside each group (§39(1) Insolvenzordnung). Certain post-commencement and pre-commencement debts are subordinated. Post-commencement debts that are subordinated are interest and penalties for late payment accruing after the opening of the insolvency proceedings (§39(1)No.1 Insolvenzordnung) and costs of ordinary creditors due to their participation in the proceedings (§39(1)No.2 Insolvenzordnung). Pre-commencement debts that are subordinated are fines and other legal consequences of a criminal or administrative offence binding the debtor to pay money (§39(1)No.3 Insolvenzordnung), claims to the debtor's gratuitous performance of a consideration (§39(1)No.4 Insolvenzordnung), and claims for restitution of shareholder loans or for transactions corresponding in economic terms to such a loan (§39(1)No.5 Insolvenzordnung). The latter – shareholder loans rank after ordinary creditors and all other groups of subordinated creditors – is of significant importance in many insolvency proceedings. Subordinated creditors may not file their claims with the Insolvency Practitioner (since they will normally come out empty-handed) unless they are summoned by the court to do so (§174(3) Insolvenzordnung). Besides, shareholders as such (i.e. without any claims for payment) do not participate in the distribution of liquidation proceeds unless all creditors (including subordinated creditors) are paid in full (§199 Insolvenzordnung).

7.37 In the **USA**, subordination is not prescribed in statute. The only exception is the subordination of claims resulting from a purchase or sale of securities of the debtor which typically arise where the purchaser was defrauded by the debtor (§510(b) Bankruptcy Code).[83] Apart from that, subordination is left at the discretion of the court, which may, under principles of equitable subordination, subordinate for purposes of distribution all or part of an allowed claim to all or part of another allowed claim or all or part of an allowed interest to all or part of another allowed interest and order that any lien securing such a subordinated claim be transferred to the

---

[83] At its core, this rule "serves to effectuate one of the general principles of corporate and bankruptcy law: that creditors are entitled to be paid ahead of shareholders in the distribution of corporate assets", *Seaquest Diving LP v. S & J Diving Inc. (In re Seaquest Diving LP)*, 579 F.3d 411 (5th Cir. 2009).

estate (§510(c) Bankruptcy Code). However, this authorisation is rarely executed. For such measures, courts require inequitable conduct of the claimant (e.g. fraud, breach of fiduciary duties, undercapitalisation, instrumentalisation of the debtor), injury to the general body of creditors (or unfair advantage of the claimant), and consistency with the provisions of the Bankruptcy Code.[84] These conditions are typically met where insiders (shareholders, directors, etc.[85]) are involved. Subordinated are also tardily and unexcused filed claims (§726(a)(3)/(2)(C) Bankruptcy Code) and – ranking after them – claims for non-compensatory penalties or multiple damages (§726(a)(4) Bankruptcy Code). The last class comprises interest claims for the time period after the commencement of insolvency proceedings (§726(a)(5) Bankruptcy Code).

Example: Creditor C files her claim against D with the Insolvency Practitioner (or court respectively), including interest for the time before and after the commencement of the insolvency proceedings. This will be disputed as far as the post-commencement interest is concerned, since such claims are subordinated in all jurisdictions evaluated here except for France. Under French law, no such claims exist, since interest is suspended by the opening of the proceedings (Art. L. 622-28, 631-14, 641-3 Code de Commerce). 7.38

VI. DISTRIBUTION OF THE PROCEEDS

Satisfying the creditors' claims is the final step in insolvency proceedings. 7.39 It requires the **realisation of the estate**, since creditors are not entitled to the debtor's assets but only to the proceeds of such assets. As elaborated extensively above,[86] the realisation of the estate is typically the task of the Insolvency Practitioner, with some exceptions for collateral.[87] Hence, assets must be sold – singly or together with others of the same kind or as part of the completely transferred estate –, receivables must be collected, real estate must be sold or put up for compulsory sale, etc. The details

84 A leading case is *In re Mobile Steel Co.*, 563 F.2d 692 (5th Cir. 1977).
85 See for transactions avoidance law also above at para. 6.19.
86 Cf. at para. 5.2, 5.4, 5.19 et seq.
87 For the latter, see above at para. 7.13 et seq.

of realisation rules are dependent on the nature of the asset in question on the one hand (the realisation of real estate may differ widely from the realisation of receivables or shares) and of the rules in national insolvency laws on the other hand. At any rate, the Insolvency Practitioner who has to safeguard the interests of the creditors is obliged to realise the estate as favourably as possible and collect as much money for distribution as possible.

7.40 Once the estate is realised, the Insolvency Practitioner can start with the distribution of the proceeds, following the order of **ranking of claims.**[88] This order is typically as follows: in the first rank, secured creditors are satisfied from the proceeds of the collateral, followed by – as the case may be: various groups of – preferential creditors[89] (second rank), ordinary creditors (third rank), and subordinated creditors (fourth rank). In the – rare – event there is a surplus after all claims have been satisfied in full, this is to be returned to the debtor. However, this typical ranking is not always strictly provided for, since national laws break these rules by establishing exceptions and modifications.

7.41 One class ranking ahead of another means that the proceeds of the estate are primarily paid *pari passu* to the higher ranking creditors until they are all paid in full. This is expressed in the **absolute priority rule** according to which no distribution can be made to a lower ranking class – let alone the debtor – before all creditors of a higher ranking class are satisfied in full.[90] Only then can the remaining proceeds be distributed to the lower ranking creditors on a *pro rata* basis (unless the proceeds suffice to pay both classes in full).[91] Exceptions can be necessary, particularly regarding restructuring attempts,[92] but in principle the absolute priority rule is strictly applied.

7.42 Normally, ordinary creditors are not fully satisfied and that brings up the question as to the fate of the **unsatisfied rest** of the claims. Principally,

---

88 See also UNCITRAL Legislative Guide, p. 266 para. 51 et seq. with Recommendations 185 et seq.

89 Typically: creditors of the estate (regarding costs and expenses of the proceedings) before privileged ordinary creditors.

90 *Bank of America Natl. Trust & Savings Assn. v. 203 North LaSalle St. Partn.*, 526 U.S. 434, 119 S. Ct. 1411, 143 L. Ed. 2d 607, 67 U.S.L.W. 4275 (1999).

91 Cf. UNCITRAL Legislative Guide, p. 276 Recommendation 191.

92 See, however, below at para. 8.37.

this part of the claims continues to exist and the creditor can demand satisfaction if the debtor achieves a new fortune after the termination of the insolvency proceedings. However, this is subject to two serious restrictions. First, where the debtor is not a natural person but a legal entity (company), liquidation of the assets normally entails liquidation of the legal person; hence, the debtor extinguishes[93] and with it, its debts extinguish. Second, where the debtor is a natural person, many jurisdictions provide for a discharge of residual debt, which we will deal with in more detail below in Chapter 9.

In **England and Wales**, the ranking of creditors is much more complicated than in other jurisdictions. According to a leading decision of the UK Supreme Court,[94] the order is as follows: first-ranking are creditors secured by fixed charges who are satisfied outside the proceedings.[95] They are followed by the expenses of the proceedings (sec. 175(1A) Insolvency Act 1986) and, third-ranking, other preferential creditors[96] (sec. 175(1) Insolvency Act 1986). Only the fourth rank is assigned to floating charge creditors[97] (sec. 175(2)(b), 176ZA(1) Insolvency Act 1986) who are followed by ordinary creditors with unsecured provable claims,[98] post-commencement interest claims, and non-provable claims. At the end of line are other subordinated creditors[99] and finally shareholders. Within each class, creditors rank equally and are satisfied on a *pro rata* basis (sec. 107, 175, 189(3) Insolvency Act 1986, rule 14.12(2), 14.23(7) Insolvency Rules 2016). 7.43

French law protects certain pre-commencement claims of employees with a *super-privilège* which outranks all other creditors, no matter whether they are secured or not.[100] Apart from this, secured creditors are satisfied 7.44

---

93 Cf. §13.2(2) PEIL: "When the debtor is a legal person, it will cease to exist following the closure of liquidation."

94 *Re Nortel GmbH* [2013] UKSC 52; see also *Re Lehman Brothers International (Europe) ('Waterfall I')* [2017] UKSC 38.

95 Above at para. 7.17.

96 For them, see above at para. 7.26.

97 See again above at para. 7.17 (also for the "prescribed part", benefitting the ordinary creditors).

98 Cf. above at para. 7.8.

99 More above at para. 7.34.

100 Details above at para.7.27.

from the proceeds of the collateral.[101] Among unsecured creditors, some claims enjoy priority over others:[102] first come the costs and expenses of the proceedings, after them certain tax claims and pre-commencement employee claims (Art. L. 622-17(3), 641-13(3) Code de Commerce). All other unsecured creditors rank lowest but equally (the category of subordinated creditors is unknown to French law[103]); they are entitled to distribution on a *pro rata* basis (Art. L. 643-8 Code de Commerce).

7.45 In **Germany**, the ranking of claims strictly follows the order explained above.[104] Secured creditors are satisfied from the proceeds of the collateral independent and separated from the general distribution of the estate.[105] Preferential creditors are also not bound to wait for the general distribution but can collect their claims continuously during the proceedings.[106] As opposed to that, ordinary creditors have to wait for instalments or final payments from the proceeds of the estate. There is only one group of ordinary creditors and they are paid on a *pro rata* basis.[107] Only if a surplus is left for subordinated creditors, these are paid according to the ranking of the groups of subordinated creditors and again on a *pro rata* basis.[108]

7.46 Similar rules apply in the **USA**. According to §725 Bankruptcy Code, secured creditors come first. They have to be satisfied from the proceeds of the collateral before any other distribution to the ordinary creditors can be made. For all other creditors, ranking is regulated in §726 Bankruptcy Code. First rank is assigned to privileged ordinary creditors who enjoy priority over other claims according to §507 Bankruptcy Code. They are entitled to payments from the proceeds of the estate in the order of priority groups and are followed by ordinary creditors who have filed their claim in a timely manner (or not timely, but "excused"). Third ranking are subordinated creditors as described above at para 7.37. According

101 See above at para. 7.18.
102 More above at para. 7.27.
103 Cf. above at para. 7.35.
104 At para. 7.40.
105 See above at para. 7.19, also for the reimbursement of costs where the Insolvency Practitioner has realised the collateral.
106 Cf. above para. 7.28.
107 See above at para. 7.10.
108 In detail above at para. 7.36.

to §726(b) Bankruptcy Code, lower ranking groups are not entitled to participate in the proceeds unless higher ranking groups are fully satisfied, and in each group the distribution must be made on a *pro rata* basis.

For further reading: *Bork*, Einführung, §§25, 26; *Bork*, Rescuing Companies, para. 13.01 et seq.; *Fletcher*, Law of Insolvency, para. 9-001 et seq., 10-001 et seq.; *Saint-Alary-Houin*, Droit des enterprises en difficulté, para. 764 et seq.; *Tabb*, Law of Bankruptcy, §7.1 et seq.; *van Zwieten*, Principles of Corporate Insolvency Law, para. 8-35 et seq. 7.47

CHAPTER 8
RESTRUCTURING PROCEEDINGS

In the eighth chapter we will deal with restructuring proceedings which, as an alternative to liquidation proceedings, aim at rescuing the insolvent debtor company or at least the business. We will cover the policy behind rules on restructuring and will learn that all jurisdictions covered by this book provide for one or more kinds of reorganisation proceedings. We will be informed about the prerequisites and main features of these proceedings and will particularly encounter the special appearance of debtor-in-possession proceedings. Finally, we will cover restructuring plans, i.e. agreements between the debtor and at least a majority of its creditors, as a special instrument to overcome insolvency and to make the business viable again. 8.1

I. BASICS

Thus far, we have primarily dealt with **liquidation proceedings** in this book. However, where insolvency of businesses is concerned, liquidation is mostly the least favourable option, since it results in the loss of all jobs, destroys the remaining value of the business, diminishes the return to the creditors, extinguishes a competitor in the market, may have severe consequences for the municipality the company is doing business in, and may cause further insolvencies of business partners (domino effect). Despite such detrimental consequences, liquidation is often unavoidable – where a badly qualified cook has an uninspired restaurant in a low frequented area of the town, the situation is hopeless – and in many cases the business is already shut down when insolvency proceedings are commenced. 8.2

On the other hand, every insolvency law must take **restructuring** (or reorganisation) into account. Where the company – or at least the 8.3

business[1] – can be rescued, jobs can be preserved, the market upholds a competitor and the municipality a tax payer, and the return for the creditors is significantly higher than in liquidation, since the going concern value (including "good will") instead of the divestiture value can be realised to the benefit of the creditors. Furthermore, where not only the business but also the company is rescued, the debtor keeps their enterprise and shareholders keep their investment.[2] Hence, where restructuring is possible, it is, in most cases, the better option.

8.4 It is for this reason that almost all jurisdictions include **rules on restructuring** for debtors or businesses in their law, sometimes in company law but typically in insolvency law. Of course, the avoidance of insolvency and the overcoming of financial crises can be negotiated and regulated between all stakeholders in out-of-court settlements, but frequently legal support is necessary, especially against opposing minorities who sabotage restructuring efforts by enforcing their claims or refusing to compromise and to contribute to the restructuring. Hence, reorganisation rules are nowadays an important feature of insolvency law[3] – so important that some authors observe a "shift from liquidation to restructuring" which describes the focus of current academic discussion rather than the reality in practice.[4] However, national laws differ widely regarding the details of restructuring law. Some jurisdictions provide for autonomous restructuring-related proceedings which are available alongside insolvency proceedings (II.). Others have special legal instruments in their insolvency proceedings on hand which are predominantly designed for rescuing companies (III.). In any case, this deserves a closer look.

II. PROCEEDINGS

8.5 National laws provide for **various kinds** of restructuring proceedings. Some are shaped to assist debtors who are already insolvent, and therefore require substantive insolvency as a prerequisite for opening such proceedings.[5]

---

1 The business as the organisational entity (pooling of assets and human resources, i.e. the enterprise) must be distinguished from the debtor company which is the holder of the business (entrepreneur); see also above at para. 1.4. – For consumers, see below at para. 9.31 et seq.

2 Comprisingly *United States v. Whiting Pools, Inc.*, 462 U.S. 198 (1983).

3 See also UNCITRAL Legislative Guide, p. 26 para. 19 et seq.

4 Cf. above at para. 8.2.

5 On this already above at para. 3.19.

In this case, the proceedings are insolvency proceedings which, on the one hand, are marked with the "stigma of insolvency" but, on the other hand, offer the instruments of insolvency law[6] to support restructuring efforts. As opposed to this, other proceedings can only be commenced where the debtor is not insolvent but is likely to become insolvent in the foreseeable future. A third group of proceedings is tagged by indifference as to the insolvency of the debtor and does not mention insolvency at all. In the present context, it is not possible to expound all these proceedings in detail. An overview over the most important features must suffice.

Interestingly, the **European Union** has bound its Member States by Art. 1(1)(a) Directive 2019/1023[7] to establish "preventive restructuring frameworks available for debtors in financial difficulties when there is a likelihood of insolvency, with a view to preventing the insolvency and ensuring the viability of the debtor". As we will see in the following paragraphs, such "pre-insolvency restructuring proceedings" are already available in many, but not yet in all jurisdictions.[8] Member States are obliged to adopt the laws, regulations, and administrative provisions necessary to comply with this Directive only by 17 July 2021 (Art. 34(1) Directive 2019/1023). Hence, it must be left for the next edition of this book to report on the amendments of national laws regarding pre-insolvency restructuring proceedings. Until then, it will stick to the legal *status quo*. 8.6

A. GERMANY

To start with Germany, there is currently **only one single set of proceedings** serving all purposes, leaving it to the parties involved whether the proceedings should aim at restructuring rather than liquidation.[9] 8.7

---

6 More on this below at para. 8.27 et seq.

7 Directive (EU) 2019/1023 of the European Parliament and of the Council of 20 June 2019 on preventive restructuring frameworks, on discharge of debt and disqualifications, and on measures to increase the efficiency of procedures concerning restructuring, insolvency and discharge of debt, and amending Directive (EU) 2017/1132 (Directive on restructuring and insolvency, OJ 2019 L 172/18).

8 General remarks in the UNCITRAL Legislative Guide, p. 21 para. 1 et seq. and p. 238 para. 76 et seq. with Recommendations 160 et seq.

9 Cf. §1 Insolvenzordnung: "The insolvency proceedings shall serve the purpose of collective satisfaction of a debtor's creditors by liquidation of the debtor's assets and by distribution of the proceeds, or by reaching an arrangement in an insolvency plan, particularly in order to maintain the enterprise."

In most cases, restructuring is the task of the Insolvency Practitioner who is empowered by §80 Insolvenzordnung[10] to take all necessary measures to bring the business back to life and to either rescue the debtor company which keeps its business or transfer the business to a third party by way of an asset deal,[11] which requires the consent of a creditors' committee.[12] Within insolvency law, there are not only the general tools[13] which can be useful for rescuing the business but also special instruments designed for supporting restructuring efforts, especially rules on an "insolvency plan"[14] and on debtor-in-possession proceedings (self-administration).[15] In any case, these measures are embedded in insolvency proceedings and thus require inability to pay debts or overindebtedness to be opened.[16]

8.8 Pure pre-insolvency proceedings are currently not available. However, since there is normally an extensive application stage between the application for and the opening of insolvency proceedings,[17] this can be used in combination with debtor-in-possession proceedings to prepare for restructuring decisions. This especially holds true for the so-called "**Protective Umbrella Procedure**" (*Schutzschirmverfahren*),[18] governed by §270b Insolvenzordnung which lays the groundwork for a restructuring preparation procedure within the application stage of insolvency. The objective is to give the debtor who has to apply for formal insolvency proceedings time to prepare for a restructuring in self-administration. If he or she asks for it, they may be granted a period of up to three months under the umbrella of the protection of the court and the preliminary Insolvency Practitioner (insolvency monitor, *Sachwalter*). During this time an "insolvency plan" can be negotiated and it can be executed quickly upon the opening of proceedings in a pre-packaged fashion.

---

10 Extensively above at para. 5.19 et seq.
11 Again, see above at para. 1.4.
12 Cf. above at para. 2.35.
13 More on this below at para. 8.27 et seq.
14 More on this below at para. 8.32 et seq.
15 Details below at para. 8.21 et seq.
16 In detail, above at para. 3.18.
17 Cf. above at para. 3.6.
18 Extensively *Bork*, The "Protective Umbrella Procedure" – a New German Restructuring Tool, Insolvency Intelligence 25 (2012), 22–24.

B. ENGLAND AND WALES

In England and Wales, various procedures which aim mainly at restructuring are available.[19] The first are **Company Voluntary Arrangement** proceedings (CVA), regulated in sec. 1-7B Insolvency Act 1986.[20] This is a procedural instrument chiefly intended to enable a compromise agreement between debtor and unsecured creditors: it allows only for debt restructuring, not operational reorganisation.[21] The CVA procedure is begun by the debtor's submission of a proposal, which must include declarations about the size and compound of the estate. Substantive insolvency is not required, nor does access to the procedure depend on convincing a court of some sort of crisis or financial difficulty. The procedure aims exclusively at coming to an agreement with the debtor's creditors. It can be embedded in insolvency proceedings but also stand alone, in which case the instruments of insolvency law (such as transactions avoidance law or rules on executory contracts) are not available. The proposal must contain either a composition of debts or a Scheme of Arrangement (sec. 1(1) Insolvency Act 1986).[22] It is generally prepared with the assistance of an insolvency professional, whom the debtor then designates as its nominee in court. The nominee reviews the proposal within 28 days of the involvement of the court, and invites the shareholders and creditors to meetings that vote on the proposal which needs a majority of 75% but no court sanctioning. Once accepted, the plan is binding on all creditors entitled to vote.[23] 8.9

From company law comes the **Scheme of Arrangement** procedure, set out in sec. 895 et seq. Companies Act 2006.[24] It seeks a compromise between the company and creditors as well as among shareholders, 8.10

---

19 Extensively *Bork*, Rescuing Companies in England and Germany, Chapter 6.

20 For individuals, Individual Voluntary Arrangement proceedings (IVA) are available, sec. 252–263G Insolvency Act 1986. See for details below at para. 9.32.

21 This may be the reason for the fact that the CVA is not used very frequently (only 23 cases between 2016 and 2019) and that more than 50% of all CVA cases have resulted in failure.

22 The latter would lead to a combination of CVA and Scheme of Arrangement, cf. below at para. 8.10.

23 For details, see below at para. 8.36.

24 Note, that the use of a Scheme of Arrangement is not limited to restructuring but can also be used to facilitate liquidation proceedings. Cf. *Lehmann Brothers International (Europe) (in administration)* [2018] EWHC 1980 (Ch), regarding the distribution of surplus funds remaining after satisfaction of ordinary creditors, see above at para. 7.43.

dividing them into classes based on how they are affected by the proposed arrangement. The procedure, for which insolvency is not a requirement, is begun on application to the court by the company, a creditor, or a shareholder. A statement on the effects of the plan and all possible conflicts of interest must accompany an invitation to a general meeting of the creditors (sec. 897 Companies Act 2006). There is no mandatory appointment of an insolvency practitioner: the procedure is carried out without administrators or officially designated restructurers, unless it is embedded in insolvency – mostly: administration – proceedings. It can be deduced from statute that the law intends this procedure to be used to restructure the company and its capital, whether within or without insolvency, rather than to serve as a pre-insolvency restructuring procedure. The Scheme of Arrangement is designed to be used at any stage of a business crisis. In the further course of proceedings, the court calls a separate assembly of each individual creditor group who can in turn approve the compromise with a simple majority of votes constituting at least three-quarters of the sum outstanding. If the necessary majority is reached, the court must then approve the agreement, checking its procedural integrity as well as whether it is fair and reasonable. If the court approves the compromise, it is binding on all the creditors, including secured creditors, shareholders, and the debtor. These rules have recently been supplemented by Part 26A Companies Act 2006 which provides for arrangements for companies in financial difficulty. It is modelled on the scheme of arrangement but introduces a restructuring plan which must be approved by creditors affected by the plan and can be confirmed by the court even where not all classes have given their consent (cross-class cram-down). It is for this reason that the arrangement is labelled as the **Cross-Class Cram-Down Scheme**.

8.11 The most important option for companies that are looking to restructure are **administration** proceedings, regulated in Sch. B1 Insolvency Act 1986. Administration is designed by statute to last for one year (para. 76(1) Sch. B1 Insolvency Act 1986). There are two types: administered by the court or administered out of court. The court-administered variety is begun by an administration order on application of the debtor, its management, or one or more creditors. The order names an administrator (para. 10, 12 Sch. B1 Insolvency Act 1986). An out-of-court administration can be initiated by the holder of a qualifying floating charge, the debtor company, or its management naming an administrator and registering the nomination with the court (para. 22 et seq., 31 Sch. B1 Insolvency Act 1986). Administration requires either cash-flow insolvency (inability to pay debts) or the likelihood of it (para. 11(a), 27(2)(a) Sch. B1 Insolvency Act 1986). The beginning of either type of administration automatically leads to a moratorium (para. 42 Sch. B1 Insolvency Act 1986). While the administration is running, the management of the business can no longer act without the administrator's (or the court's) permission (para. 64 Sch. B1 Insolvency Act 1986), and the administrator, as both agent of the company and officer of the court (para. 5, 69 Sch. B1 Insolvency Act 1986), has far-reaching powers, based in statute or conferred by the court (para. 1, 59 et seq. Sch. B1 Insolvency Act 1986), including transactions avoidance actions.[25] He or she has a duty to lay out a restructuring proposal which must be laid before a creditors' meeting within ten weeks for them to vote on it.[26] Restructuring plans often call for an agreement with the creditors, either in the form of a Scheme of Arrangement or a CVA, and the rules on voting for these provisions are imported from their respective regulatory bases. The carrying out of the restructuring is the decision and responsibility of the administrator. Where restructuring attempts fail, administration proceedings can be moved to winding-up proceedings.[27]

C. FRANCE

Book VI of French Code de Commerce offers a variety of restructuring proceedings, the application of which depends on the level the crisis of the company has reached and of the amount of support the company needs. The first to be mentioned here is the ***mandat ad hoc*** as regulated in Art. L. 611-1 et seq. Code de Commerce. In these proceedings, the debtor may join a state-organised prevention group which is tasked with providing its members with a confidential analysis of the debtor's economic, accounting, and financial data and which will inform the management and may suggest that an expert provide assistance where signs of difficulty are identified (Art. L. 611-1 Code de Commerce). Also, where it comes to the knowledge of the presiding judge of the Commercial Court that a debtor is encountering difficulties that may undermine the continuation of their business operations, he or she may summon the managers to determine the appropriate steps necessary to remedy the situation 8.12

25 However, the rules on executory contracts (above at para. 5.25 et seq.), which are seen as liquidation tools under English law, are not applicable in administration proceedings.
26 More below at para. 8.36 et seq.
27 See para. 79(4)(d), 83 Sch. B 1 Insolvency Act 1986.

(Art. L. 611-2 Code de Commerce). In both cases, the court may appoint a special commissioner (*mandataire ad hoc*) and define their duties, albeit at the debtor's request only who may also propose a concrete person to be named special commissioner (Art. L. 611-3 Code de Commerce). These rather preventative proceedings aim more at expert counselling for a not yet insolvent debtor at a very early stage of the crisis than at interfering in the debtor's business to the benefit of the creditors. However, the special commissioner may be tasked to negotiate a compromise between the debtor and some or all creditors. Such negotiations are not official proceedings and the compromise is a private contract which is neither sanctioned by the court nor privileged in future insolvency proceedings.

8.13 The next step on the "escalation ladder" is the ***procédure de conciliation*** (Art. L. 611-4–611-15 Code de Commerce). It must be applied for by the debtor (Art. L. 611-6 Code de Commerce) and aims at negotiating a compromise – i.e. a consensual contract – between the debtor and its main creditors and business partners (Art. L. 611-7 Code de Commerce) under the mediation of a *conciliateur* proposed by the debtor but chosen and appointed by the court (Art. L. 611-6 Code de Commerce).[28] It is open to debtors who are faced with actual or foreseeable legal, economic, or financial difficulty and whose state of cessation of payments has not lasted longer than 45 days (Art. L. 611-4 Code de Commerce). The proceedings, which are not collective enforcement proceedings and therefore not insolvency proceedings (despite the debtor being possibly insolvent), are limited to a time period of four months, extendable to five months (Art. L. 611-6(2) Code de Commerce).[29] They are conducted strictly confidentially and do not trigger a moratorium.[30] Where a compromise agreement is reached, it can be recorded and made enforceable by the court (Art. L. 611-8(1) Code de Commerce), but also formally approved by the court if the debtor is not in a state of cessation of payments or the agreement puts an end to it, the terms of the agreement should normally ensure the continuity of the business's activity and the agreement is not harmful to the interests of the creditors (Art. L. 611-8(2) Code de Commerce). The approval decision (*homologation*), which makes the proceedings public, does not bind creditors who have not participated in the compromise.

---

28 In practice, it is frequently the previous *mandataire ad hoc*, see above at para. 8.9.

29 This is quite short und debtors therefore tend to start with a *mandat ad hoc* before they switch to conciliation proceedings.

30 However, the court may grant a respite for claims of obstructing creditors, Art. L. 611-7(5) Code de Commerce, Art. 1244-1 Code Civil.

But it privileges the claims resulting from the investment of fresh funds, assets, or services (Art. L. 611-11 Code de Commerce) and also protects payments based on the agreement against transactions avoidance in future insolvency proceedings. Besides, in case of non-performance or ensuing insolvency proceedings the agreement will be rescinded or terminated (Art. L. 611-10-3, 611-12 Code de Commerce). If an agreement cannot be reached, the court will terminate the conciliation proceedings and commence insolvency proceedings (Art. L. 611-7, 631-4(2) Code de Commerce).

The main appearance of French restructuring law – and the centrepiece 8.14 of French insolvency law as a whole – is the ***procédure de sauvegarde*** (safeguard proceedings), regulated in Art. L. 620-1–628-3 Code de Commerce. According to Art. L. 620-1(1)(2) Code de Commerce, the purpose of this procedure is to facilitate the reorganisation of the business in order to allow the continuation of the economic activity, the maintenance of employment, and the settlement of liabilities. It needs an application by the debtor[31] who can prove that although it is not faced with a cessation of payments, it has difficulties that it is unable to overcome[32] (Art. L. 620-1(1)(1) Code de Commerce).[33] With the opening decision of the court, an observation period starts which is limited to an (extendable) time period of six months (Art. L. 621-3 Code de Commerce) and aims at preparing either a restructuring plan (Art. L. 620(1) Code de Commerce) or an asset deal (Art. L. 642-1 Code de Commerce). The law states expressly that the management of the business shall be carried out by its manager (Art. L. 622-1(1) Code de Commerce), but the court may appoint a receiver (*mandataire judiciaire*), who acts on behalf of and in the general interest of the creditors (Art. L. 622-20(1) Code de Commerce), and an administrator (*administrateur judiciaire*; Art. L. 621-4 Code de Commerce) who may be proposed by the debtor and who is tasked to supervise the debtor's management operations or to assist the debtor in all or some of such operations (Art. L. 622-1(2) Code de Commerce). Although the debtor is not substantively insolvent, many features of insolvency law

31 A previous application for appointing a *mandataire ad hoc* or a *conciliateur* does not hinder the application for safeguard proceedings. On the contrary, pending conciliation proceedings open the way to accelerated proceedings (*procédure de sauvegarde accélérée*, Art. L. 628-1 et seq. Code de Commerce).

32 Examples: loss of the main customer, production not cost-covering, termination of overdraft facility.

33 If the debtor has already ceased payments – or does so during the safeguard proceedings – the *procédure de sauvegarde* is converted into a *procédure de redressement judiciaire* or into liquidation proceedings, Art. L. 621-12, 622-10(2) Code de Commerce.

appear in these proceedings: the opening decision leads to a moratorium (Art. L. 622-21 et seq. Code de Commerce);[34] contracts must be performed by the counterparty despite the debtor's non-performance unless the administrator requires the performance of an executory contract (Art. L. 622-13 Code de Commerce);[35] creditors must file their claims with the receiver (Art. L. 622-24, 624-1 et seq. Code de Commerce);[36] etc. Only transactions avoidance law is not applicable, since the debtor is not yet insolvent.[37] The safeguard proceedings result in a restructuring plan provided there is a serious likelihood of saving the business (Art. L. 626-1 Code de Commerce). The plan is drafted by the debtor who is assisted by the administrator (Art. L. 626-2 Code de Commerce). The draft plan is sent to the receiver who asks every creditor whose rights shall be affected for consent (Art. L. 626-5 Code de Commerce). If the creditor does not reply within 30 days, consent is presumed. However, the plan does not need the consent of those creditors who are represented in the two creditors' committees;[38] insofar the approval by a majority of two thirds of the claims represented by the members of the two creditors' committees present and voting suffices (Art. 626-30-2 Code de Commerce). On the basis of the creditors' committees' voting and of a hearing, the court decides on the confirmation of the plan which is then binding on all creditors (Art. L. 626-11 Code de Commerce).[39]

8.15 The same rules as for safeguard proceedings apply for the ***procédure de redressement judiciaire*** which is governed by Art. L. 631-1–632-4 Code de Commerce. The main difference between the *procédure de sauvegarde* and the *procédure redressement judiciaire* is the precondition for the opening of the latter: these proceedings require cessation of payments (Art. L. 631-1(1) Code de Commerce) and are therefore restructuring-oriented insolvency proceedings which can be conducted by the management in self-administration but also, depending on a decision of the court, by the administrator (Art. L. 631-12(2) Code de Commerce). According to Art. 631-4(1) Code de Commerce, the commencement of these proceedings must be requested by the debtor at the latest within the 45 days following the cessation of payments if the debtor has not, within this time limit, requested the commencement of conciliation

---

34 Details above at para. 5.17, 5.47.
35 See above at para. 5.28.
36 More above at para. 7.9.
37 See above at para. 6.26.
38 For them, see Art. L. 626-30 Code de Commerce and above at para. 2.34.
39 More below at para. 8.32 et seq.

proceedings, but creditors are also entitled to apply (Art. L. 631-5(2) Code de Commerce). Beyond that, more or less the same rules apply for the *redressement judiciaire* as for safeguard proceedings. An important exception is, among others, transactions avoidance law[40] which is applicable because the *procédure redressement judiciaire* is an insolvency procedure which justifies the application of claw-back provisions.[41]

D. USA

In the USA, the law distinguishes liquidation (chapter 7 Bankruptcy Code) 8.16
from reorganisation (chapter 11 and 13 Bankruptcy Code). Restructuring proceedings under **chapter 11** require an application which is typically filed by the debtor[42] and it is therefore regularly a voluntary case (§301 Bankruptcy Code).[43] Hence, insolvency of the debtor is not required.[44] The application leads to debtor-in-possession proceedings[45] which are nevertheless insolvency proceedings. As a consequence, the rules on the automatic stay (§362 Bankruptcy Code)[46] and executory contracts (§365 Bankruptcy Code)[47] apply. Under the protection of this stay, the debtor carries on business (§1108 Bankruptcy Code) with the duty to preserve its value and the intention to finally keep the (reorganised) enterprise, although an asset deal is permissible under §1123(b)(4) Bankruptcy Code (and sometimes is executed under §363(b) Bankruptcy Code at a very early stage of the proceedings[48]). At the same time, the debtor performs the tasks of an Insolvency Practitioner (§§1101, 1107(a) Bankruptcy Code)[49]

---

40 As explained above at para. 6.26.

41 Cf. above at para. 6.2.

42 Debtors in chapter 11 proceedings are mostly companies. Individuals are also eligible, but for them chapter 13 proceedings (see for them below at para. 9.25) are more favourable which leads to very low applications of individuals under chapter 11. Note, that special rules for small business debtors are available in §§1181 et seq. Bankruptcy Code. These rules will be neglected in the further course of this chapter.

43 Involuntary cases are possible (arg. §303 Bankruptcy Code) but rare, since it is not very promising to force a debtor into debtor-in-possession proceedings against their will.

44 See above at para. 3.18.

45 More below at para. 8.21 et seq.

46 In detail above at para. 3.9.

47 See for them, above at para. 5.28 and below at para. 8.28.

48 *Elliott v. Gen. Motors LLC (In re Motors Liquidation Co.)*, 829 F.3d 135 (2nd Cir. 2016); Cf. *In re Trans World Airlines, Inc.*, No. 01-0056 (PJW), 2001 BL 13387 (Bankr. D. Del. Mar. 27, 2001).

49 An independent trustee or examiner is only appointed if the requisite need is shown, §1104 Bankruptcy Code.

which include administering the estate, examining the proofs of claims, and bringing avoidance actions.

8.17 The main instrument, however, is the **reorganisation plan** (§§1121 et seq. Bankruptcy Code).[50] The debtor drafts and negotiates such a plan, primarily with respect to the fate of pre-insolvency claims and security rights, and puts it to a vote of the creditors. On adoption by the creditors and confirmation by the court, the plan replaces the old debts with the new (§1141 Bankruptcy Code) which affords the debtor a fresh start. However, where the debtor is unable to continue the business, to administrate the estate, to preserve the value of the estate, or to obtain the consent of the creditors, chapter 11 proceedings can be converted to chapter 7 liquidation proceedings (§1112 Bankruptcy Code).

8.18 **Example:** D company is in financial difficulties and intends to start negotiations with its creditors. However, since C, one of the pushing creditors, starts individual enforcement proceedings, D needs a moratorium which grants D some breathing space and protects the negotiations against creditors who are not prepared to participate in the negotiations. In England and Wales, a moratorium is only available in small CVA cases and in administration proceedings, which are insolvency proceedings. In France, a moratorium comes with the *procédure de sauvegarde* and the *procédure de redressement judiciaire*. In Germany, it is only possible within the framework of insolvency proceedings, and the same holds true for the US.[51]

III. SPECIAL INSTRUMENTS

8.19 As already mentioned above,[52] some jurisdictions trust completely in **insolvency law** when it comes to reorganising businesses. And indeed, insolvency law offers many tools which are apt to support restructuring efforts. To name but a few,[53] a moratorium, triggered by the

---

50 Extensively below at para. 8.32 et seq.

51 See also below at para. 8.27.

52 At para. 8.5.

53 I have dealt with this subject extensively in "Rescuing Companies in England and Germany".

commencement of the proceedings[54] and continued after the opening of formal proceedings,[55] assists the debtor and the Insolvency Practitioner against creditors who do not comply with restructuring requests and wish to enforce their claims. Rules on executory contracts[56] help to get rid of onerous contractual relationships, thereby preserving liquidity which is urgently needed for continuing and improving the business, to endorse the adjustment of workforce, and to allow for the continuance of advantageous contracts. The reference of ordinary creditors to a *pro rata* distribution is useful for clearing the liability side of the balance sheet, and liquidity is also enhanced by transactions avoidance.[57]

However, it is generally agreed that such insolvency law based instruments are useful but not sufficient. When the reorganisation of companies and businesses is at stake, special tools of **restructuring law** are necessary. In the following text, we will therefore deal with this special equipment, elaborate on the policy behind it and describe its appearances in national laws. In particular, we will deal with the two main features of restructuring law, which can be found in nearly all the restructuring procedures introduced before: rules on debtor-in-possession proceedings (A.) and on restructuring plans (B.) 8.20

A. DEBTOR-IN-POSSESSION PROCEEDINGS

Debtor-in-possession proceedings can be found in many jurisdictions[58] and there are various **reasons** for this. First, it has been described earlier in this book that most insolvency proceedings start far too late.[59] One of the causes is that the directors must fear to lose influence, if not their jobs, as soon as insolvency proceedings are commenced.[60] It is therefore a strong incentive for starting proceedings in good time if the management 8.21

---

54 See above at para. 3.7.
55 In detail above at para. 5.3 et seq., 5.16 et seq.
56 Above at para. 5.31 et seq.
57 Extensively above in Chapter 6.
58 See also §14.1 PEIL: "The debtor may, subject to supervision, be allowed to manage and dispose of the assets. In this case the proceeding follows the Principles of §§1–13, except to the extent that they presuppose an administrator." General remarks in the UNCITRAL Legislative Guide, p. 161 para. 2 et seq. with Recommendation 112 et seq.
59 Cf. above at para. 3.3.
60 This is due to the shift of responsibility from debtors to Insolvency Practitioners; see above at para. 5.19 et seq.

can stay in charge and the debtor (or the directors respectively) do not only keep their jobs but can also decide on the business's affairs. This is one of the reasons for providing for debtor-in-possession proceedings (self-administration). A second reason is the effect that such proceedings avoid general publicity of the debtor's financial distress and the need for restructuring. Markets, banks, suppliers, customers, and employees tend to withdraw their support once the debtor's financial problems become public which may lead to a "sudden death" of the company. It is therefore helpful if nothing changes in the outward appearance, if stakeholders are not confronted with an Insolvency Practitioner but are dealing with the same persons they have dealt with before. This demonstrates to the outward world that the business continues, that the debtor has started to tackle the financial problems and that the main stakeholders support the restructuring efforts at least for an evaluation phase. All this enhances restructuring chances. Third, debtor-in-possession proceedings allow for making use of the expertise and personal qualification[61] of the debtor in the further running of the estate. Fourth, leaving the debtor in charge can spare the costs of an Insolvency Practitioner (although hiring an insolvency expert for the management and paying the fees of an official monitor[62] may cause costs of a similar amount). Finally, the idea of restructuring proceedings is to make the business viable again and to release it to the market once reorganisation has been successful. Hence, it does not make much sense to deprive the debtor of their administration powers if the proceedings aim at a restructured business with the debtor in charge.

8.22 Before taking a closer look, a **definition** of the term "debtor-in-possession proceedings" (or self-administration) is due. Using this expression is only meaningful in the context of insolvency. If the debtor is not insolvent, the appointment of an Insolvency Practitioner and the shift of administration from debtor to the office holder are off the cards. Hence, in the state of pre-insolvency, all debtors administrate their affairs themselves and all proceedings designed exclusively for pre-insolvency restructuring are necessarily debtor-in-possession proceedings. It is not until the debtor is insolvent that self-administration as an alternative to normal insolvency

[61] E.g. trading certificates for innkeepers or concessions for doctors, lawyers, architects, etc. which are not connected to the business but to the debtor in person and are not performable by an Insolvency Practitioner.

[62] CF. for Germany below at para. 8.25.

proceedings is a topic. It is then for the person or institution commencing the proceedings to decide whether the debtor should stay in charge, albeit under the supervision of a monitor, or whether an Insolvency Practitioner should take over. Hence, debtor-in-possession proceedings can be collective enforcement proceedings as an alternative to liquidation proceedings, albeit mostly with the special purpose to valorise the estate not by liquidation but by restructuring.[63] But they can also be pure restructuring proceedings provided these proceedings are open for insolvent debtors and the debtor is really insolvent.

1. *Overview*

Against this background, it is not surprising that national laws provide for such debtor-in-possession proceedings, albeit in quite diverging shapes. In **England and Wales**,[64] for example, self-administration is not formed as a special kind of insolvency procedure. For insolvent debtors, only administration or liquidation are available and both are not debtor-in-possession proceedings. Restructuring related Company Voluntary Arrangement, Scheme of Arrangement, and Cross-Class Cram-Down Scheme are instruments for reaching agreements with creditors rather than self-administration proceedings. They can be used both within and outside insolvency proceedings, do not require the substantive insolvency of the debtor, and are therefore not *per se* collective enforcement proceedings as an alternative to an insolvency procedure under the command of an Insolvency Practitioner. Only where the debtor is insolvent and commences CVA or Scheme proceedings, it is correct to use the term debtor-in possession proceedings. 8.23

The same holds true for **France**[65] as far as the *mandat ad hoc* is concerned, since it is not open for insolvent entities and the *mandataire* is a mediator rather than an Insolvency Practitioner. This is not so clear for the *procédure de conciliation* because it is also available where the debtor has ceased payments (albeit no longer than 45 days). Although they are, by their very nature, not insolvency proceedings in the strict sense of the term, i.e. not collective enforcement proceedings, they can be assessed as self-administration if the debtor is insolvent. This is not different for the *procédure de sauvegarde*. Although it shows many features of 8.24

63 Cf. above at para. 1.4.
64 See for the details above at para. 8.9 et seq.
65 Cf. above at para. 8.12 et seq.

collective enforcement proceedings and self-administration is expressly stated (Art. L. 622-1(1) Code de Commerce), it is not an example of self-administration, if the debtor is not insolvent and insolvency proceedings under the lead of an Insolvency Practitioner are not an option. Hence, only the *procédure de redressement judiciaire* can be classified as pure debtor-in-possession proceedings provided that the court does not oblige the administrator to take over (Art. L. 631-12 CdC).

8.25 Things are much easier to assess in **Germany**[66] where only pure insolvency proceedings are available. Within these insolvency proceedings, §§270 et seq. Insolvenzordnung entitle the – necessarily insolvent – debtor to apply for debtor-in-possession proceedings. The court will order such proceedings if it is advantageous for the insolvency estate to continue to make use of the expertise and personal qualification of the debtor in the further running of the estate. The insolvency court has to give particular attention to any circumstances that may arise in which self-administration could be detrimental to the creditors. In many cases, a debtor brings an unencumbered restructuring expert into its management, who possesses the necessary experience in insolvency law and reduces the risk of such detriment. Under German law, debtor-in-possession proceedings are still collective enforcement proceedings but the tasks of the Insolvency Practitioner are performed by the debtor.[67] The insolvency court appoints a monitor (*Sachwalter*) in place of an Insolvency Practitioner, whose role is to oversee the activities of the debtor-in-possession.

8.26 Under **US law**,[68] chapter 11 proceedings are shaped as debtor-in-possession proceedings and it is correct to use this term if the debtor is really insolvent. Although substantive insolvency is not a prerequisite, the Bankruptcy Code takes this as the regular case and treats restructuring proceedings under chapter 11 as insolvency proceedings.

2. *Details*

8.27 Restructuring efforts can be supported by supplying the debtor-in-possession with additional legal instruments. Among those mentioned above at para. 8.19, a **moratorium** (or stay), which – among others –

66 See above at para. 8.7 et seq.

67 An important exception is the enforcement of transactions avoidance, §280 Insolvenzordnung.

68 Cf. above at para. 8.16 et seq.

prevents creditors from enforcing their rights irrespective of the debtor's endeavour to rescue the business, is of special importance. Such a moratorium is provided automatically – as a consequence of the commencement of the proceedings – under US law (automatic stay, §362 Bankruptcy Code). In Germany, the general rules apply to debtor-in-possession proceedings: the moratorium can be established through court order (§§21 et seq. Insolvenzordnung) during the application stage, especially in "Protective Umbrella Proceedings"[69] (§270b(2) Insolvenzordnung), whereas after the opening of insolvency proceedings the estate is seized.[70] In England and Wales, a Scheme of Arrangement comes without any moratorium and in CVA proceedings it is only available for small companies (sec. 1A, para. 3(2)(a) Sch. 1A Insolvency Act 1986). French law has no moratorium for the *mandat ad hoc* and the *procédure de conciliation*. This is different for the *procédure de sauvegarde* (Art. L. 622-21 et seq. Code de Commerce) and the *procédure de redressement judiciaire* (Art. L. 631-14(1), 622-21 Code de Commerce).

Rules on **executory contracts** can be very helpful for restructuring the business as they enable the debtor to abandon onerous contracts and to continue advantageous contractual relationships. However, it is not self-understood to apply these rules in debtor-in-possession proceedings. On the contrary, they are typically reserved for real insolvency proceedings. The restructuring law of England and Wales, for example, provides only for the adjustment of debts but not for interference in contractual relationships which is only possible in liquidation proceedings. As opposed to that, French law recognises the need for such rules in restructuring proceedings, albeit only in the *procédure de sauvegarde* (Art. L. 622-13 Code de Commerce) and the *procédure de redressement judiciaire* (Art. L. 631-14, 622-13 Code de Commerce). In Germany, restructuring proceedings, even where they are debtor-in-possession proceedings, are insolvency proceedings and therefore the rules on executory contracts apply (§§103 et seq. Insolvenzordnung). The same holds true for chapter 11 proceedings in the United States (§365 Bankruptcy Code), which is not natural, since the debtor needs not to be substantively insolvent;[71] this opens the door to fraudulent use. 8.28

69 Cf. above at para. 8.8.
70 See above at para. 5.3, 5.5.
71 Cf. above at para. 8.16.

8.29 A special problem of contract law in restructuring proceedings are ***ipso facto* clauses**, i. e. contractual terms which provide for the automatic termination of the contract upon the opening of insolvency proceedings.[72] Such clauses can undermine all restructuring efforts where they automatically deprive the debtor of necessary contractual relationships. It is for this reason that many insolvency laws declare such clauses void, thereby protecting the rules on executory contracts. However, legislators are reluctant to extend the scope of rules on *ipso facto* clauses to debtor-in-possession proceedings. Such rules are available in England and Wales (sec. 233B Insolvency Act 1986), Germany (§119 Insolvenzordnung), and the US (§365(e) Bankruptcy Code[73]). They render *ipso facto* clauses toothless in self-administration as well as in liquidation proceedings. For France, this again holds only true for the *procédure de sauvegarde* (Art. L. 622-13(1) Code de Commerce) and the *procédure de redressement judiciaire* (Art. L. 631-14, 622-13(1) Code de Commerce).

8.30 Jurisdictions are even more reluctant to enable the application of **transactions avoidance law** to debtor-in-possession proceedings.[74] Such application is not possible in England and Wales, and in France it is only in the *procédure de redressement judiciaire* that transactions are challengeable by the administrator under Art. L. 632-1 et seq. Code de Commerce. As opposed to this, transactions avoidance law (§§129 et seq. Insolvenzordnung) is also part of restructuring law in Germany yet executed by the monitor (*Sachwalter*) in self-administration (§280 Insolvenzordnung). In the US, transactions avoidance law is applicable in chapter 11 proceedings, but here avoidance actions are brought by the debtor-in-possession under §1107(a) Bankruptcy Code.[75]

8.31 All in all, it turns out that the **focus** of debtor-in-possession proceedings is frequently on alleviating debt restructuring agreements between the debtors and their creditors rather than to provide for the optimal satisfaction of the claims of the ordinary creditors. Most of these proceedings are of a preventive nature and are not insolvency proceedings in a strict sense. It is therefore not surprising that legislators are reluctant to provide the

---

72 See also above at para. 5.29.

73 *See Bonneville Power Admin. v. Mirant Corp. (In re Mirant Corp.)*, 440 F.3d 238 (5th Cir. 2006).

74 Cf. §14.3 PEIL: "The debtor does not have the power of the administrator to obtain reversal of a juridical act."

75 *Gandy v. Gandy (In re Gandy)*, 299 F.3d 489 (5th Cir. 2002).

debtor-in-possession with typical liquidation-related instruments of insolvency law and reserve them for reorganisation proceedings which are designed to overcome rather than to prevent the debtor's insolvency.

B. RESTRUCTURING PLAN

This leads us to the legal institute "restructuring plan" (or "reorganisation 8.32 plan") and here first to the question as to the **policy** of such agreements. Naturally, a debtor can, at any time, negotiate a debt restructuring with all or at least the main creditors out of court and without entering into any kind of formal proceedings. However, as already mentioned above,[76] in many cases legal support is necessary, particularly against opposing minorities who do not wish to join restructuring negotiations or do not accept the proposal supported by the majority. In such cases, the only way to include the opposing minority into the restructuring agreement is a formal procedure which aims at the passing and sanctioning of a restructuring plan which deploys binding force for all – including dissenting – creditors.[77]

Nearly all **national laws** provide for rules on a restructuring plan.[78] 8.33 In England and Wales, the CVA as well as the Scheme proceedings aim at adopting an agreement designed to solve the financial problems of the debtor. In France, such agreements are the target of all procedures introduced above at para. 8.12 et seq.[79] Likewise, in the USA the reorganisation plan is a central tool in chapter 11 proceedings. In Germany, §§217 et seq. Insolvenzordnung provide for rules on an "insolvency plan" which can be used in all insolvency proceedings, no matter whether

---

76 At para. 8.4.

77 It is for this binding force, that the thesis, restructuring law was based on contract law (promoted by, among others, *Madaus*, Leaving the Shadows of US Bankruptcy Law, 19 (2018) Eur Bus Org Law Rev 615, 624 et seq., 632 et seq.), seems vulnerable. Also, all explanations based on bargaining theories come to an end at this point; cf. *Casey*, The New Bargaining Theory, SSRN 3353871, p. 1 et seq.

78 See also §11.1 PEIL: "In a reorganisation, the liabilities of the debtor are restructured on the basis of a reorganisation plan, stating the extent and the manner of such restructuring. A reorganisation plan may include further measures." Extensively UNCITRAL Legislative Guide, p. 209 para. 1 et seq. with Recommendations 139 et seq.

79 The agreement is not particularly mentioned in the rules on the *mandat ad hoc* (Art. L. 611-3 Code de Commerce) which will therefore not be dealt with in great detail in the following text.

they aim at liquidation or restructuring and no matter whether they are conducted by an Insolvency Practitioner or a debtor-in-possession. However, national laws differ in decisive details, the most important of which shall be described in the following paragraphs.

8.34 The first issue concerns the **standing** to make a proposal for the restructuring agreement.[80] At least where formal plan proceedings are established, the principle of efficiency of proceedings requires avoiding a "battle of plan proposals", i. e. ensuring that not too many competing plans are put forward to discussion and voting. In all procedures discussed here, the debtor is entitled to submit a plan. Additionally, proposals can be made by the Insolvency Practitioner in England and Wales (where CVA or Scheme of Arrangement proceedings are used as a tool in the context of administration or liquidation, sec. 1(3) Insolvency Act 1986, sec. 896(2)(c)/(d) Companies Act 2006), France (Art. L. 611-7(1) Code de Commerce for the *procédure de conciliation* and Art. L. 631-19(1) Code de Commerce for the *procédure de redressement judiciaire*[81]), Germany (§218(1) Insolvenzordnung) and, albeit subsidiarily only, the USA (§1121(c) Bankruptcy Code). Also, in some exceptional cases, single creditors or the creditors' committee may submit a plan.[82]

8.35 The next topic is the possibility to group creditors in **classes** and treat these classes differently. In restructuring, it is frequently not necessary to include all creditors in the reorganisation plan. Some of them – e.g. employees, suppliers – may be supposed to be paid in full, since the business continues. Others – e.g. banks, bond holders, but also suppliers, as the case may be – are required to waive their claims partially or entirely, which may be economically reasonable as these creditors keep a customer they can do business with as soon as the debtor is restructured. Finally, it may be appropriate to treat creditor groups differently, e.g. propose a debt-to-equity swap for some, ask for a waiver of 20% for others and suggest the reduction of interest rates for a third group. These economic necessities can only be transformed in an acceptable restructuring plan if

80 On this, see §11.2 PEIL: "A reorganisation plan can be presented by the debtor or the administrator."

81 Differently for the *procédure de sauvegarde* Art. 626-2 Code de Commerce: debtor only.

82 See for the English Scheme of Arrangement sec. 896(2)(b) Companies Act 2006; for the French *procédure de sauvegarde* and the *procédure de redressement judiciaire* Art. 626-30-2(2), 631-19(1) Code de Commerce; for chapter 11 proceedings §1121(c) Bankruptcy Code.

the law permits such grouping of creditors and the diverging treatment of the groups. Fortunately, that is the case in most jurisdictions. Although in England and Wales the CVA is explicitly limited to dealing with legal relationships between debtor and unsecured creditors (sec. 1(1) Insolvency Act 1986), meaning in practice that there is only one creditor group as a rule and that dividing creditors into different classes is almost always out of the question, sec. 895(1)(a), 899(1) Companies Act 2006 permit for the Scheme of Arrangement the division of creditors into separate groups according to their various interests, with different consequences permissible for each.[83] The same holds true for the Cross-Class Cram-Down Scheme (sec. 901C Companies Act 2006). German law also permits grouping unsecured creditors into various classes (§222(2) Insolvenzordnung) and applying different legal consequences to each (§§222 (1), 224 Insolvenzordnung). The same holds true for the US (§§1122, 1123(a)(1)-(4) Bankruptcy Code). Only French law is completely silent on this matter. This is no surprise for the *mandat ad hoc* and the *procédure de conciliation*, since these procedures end with a completely voluntary agreement of the debtor with the (main) creditors. Hence, it is up to each creditor to agree to the legal consequences proposed to them by the debtor or the mediator. However, as regards the *procédure de sauvegarde* and the *procédure de redressement judiciaire*, the plan cannot group creditors and provide for diverging effects for each group.

In nearly all restructuring proceedings, the restructuring plan is put to a 8.36
vote of the creditors. However, voting rules and necessary majorities are quite divergent.[84] As regards the English CVA, a decision of a creditors' meeting is necessary which requires a majority of 75% in value of those present and voting (para. 15.34(3) Insolvency Rules 2016). The same holds true for the Schemes where in each class 75% in value of those present and

83 The proper composition of classes is subject to control of the court. For examples, see *Re Realm Therapeutics Plc* [2019] EWHC 2080 (Ch); *Re Syncreon Group B.V. and Syncreon Automotive (UK) Ltd* [2019] EWHC 2068 (Ch).

84 Cf. §11.3 PEIL: "A reorganisation plan is approved or rejected by a vote of the persons affected by it, or by the court. The approval of the reorganisation plan by a vote of the persons affected by it may be subject to:

a) quorum requirement;
b) the requirement of a qualified majority;
c) the persons affected by the reorganisation plan voting in separate categories;
d) certain categories of affected persons having blocking votes.

A reorganisation plan approved by a vote of the persons affected by it needs the confirmation of the court."

voting are necessary (sec. 899(1), 901F Companies Act 2006). In Germany, under §244 Abs 1 Insolvenzordnung the approval of the insolvency plan in a creditors' meeting requires a simple head-count majority and a simple value majority within every voting group, and – subject to a ban on obstruction[85] – the plan must be approved by all of the groups voting separately under §243 Insolvenzordnung. Under US law, §1126(c) Bankruptcy Code requires in each class a majority of two-thirds by value and a simple majority in number of the allowed claims. France, however, is different. While under the rules for the *mandat ad hoc* and the *procédure de conciliation* no voting takes place and each affected creditor has to agree, in the *procédure de sauvegarde* and the *procédure de redressement judiciaire* the voting is not for a creditors' meeting but for the two creditors' committees. Art. L. 626-30-2(5) Code de Commerce requires a majority vote of the committees' members, representing two-thirds of the total amount of the claims of all the members of the committee who have voted. Only if the creditor committees have not been established, the court decides on the basis of the creditors' responses to the plan-proposal sent to them, using equitable discretion.[86]

8.37 Rules which require the consent of all classes give the members of each class a hold-up position: they may make their consent dependent on receiving a larger piece of the cake. In order to prevent such obstruction, some jurisdictions provide for rules on **cross-class cram-down**: the court may sanction the plan despite the denial of a group if it is satisfied that concrete prerequisites are met, particularly the "best interest of creditors test" which is passed if the plan does not put the members of the respective group in a worse position than they would be in regular insolvency (liquidation) proceedings. Such cross class cram-down, which is not necessary in France,[87] has first been regulated in the US, where §1129(b)(1) Bankruptcy Code enables the court to confirm the plan if (a) at least one impaired class of claims has accepted the plan, (b) it does not discriminate unfairly against any non-assenting class, and (c) is fair and equitable, with respect to each class of claims that is impaired under, and has not accepted, the plan. The term "fair and equitable" is described for ordinary creditors in detail in §1129(b)(2)(B) Bankruptcy Code: a plan meets this requirement if (a) it provides that each class member receives property of a value equal to the allowed amount of such claim or

---

85 Discussed immediately below in para 8.37.

86 Cf. above at para. 8.14.

87 Since grouping of creditors is not permissible, cf. above at para. 8.35.

(b) no payments are made to creditors junior to the member of this class ("absolute priority rule"[88]). Similar rules are available in England and Wales (sec. 901G Companies Act 2006). Stricter requirements can be found in German law where §245(1) Insolvenzordnung puts the cram-down under the conditions that (a) the majority of groups has given their consent, (b) the group members are likely not to be placed at a disadvantage by the insolvency plan compared with their situation without such plan ("best interest of creditors test"), and (c) the group members participate to a reasonable extent in the economic value devolving on the parties under the plan. The latter is explained in more detail in §245(2) Insolvenzordnung, according to which reasonable participation requires that (a) no other creditor receives economic values exceeding the full amount of his claim, (b) neither a lower-ranking creditor nor the debtor nor a shareholder receives any economic value ("absolute priority rule"), and (c) no creditor to be satisfied on an equal footing outside plan proceedings receives more than the group members. The latter, however, torpedoes the advantage of treating certain groups of ordinary creditors better than others,[89] because on treating various groups differently, the denial of the disadvantaged group cannot be overruled by a cross-class cram-down.

Restructuring agreements can be binding where all stakeholders signed the contract. In this case the legal consequences are based on the stakeholders consent. However, where the inclusion of dissenting minorities is at stake, a **court sanctioning** is necessary.[90] Laws must then provide for a court decision which, on the one hand, assesses whether the plan and the decision of the majority meets the legal requirements and is fair and equitable regarding dissenting creditors,[91] and which, on the other hand, is the basis for including such creditors. Although French law trusts in voluntary consent in the *mandate ad hoc* and the *procédure de conciliation* (here the court approval does not force dissenting creditors under the restructuring agreement[92]), nearly all other proceedings end with such 8.38

88 See above at para. 7.41 and *Bank of America Natl. Trust & Savings Assn. v. 203 North LaSalle St. Partn.*, 526 U.S. 434, 119 S. Ct. 1411, 143 L. Ed. 2d 607, 67 U.S.L.W. 4275 (1999).

89 E.g. where the plan offers 100% to employees but only 20% to suppliers, cf. above at para. 8.35.

90 For §11.3 PEIL, see above at fn. 84.

91 Details below at para. 8.39.

92 It is only the basis for enforcing the claims as established in this agreement (Art. L. 611-8 Code de Commerce: *contestation*), confirms the viability of the business and

a sanctioning. In England and Wales, while there is no need for the court's approval of a CVA, the Schemes must be sanctioned by the court (sec. 899(1), 901F Companies Act 2006) and so does the restructuring plan under French law (in *sauvegarde* and *redressement judiciaire* proceedings, Art. L. 626-9 et seq., 631-19(1) Code de Commerce), under German law (§248 et seq. Insolvenzordnung) and under US law (§1128 et seq. Bankruptcy Code).

8.39 The decisive question in the context of the court sanctioning regards the prerequisites of this decision and particularly the **protection of dissenting minorities**. If the dissenting creditors are subjected to the plan, it is necessary to safeguard the legitimate interests of such creditors. It must be ensured that the plan treats the dissenting creditors in a fair and equitable way, in particular does not deprive them of the liquidation value of their claims, and that it meets the statutory requirements, which includes an examination of whether the decision was correctly arrived at, especially whether the proceedings were correctly announced, whether invitations were correctly issued to the creditors' meetings, and whether the majorities were reached and calculated correctly. In England and Wales, this is guaranteed by entitling each creditor to challenge a CVA under sec. 6 Insolvency Act 1986 for material irregularity in the proceedings or unfair prejudice of the creditor's interests. For confirmation of a Scheme the court reviews the scheme mainly with respect to four points:[93] firstly, whether the law's procedural requirements were met, and especially whether the necessary majority has been reached; secondly, that the majority in a given group has fairly represented the interests of the members of that group;[94] thirdly, the court examines whether the decision is fair and reasonable which is, according to a well-known formula, the case when "the proposal is such that an intelligent and honest man, a member of the class concerned and acting in respect of his interest, might

through Art. L. 611-11 Code de Commerce privileges creditors who provided the debtor with fresh money in future insolvency proceedings (Art. L. 611-8(2) Code de Commerce, *homologation*); cf. above at para. 8.13.

93 Recent decisions are *Re NN2 NewCo Ltd* [2019] EWHC 2532 (Ch); *Re Ophir Energy Plc* [2019] EWHC 1278 (Ch); *Re Realm Therapeutics Plc* [2019] EWHC 2080 (Ch); *Re Syncreon Group B.V. and Syncreon Automotive (UK) Ltd* [2019] EWHC 2412 (Ch).

94 This may not be the case where only a small minority of creditors have participated in the voting but nonetheless voted with the necessary majority in favour of the proposal. In such cases, it is possible that the voting creditors have failed to represent the interests of the "silent majority" for selfish purposes.

reasonably approve";[95] and fourthly, it is checked whether there is a blot on the scheme. In France, the court has wide discretion when sanctioning the plan and is particularly entitled to amend the plan in order to ensure a fair and equitable balance of interests. *Inter alia*, it fixes the duration of the plan (Art. L. 626-12 Code de Commerce), can prohibit the alienation of assets indispensable for the continuation of the business (Art. L. 626-14 Code de Commerce), can reduce deferrals and waivers accepted by the creditors, and impose uniform payment terms on those who are not represented in the creditors' committees and have not approved of the plan (Art. L. 626-18 Code de Commerce with exceptions in Art. L. 626-20, R. 626-34 Code de Commerce). In Germany, the court's approval shall be denied where the procedural rules were not complied with (§250 Insolvenzordnung) or – on the request of an opposing creditor – where this creditor is likely to be placed at a disadvantage by the plan compared with their situation without a plan (§251 Insolvenzordnung). Similarly, US law puts the confirmation of the plan under various conditions, amongst others that the plan complies with the applicable law, has been proposed in good faith, that the debtor can meet the plan obligations, and that dissenting creditors are not put in a worse position than they would be in in liquidation proceedings (§1129 Bankruptcy Code).

A last topic necessary to discuss is the legal **effect** of the (court confirmed) plan: does it only apply to consenting parties or are dissenting or passive stakeholders also bound by the plan?[96] Against the background of what has been explained in the previous paragraphs, restructuring agreements have only contractual consequences between the contracting parties where the plan is not subject to judicial review or confirmation. This holds especially true for the agreements reached in French *mandat ad hoc* and *conciliation* proceedings.[97] As opposed to that, most restructuring plans have *inter omnes* effect, since they either need court confirmation or are subject to judicial review. That such plans are binding on everyone or at least on all creditors entitled to vote, is expressly stated for the English CVA in sec. 5 Insolvency Act 1986 and for the Schemes in sec. 899(3), 901F(5) Companies Act 2006, for the French *procédure de sauvegarde* and 8.40

95 *Re Dorman Long & Co Ltd* [1934] Ch 635.

96 On this, see §11.4 PEIL: "The confirmed reorganisation plan binds all persons affected by it, including persons who have not agreed and creditors who have not submitted their claims."

97 Cf. above at para. 8.38.

procédure de redressement judiciaire in Art. L. 626-11, 631-19(1) Code de Commerce, for the German insolvency plan in §254(1) Insolvenzordnung and for reorganisation plans under US law in §1141(a) Bankruptcy Code. A usual and necessary exception is the effect for third parties: sureties or guarantors do normally not benefit from the claim-reducing effect of a restructuring plan[98] unless they are expressly included in such a plan (§254(2) Insolvenzordnung[99]).[100]

8.41 **Example**: D company proposes a restructuring plan to its creditors, suggesting a "haircut" of 20% and a deferment of payment for six months. It turns out, that most creditors are prepared to give their consent except for some suppliers who hold 10% of all claims. If D aims for the court's sanctioning, the plan must be drafted in a way that leaves the suppliers without a hold-up position. The easiest way might be to assign all unsecured creditors to one single class, since in this class the necessary majority[101] can be reached against the vote of the suppliers.[102] Another way might be to put the suppliers in a sepratae class. This class will not accept the plan but can be crammed down provided a cross class cram-down is available.[103]

8.42 ***For further reading***: *Bork*, Einführung, §§29-32, 35; *Bork*, Rescuing Companies, passim; *Fletcher*, Law of Insolvency, para. 15-001 et seq., 16-001 et seq.; *Saint-Alary-Houin*, Droit des enterprises en difficulté, para. 331 et seq., 410 et seq., 923 et seq.; *Tabb*, Law of Bankruptcy, §11.1 et seq.; *van Zwieten*, Principles of Corporate Insolvency Law, para. 11-01 et seq., 12-01 et seq.

---

98 Cf. §11.4 PEIL: "The reorganisation plan does not affect the rights of creditors against third parties."

99 For the US, see *Stoll v. Gottlieb*, 305 U.S. 165, 59 S. Ct. 134, 83 L. Ed. 104 (1938). Under English law, this effect is recognised for a Scheme of Arrangement in case law, see *Re Garner's Motors Ltd* [1937] Ch. 594.

100 See for the effects of a discharge below at para. 9.21 et seq.

101 On this, see above at para. 8.36.

102 This is the only way in France, where grouping creditors in classes is not possible, cf. above at para. 8.35.

103 This is the case in Germany and the USA, see above at para. 8.37.

CHAPTER 9

DISCHARGE AND CONSUMER PROCEEDINGS

In the ninth chapter, regular insolvency proceedings will be distinguished from proceedings which are designed for surmounting financial crises of individuals, particularly consumers. We will learn in the second part of this chapter that many jurisdictions provide for special consumer insolvency proceedings which aim at discharging the debtor from residual debt rather than at liquidating the debtor's estate. However, discharge of residual debt is not reserved for consumers but also available for entrepreneurs and, under certain conditions, even for companies. Hence, the general rules on discharge will be introduced first before their interweaving with consumer insolvency proceedings can be dealt with. 9.1

I. DISCHARGE

We have seen above in Chapter 7[1] that liquidation proceedings normally only result in a partial satisfaction of the creditors' claims which raises the question as to the fate of the **residual debt**. Principally, the unsatisfied part of the claims continues to exist and the creditor can demand performance if the debtor achieves a new estate after the termination of the insolvency proceedings, provided the debtor is not a legal entity (company) which is liquidated after the termination of the insolvency proceedings.[2] However, such continuity of claims is in most cases useless. Facing the obligation to 9.2

---

1 In detail above at para. 7.41.

2 However, discharge for legal entities is possible in restructuring plans, cf. below at para. 9.8.

pay not only new but also a significant part[3] of old debts, debtors have no incentive to start a new economic life. They are forced into black labour or are content with unemployment and support by social security. From an economic point of view, it is more reasonable to allow for a fresh start by granting a discharge for the remaining debts, enable debtors to build up a new economic existence, and thus to contribute to the economic welfare of the society.

9.3 There are **two ways** of discharging a debtor from the residual debt. First, debtors may negotiate with their creditors and propose a waiver of the remaining claims, either in voluntary agreements or on the basis of an insolvency or restructuring plan.[4] However, creditors are mostly reluctant to waive residual debts voluntarily, since they hope for an improvement of the debtor's economic situation and for an additional satisfaction of – at least part of – their remaining claims. It is therefore part of most modern insolvency laws to provide for a statutory discharge[5] which is granted to debtors who have met certain prerequisites. First and foremost, they must have entered into insolvency proceedings properly (particularly in a timely manner and without wasting assets), have cooperated with the Insolvency Practitioner, and have contributed to the satisfaction of creditor claims in a reasonable way.

A. BASICS

9.4 However, overlooking national laws, the **typical prerequisites** for a discharge of residual debt differ widely. Some restrict statutory discharge to consumers (which excludes entrepreneurs). Frequently, dishonest debtors – e.g. those who committed insolvency related crimes or wasted their assets instead of furnishing them for the creditors – are banned from the benefits of discharge proceedings. Many laws require the debtor's cooperation during the insolvency proceedings and some even demand

---

3 Typically, ordinary creditors receive between 3 to 5% of their claims in insolvency proceedings.

4 For the latter, see above at para. 8.32 et seq.

5 Cf. §13.2(1)(1) PEIL: "The debtor, if a natural person, may be discharged from debts remaining after liquidation." See also UNCITRAL Legislative Guide p. 281 para. 51 et seq. with Recommendations 194 et seq.

for a minimum percentage of satisfaction (e.g. 10 or 30% of the ordinary creditors' claims[6]). In addition, some national laws tie the discharge to a compliance period subsequent to insolvency proceedings during which the debtor is required to seek employment and to hand the leviable part of the income over to the (ordinary, pre-commencement) creditors.

The fact that discharge prerequisites vary significantly between jurisdictions has incentivised a "discharge tourism": debtors tend to move their domicile to countries with easier discharge requirements in order to be freed of their debts as early and easily as possible. It is for this reason, that the **European Union** has bound its Member States by Art. 20 et seq. Directive 2019/1023[7] to ensure that insolvent entrepreneurs have access to at least one procedure that can lead to a full discharge of debt within a discharge period of no longer than three years. As we will see in the following paragraphs, such discharge rules are already available in many, but not yet in all jurisdictions. Member States are obliged to adopt the laws, regulations, and administrative provisions necessary to comply with this Directive only by 17 July 2021 (Art. 34(1) Directive 2019/1023). Hence, it must be left for the next edition of this book to report on the amendments of national laws regarding discharge proceedings. Until then, it will stick to the legal *status quo*. 9.5

B. DETAILS

All **national laws** covered by this book provide for discharge proceedings, albeit under diverging conditions. In England and Wales, discharge for individuals can be reached in two ways. In small cases (debts not exceeding £20,000, total value of property not exceeding £1,000, monthly surplus income not more than £50[8]), the debtor can apply for a debt relief order (sec. 251A et seq. Insolvency Act 1986). In all other cases, 9.6

---

6 See below at para 9.14: premature discharge in Germany where 35% of the debts have been paid.

7 Directive (EU) 2019/1023 of the European Parliament and of the Council of 20 June 2019 on preventive restructuring frameworks, on discharge of debt and disqualifications, and on measures to increase the efficiency of procedures concerning restructuring, insolvency and discharge of debt, and amending Directive (EU) 2017/1132 (Directive on restructuring and insolvency, OJ 2019 L 172/18).

8 See para. 6-8 Sch. 4ZA Insolvency Act 1986 together with the Insolvency Proceedings (Monetary Limits) (Amendment) Order 2009 (SI 2009/465), Sch. Pt. II, as amended by SI 2015/26.

bankruptcy proceedings are necessary and the discharge is the automatic statutory consequence one year after the opening of such proceedings (sec. 279 et seq. Insolvency Act 1986[9]). In France, various procedures are available. First, discharge is the regular result of liquidation proceedings (Art. L. 643-11 Code de Commerce). Second, individual entrepreneurs whose estate is not sufficient to cover the costs of insolvency proceedings and who acted in good faith can apply for the *procédure de rétablissement professionnel* which leads to an immediate discharge without liquidation proceedings (Art. L. 645-1 et seq. Code de Commerce). Third, the same holds true for consumers who can apply for a *procédure de rétablissement personnel* under Art. L. 741-1 et seq. Code de la Consommation, which is only followed by a liquidation procedure where the debtor did not act in good faith and exploitable assets are available. German law provides for discharge proceedings which are connected to insolvency proceedings. All honest individuals who cooperate during the insolvency proceedings and pass through a compliance period of (typically[10]) six years during which they have to seek employment and deliver the leviable part of the income to a trustee can be discharged of their residual debt by the court under §§286 et seq. Insolvenzordnung. Under US law, there are three ways to receive a discharge (all subject to the general rules in §§523 et seq. Bankruptcy Code). Honest individuals are granted discharge by the court at the end of liquidation proceedings (§727 Bankruptcy Code). However, discharge can also be the result of restructuring proceedings (§1141(c) Bankruptcy Code). And finally, §1328 Bankruptcy Code provides for the adjustment of debts of an individual with manageable debts[11] and regular income who has met their payment obligation called for by a payment plan confirmed by the court.

9.7 In this book, it is not possible to describe all these proceedings in great detail. However, it seems appropriate to cover the most **important features** and compare the national rules on these topics. This regards the addressees of such rules, the connection to insolvency proceedings,

9 An exception is the discharge by order of court (sec. 280 Insolvency Act 1986). However, this is of no practical relevance.

10 Cf. below at fn. 19.

11 According to §109(e) Bankruptcy Code, chapter 13 proceedings are reserved for debtors with non-contingent, liquidated, unsecured debts of less than $250,000 and non-contingent, liquidated, secured debts of less than $750,000. These values are subject to triannual adjustment to the consumer price index (§104 Bankruptcy Code). Currently, the figures are $419,275 and $1,257,850 respectively.

possible compliance periods and debtors' obligations during such a period, court involvement, and finally the effects of a discharge.

1. *Addressees*

The first question to be answered here is: who is **eligible** for a discharge? As we will see in the next paragraph, most rules on discharge are confined to individuals (natural persons). Legal entities (companies) can be discharged from residual debt in insolvency or restructuring plans under the conditions prescribed in the law and in the plan. §1141(c) Bankruptcy Code puts this in a nutshell. But besides from this, legal persons will be liquidated after the termination of insolvency proceedings which renders any discharge superfluous. Among individuals, discharge can be constrained either to entrepreneurs or to consumers. Finally, laws can restrict the effects of discharge proceedings to honest debtors and provide for protection against repeated discharge applications. 9.8

Nearly all national laws analysed here offer statutory – i.e. not restructuring plan-based – discharge for **individuals** only but include both **consumers and entrepreneurs**. In England and Wales, it follows from sec. 251A(1), 279 et seq. Insolvency Act 1986 that discharge is available for "individuals" (or "bankrupts" respectively) which covers consumers as well as entrepreneurs. Under French law, discharge is also available for natural persons only[12] and includes consumers and entrepreneurs but offers different procedural regimes: discharge for entrepreneurs after regular liquidation proceedings (Art. L. 643-11 Code de Commerce) or in a *procédure de rétablissement professionnel* (Art. L. 645-1 et seq. Code de Commerce) and the *procédure de rétablissement personnel* for consumers (Art. L. 741-1 et seq. Code de la Consommation). Germany has only one type of insolvency proceedings, no matter whether the debtor is a legal entity or a natural person and no matter whether a consumer or an entrepreneur is insolvent, but entitles all debtors to discharge proceedings only if they are natural persons (§286 Insolvenzordnung). In the USA, discharge is also restricted to individuals, not distinguishing consumers from entrepreneurs (§727(a)(1), 1301(1) Bankruptcy Code).[13] 9.9

12 An exception is made by Art. L. 643-11 Code de Commerce, since this rule covers all debtors and does not distinguish between individuals and legal entities.

13 However, when it comes to the details, particularly regarding denial of discharge, lesser expectations apply to consumer debtors who are not conducting a business; cf.

9.10 Discharge rules tend to exclude **dishonest debtors** from the entitlement to statutory debt relief. In France, for example, the *procédure de rétablissement* without any liquidation proceedings is only available where the debtor acted in good faith (Art. L. 645-9(1) Code de Commerce, Art. L. 724-3(1) Code de la Consommation). Additionally, Art. L. 643-11(3)/(4) Code de Commerce denies the entitlement to discharge in certain cases of dishonesty. German law is more specific. Here, debtors are not entitled to a discharge if they have received a final verdict for commission of an insolvency related criminal offence, have given a false or incomplete statement on their economic condition in writing in the last three years prior to the application for insolvency proceedings in order to obtain a loan or grants from public funds or to avoid making payments to public funds, or have impaired the satisfaction of the insolvency creditors in the last year prior to the application for insolvency proceedings by entering into inappropriate obligations, by wasting property or by delaying the opening of the insolvency proceedings without any expectancy of an improved economic condition (§290(1)No. 1-4 Insolvenzordnung). Similar rules can be found in the US (§727(a) Bankruptcy Code). English law, however, is different. Here, the court may either extend the compliance period of one year or suspend the discharge, but only if the debtor has failed to comply with an obligation under insolvency law[14] (sec. 251H(1)(b), 251M(5)–(7), 279(3)/(4) Insolvency Act 1986). The circumstances causing the bankruptcy can lead to a bankruptcy restriction order (or a bankruptcy restriction undertaking) under sec. 281A, Sch. 4A Insolvency Act 1986. However, these instruments do not hinder the discharge but impose further restrictions – such as personal disqualifications[15] – to the debtor.

9.11 Some jurisdictions provide for protection against **repeated discharge applications**. In Germany, for example, a discharge application is impermissible if a previous application of the same debtor has been granted in the past ten years or denied in the past three or five years as the case may be (§287a(2) Insolvenzordnung). Similarly, the debtor is denied

Pergament v. DeRise (In re DeRise), 394 B.R. 677 (Bankr. E.D.N.Y. 2008); *Robertson v. Dennis (In re Dennis)*, 330 F.3d 696 (5th Cir. 2003).

14 For an example, see below at para. 9.18.

15 Discharge does not overrule personal disqualifications such as exclusion from any office as an Insolvency Practitioner (sec. 390(4) Insolvency Act 1986) or from membership of the Parliament (sec. 426A Insolvency Act 1986).

discharge under US law if they have received discharge in the past eight years in chapter 7 or 11 proceedings or six years in chapter 13 proceedings (§727(a)(8)/(9) Bankruptcy Code[16]).[17] In England and Wales, the grace period is six years for debt relief orders (para. 5 Sch. 4ZA Insolvency Act 1986). French law does not provide for such a time bar.

2. *Connection to Insolvency Proceedings*

Discharge proceedings are mostly, but not always, connected to insolvency proceedings. In some jurisdictions, discharge is granted in **stand-alone proceedings** if the debtor does not have sufficient means to cover the costs of insolvency proceedings. Examples of this group are – from the proceedings mentioned above[18] – in England and Wales the debt relief order (sec. 251A et seq. Insolvency Act 1986) and in France both kinds of the *procédure de rétablissement*. As opposed to that, in Germany, discharge is always connected to insolvency proceedings which are financed by deferment of costs if the debtor is eligible for a discharge and applies for it (§§4a et seq. Insolvenzordnung). In the US, discharge is either connected to liquidation proceedings (§727 Bankruptcy Code) or to restructuring proceedings (§§1141(c), 1328 Bankruptcy Code). 9.12

3. *Compliance Period*

Creditors are typically not prepared to grant a voluntary discharge (by waiver of the residual debt) unless the debtor proves to be cooperative and particularly tries seriously to contribute to an **additional satisfaction** of the creditors' claims which exceeds the satisfaction effected by the distribution of the proceeds of the estate in liquidation proceedings. This factor is considered in some jurisdictions by providing for a compliance period as a prerequisite for the discharge. 9.13

Examples are Germany and the USA. In **Germany**, the compliance period starts with the opening of insolvency proceedings and runs for six years 9.14

---

16 See also §1328(f) Bankruptcy Code for discharge under chapter 13 proceedings.

17 The time periods are measured from filing to filing, cf. *U.S. Tr. v. Stone (In re Stone)*, No. 09-3072, 2009 BL 349748, 2009 Bankr Lexis 3348, 2009 WL 3459863 (Bankr. N.D. Ohio Oct. 06, 2009).

18 At para. 9.6.

(§287(2) Insolvenzordnung).[19] During this period, the debtor must cooperate with the Insolvency Practitioner and is particularly obliged to engage in adequate gainful employment or, in case of unemployment, to seek such employment and not refuse any reasonable activity (§287b Insolvenzordnung). The leviable part of the income resulting from such employment is to be assigned to a trustee who distributes the money among the ordinary creditors according to the schedule of claims[20] (§§287(2), 292(1) Insolvenzordnung). If the debtor does not comply, discharge can be denied by the court if an ordinary creditor applies for a rejection (§290(1) No. 5-7 Insolvenzordnung).

9.15 The situation is more complicated in the **USA**. Here, on first sight, discharge is only bound to the debtor's cooperation during the insolvency proceedings (§727(a) Bankruptcy Code). However, the court may dismiss an application for chapter 7 proceedings (and thereby the entitlement to discharge under §727 Bankruptcy Code) if granting such proceedings would be an abuse because the debtor has regular income which can be used to satisfy the creditors' claims in chapter 13 proceedings (§707(b)(1) Bankruptcy Code).[21] These proceedings oblige the debtor to present a payment plan which provides for the creditors' satisfaction from the disposable income during the next five years, starting with the first payment (§§1325(b)(1)(B), 1322(a)(4) Bankruptcy Code).[22]

9.16 The law of **England and Wales** does not oblige the debtor to add to the distribution of the proceeds of the estate. Sec. 279 Insolvency Act 1986 provides for a compliance period of one year – extendable by court decision where the debtor does not cooperate with the Insolvency Practitioner.[23] However, besides compliance with cooperation duties, discharge is not dependant on additional satisfaction from future income, since the seizable part of the debtor's income, gained during the one year period

---

19 However, the compliance period is three years if the creditors receive at least 35% of their claims, five years, if the debtor meets the costs of the proceedings, and ends immediately if (a) no creditor files a claim or (b) all creditors are satisfied completely and – in both cases – all costs and expenses of the proceedings are covered (§300 Insolvenzordnung). Beyond, the Federal Government has submitted a proposal to generally reduce the compliance period to three years.

20 See for this above at para. 7.10.

21 Example: *Advanced Control Solutions, Inc. v. Justice*, 639 F.3d 838 (8th Cir. 2011).

22 See also §1322(d)(2) Bankruptcy Code (three years only in minor cases).

23 Cf. *CJEU* Case C-493/18 *UB v. VA, Tiger SCI, WZ and Banque patrimoine et immobilier SA*, ECLI:EU:C:2019:1046 para. 16.

established by sec. 279 Insolvency Act 1986, is part of the estate anyway.[24] The same holds true for the debt relief order under sec. 251A Insolvency Act 1986.

In **France**, finally, the *procédure de rétablissement professionnel* for entrepreneurs (Art. L. 645-1 et seq. Code de Commerce) and the *procédure de rétablissement personnel* for consumers (Art. L. 741-1 et seq. Code de la Consommation) provide neither for a compliance period nor for an obligation to contribute to the satisfaction of the ordinary creditors from future income.[25] The same holds true for discharge after regular liquidation proceedings (Art. L. 643-11 Code de Commerce). 9.17

Example: Tennis great B has been declared bankrupt in England. After a while, it turns out that B withholds information about his available assets. The consequence under English law was the extension of the compliance period according to sec. 279(3) Insolvency Act 1986 in accordance with a bankruptcy restriction undertaking under sec. 281A, Sch. 4A Insolvency Act 1986 proposed by B. Under German law, discharge could be denied on application of a single ordinary creditor (§290(1)No. 5 Insolvenzordnung). The same holds true for the USA (§727(a)/(c) Bankruptcy Code). Only in France, is nothing of the kind provided for. 9.18

4. *Court Involvement*

National laws proceed very differently when it comes to the **granting of discharge**. While the debtor is occasionally discharged by force of law at the end of the compliance period (sec. 279 Insolvency Act 1986), most discharge regulations provide for a decision of the court or another official institution. This holds true in England and Wales for the debt relief order, which is granted by the official receiver (sec. 251E Insolvency Act 1986). A court decision is invariably required in Germany (§300(1) 9.19

---

24 Cf. above at para. 4.9. – This is different for the discharge by order of court (sec. 280(2)(c) Insolvency Act 1986). However, this is very rarely applied for.

25 An exception is possible in liquidation proceedings in Alsace-Lorrain (*départements* of Moselle, Bas-Rhin and Haut-Rhin) where the court may bind the discharge to further contributions under Art. L. 670-4 Code de Commerce).

Insolvenzordnung) and the USA (§§727(a), 1328(a)(1) Bankruptcy Code). In France, discharge after regular liquidation proceedings depends on a court decision (Art. L. 643-11 Code de Commerce). The same holds true for the *procédure de rétablissement professionnel* (Art. L. 645-2 Code de Commerce) while discharge in the *procédure de rétablissement personnel* is granted by a commission (*commission de surendettement des particuliers*, Art. L. 712-1 et seq., 741-1 Code de la Consommation).

9.20 It is important for creditor protection that a discharge decision is subject to **relief**. As regards automatic discharge under English sec. 279 Insolvency Act 1986, the Insolvency Practitioner can apply to the court for extension or suspension of the compliance period or for a bankruptcy restriction order, albeit before the end of the one year compliance period. A debt relief order can be challenged by every affected person to the court (sec. 251M Insolvency Act 1986). In Germany, the court decision is subject to appeal (§§296(3), 300(4)(2) Insolvenzordnung), and the same holds true for the US (§158 Code of Judiciary and Judicial Procedure). In France, the decision of the commission in *rétablissement personnel* proceedings is challengeable under Art. L. 741-4 Code de la Consommation whereas court decisions in the other proceedings that concern individuals are usually not challengeable.

5. *Effects*

9.21 Once discharge is granted, the question as to its **scope** arises. First, legislators have to decide whether only pre-commencement claims (of ordinary creditors) or also post-commencement claims (of privileged creditors) are affected. Second, the question must be answered whether all debts are released or whether exceptions are due. Legislators tend to exempt certain debts from the discharge, particularly those stemming from (intentional) tort and occasionally also fines and tax claims. Third, the effects on third parties (such as sureties or guarantors) are a topic.[26]

9.22 Analysing **national laws,** only pre-commencement claims are affected in all jurisdictions covered in this book. Among them, English sec. 281 Insolvency Act 1986 provides for some discharge exceptions, particularly for fines, debts resulting from fraudulent behaviour, and claims exempted

---

26 Cf. §13.2(1)(2) PEIL: "The discharge does not affect the rights of creditors against third parties."

by the court, and clarifies that third parties (such as guarantors or sureties) are not discharged. In France, exemptions from discharge are contained in Art. L. 643-11, 645-11 Code de Commerce for discharge after liquidation proceedings and the *procédure de rétablissement professionnel* and in Art. L. 711-4, 711-5, 741-2 Code de la Consommation for the *procédure de rétablissement personnel*. Third parties do not profit from the discharge (Art. L. 643-11(2), 645-11 Code de Commerce, 741-2(1) Code de la Consommation). Similarly, German law provides for exceptions in §302 Insolvenzordnung, again including fines and claims from intentionally committed torts. Third parties are not affected (§301(2) Insolvenzordnung). In the US, §523 Bankruptcy Code provides for a long list of exceptions (including fines, certain tax claims, and debts from fraudulent behaviour[27]) and it follows from §524(e) Bankruptcy Code that third parties (such as sureties or guarantors) do not benefit from the discharge.[28]

II. EXCURSUS: CONSUMER INSOLVENCIES

Before Chapter 9 of this book, we have dealt with insolvent entrepreneurs, 9.23 mostly companies. However, it must not be neglected that in nearly all societies insolvent consumers are a **mass phenomenon**. Figures show that many more overindebted households than businesses exist and that the number of proceedings for insolvent consumers exceed those of proceedings for insolvent entrepreneurs significantly.[29] Reasons for such insolvencies are manifold. They reach from unexpected and oppressing debts (e.g. uninsured claims for damages resulting from negligence) over illness resulting in unemployment to inability to avoid unnecessary debts (due to lack of experience, addiction to drugs or gambling, or simply craving for recognition). However, in many cases, regular insolvency proceedings as introduced in this book are not suitable for managing the economic shipwreck of the poorest. Hence, many jurisdictions offer a second way

27 See also §1328(a)(1) Bankruptcy Code.

28 *NCNB Tex. Nat'l Bank v. Johnson*, 11 F.3d 1260 (5th Cir. 1994).

29 In 2018, for example, in England and Wales 115,299 individuals and 16,090 companies went bankrupt, in Germany 67,597 consumer insolvencies were faced with 19,302 business insolvencies. In the US, figures are 22,245 (business) to 753,333 (non-business). Quite differently, in France, 92,000 consumers and 54,627 entrepreneurs went bankrupt, but this discrepancy in figures is probably due to different statistic approaches.

of surmounting the difficulties of insolvent consumers.[30] These consumer insolvency proceedings shall be shortly introduced in the following text, albeit without going too much into detail.

A. BASICS

9.24 As we have seen in the previous chapters, regular insolvency proceedings, even where they are liquidation proceedings, are quite complex, costly, and also inflexible. Insolvent consumers, however, regularly live in **simple economic circumstances**. They have no employees, few creditors, and not many – if any – assets which are worth the effort of starting sophisticated insolvency proceedings. Such proceedings are neither necessary nor always possible, since the estate of consumers is mostly not sufficient to cover the costs and expenses of the proceedings. Hence, where the debtor is not an entrepreneur but a consumer, putting emphasis on the aspect of valorising the estate instead of discharging the debtor from their residual debt misses the point. Considering all of this, simplified proceedings which at least open the chance for discharge are appropriate.

9.25 Many **national laws** offer such a lean and reasonable procedure shaped for the special needs of the poorest. In France, for example, where business insolvencies are regulated in the Code de Commerce, consumer insolvencies are dealt with in a special chapter of the Code de la Consommation (Art. L. 711-1 et seq.) which aims primarily at discharging the debtor. German law offers lean consumer insolvency proceedings in §§304 et seq. Insolvenzordnung which are liquidation proceedings in the first place but can be – and regularly are – combined with discharge proceedings. In England and Wales, Part II (sec. 251A et seq.) Insolvency Act 1986 provides for special rules on personal insolvencies (bankruptcies). Although they are not reserved for consumers but also applicable to entrepreneurs, they offer special tools for handling the needs of penniless people and lead to an automatic discharge.[31] The same holds true for the USA, where insolvent consumers are subject to the same rules as entrepreneurs. They enter

30 Cf. the National Reports in *Faber/Vermunt/Kilborn/Richter*, Commencement of Insolvency Proceedings, each at para. 3.2., and in *Kadner/Bojārs/Sajadova*, A Guide to Consumer Insolvency Proceedings in Europe, passim.

31 For a first example, see the rules on a debt relief order in sec. 251A et seq. Insolvency Act 1986 (above at para. 9.6).

either into liquidation proceedings as regulated in chapter 7 Bankruptcy Code or into chapter 13 proceedings which are open for individuals with manageable debts and regular income, both resulting in a discharge of residual debt.[32]

B. DETAILS

On a closer look, rules on consumer insolvencies show **typical features** which take account of the special needs and circumstances of non-entrepreneurs. First, where a special regime for consumer insolvencies is established, the personal scope must be set out by defining the addressees of these rules. Second, financing the proceedings is a typical issue, since consumers frequently do not have the means to cover the costs and expenses. Third, it may seem wise to set incentives for arrangements between the debtor and their creditors which can spare formal insolvency proceedings. Fourth, where such proceedings are unavoidable, a lean and – as compared to regular insolvency proceedings – simplified procedure is due. And finally, the relationship to, and connection with, discharge proceedings is an urgent topic. 9.26

1. Addressees

The first task for legislators who undertake to establish special insolvency rules for non-entrepreneurs is defining the term **consumer**. This can easily be done by distinguishing consumers from entrepreneurs, but the devil is in the detail. One of various questions is the inclusion of former entrepreneurs, at least where they are individuals and not companies. If former entrepreneurs are included, they should not be incentivised to shut down their business shortly before commencing insolvency proceedings in order to benefit from simplified consumer insolvency and discharge proceedings. Legislators should be aware of such manipulation opportunities and deal with the phenomenon of former entrepreneurs. 9.27

Looking at **national laws**, the laws of England and Wales and the United States do not distinguish between entrepreneurs and consumers but are content with special regimes for individuals; hence, no definition problems arise. An exception is sec. 112B County Courts Act 1984 which quite 9.28

32 Cf. above at para. 9.6.

elegantly reserves County Court Administration Orders[33] to debtors who do "not have any business debts", leaving former entrepreneurs who still have debts from their active business times out. As opposed to that, the delineation of the personal scope is extensively considered in German and French law. In Germany, the term "consumer"[34] is defined in §304(1)(1) Insolvenzordnung with "a natural person who pursues or has pursued no self-employed business activity". The expression "or has pursued" refers to the problem of former entrepreneurs, particularly where they had their business shut down shortly before commencing insolvency proceedings. It is explained in more detail in §304(1)(2)/(2) Insolvenzordnung: "If the debtor has pursued self-employed business activity, the first sentence" [i.e. the rules on consumer insolvencies] "shall apply if his assets are comprehensible and no claims exist against him from employment. The assets shall be comprehensible (...), only if the debtor has fewer than twenty creditors at the time the request is made to open the insolvency proceedings." In France, addressees of consumer insolvency proceedings are all overindebted individuals[35] who acted in good faith[36] and are not subject to regular insolvency proceedings under the Code de Commerce (Art. L. 711-1, 711-3 Code de la Consommation). This leads us to Art. L. 611-1 Code de Commerce which refers to all persons registered in the commercial and companies register or the trade register, and to Art. L. 620-2 Code de Commerce according to which regular insolvency law is applicable to individuals who are engaged in a retail activity or artisanal trade, farming, or an independent professional activity.[37]

2. *Financing the Proceedings*

9.29 In many cases, consumers have no or only few assets the value of which is not sufficient to cover even the minimum costs and expenses of the proceedings. Where the commencement of insolvency proceedings is only possible if the debtor is able to finance such proceedings,[38] the result might

---

33 On them below at para. 9.32.

34 Interestingly, this term is only used in the heading to Part 10 of the Insolvenzordnung, not in the rules themselves.

35 "Overindebted" is defined as evident inability to pay the non-professional mature debts, Art. L. 330-1 Code de la Consommation.

36 This proves that French consumer insolvency proceedings aim primarily at discharging the debtor from residual debt; see also above at para. 9.6.

37 This excludes former entrepreneurs.

38 Extensively above at para. 3.32.

be that they are **not accessible** for them. This is detrimental at least where discharge, forcefully strived for by consumers, is dependent on antecedent insolvency proceedings.

National laws try to avoid this, albeit in diverging ways. In Germany, where discharge can only be granted as an annex to insolvency proceedings, natural persons who apply for a discharge may also apply for deferment of costs until the moment that discharge of residual debt is awarded. Such deferment is only granted if their assets are likely not to be sufficient to cover these costs when insolvency proceedings are applied for (§4a(1) Insolvenzordnung). French law, which normally does not require sufficient means as a prerequisite for opening insolvency proceedings, offers the *procédure de rétablissement personnel* under Art. L. 741-1 et seq. Code de la Consommation, which is only followed by a liquidation procedure where the debtor acted not in good faith and exploitable assets are available. In England and Wales, the court may dismiss a bankruptcy petition under sec. 266(3) Insolvency Act 1986 where it is convinced that there are no assets distributable to the creditors or that such assets would be extinguished by the proceedings. However, in small cases, this would open the door to a debt relief order under sec. 251A Insolvency Act 1986.[39] In the USA, neither chapter 7 nor chapter 13 proceedings are dependent on sufficient means to finance them.[40] Especially chapter 7 cases can be opened as "no asset" cases,[41] resulting in a discharge after a short administration period.[42] 9.30

3. *Incentives for Arrangements*

Complex insolvency proceedings can be avoided by **debt restructuring tools** which are available in various forms. Examples are voluntary arrangements between the debtor and their creditors, "voluntary" meaning 9.31

39 See above at para. 9.6.

40 The debtor applying for the proceedings has to pay a filing fee of $335 (cf. above at para. 3.22), but this can be reduced or waived by the court under 28 U.S.C. §1930(f). Only where the debtor does not pay the fee, the case may be dismissed under §707(a)(2) Bankruptcy Code.

41 It must be taken into account that assets burdened with security rights do not belong to those distributable to unsecured creditors (§§725, 726 Bankruptcy Code) and that debtors may take certain assets from the estate under §522 Bankruptcy Code in order to enable the basic needs for them and their family.

42 In "no asset" cases (above fn. 41), creditors normally refrain from filing their claims, the Insolvency Practitioner files a final report (§704(a)(9) Bankruptcy Code), and the court, having granted discharge, closes the case (§350(a) Bankruptcy Code).

that it is at the debtor's discretion to offer a solution for overcoming the crisis. Such solutions, which typically include a clause on discharge of residual debt, can be simple agreements, binding only on those who have joined the settlement, but also payment or debt restructuring plans voted upon by the creditors and/or sanctioned by the court and binding on all creditors. Occasionally, settlement attempts are a compulsory prerequisite for insolvency proceedings. National laws have several instruments with which insolvency proceedings can be avoided.

9.32 The law of **England and Wales** offers a wide range of voluntary arrangements. We have already learned about the debt relief order, available in small cases under sec. 251A Insolvency Act 1986.[43] A future alternative is offered by the County Courts Act of 1984. It contains in sec. 112A et seq., which are not yet in force, rules on a County Court Administration Order which authorises the court to regulate the repayment of debts over the next five years for non-entrepreneurs with minor debts but a regular income. However, the most important tool under English law is the Individual Voluntary Arrangement (IVA) under sec. 252 et seq. Insolvency Act 1986. Similar to a CVA for companies,[44] a bankrupt but not discharged debtor can make a proposal to their creditors for a composition in satisfaction of debts or a scheme of arrangement of their affairs. Negotiations on this proposal can be protected by an interim order (moratorium) of the court. The proposal is put to a vote of a creditors' meeting (or by correspondence, sec. 379ZA et seq. Insolvency Act 1986) and needs a majority of three-quarters in value of those responding to the proposal (rule 15.34(6) Insolvency Rules 2016). Declination of the proposal cannot be overturned by the court (no "cross-class cram-down"[45]). In case of approval, sanctioning of the court is not necessary. However, the creditors' decision can be challenged under sec. 262 Insolvency Act 1986.[46] Where the consent of the creditors is reached, the arrangement is registered with the court and has binding effect on all those entitled to vote in the creditors' decision procedure. As a consequence, bankruptcy proceedings are no longer necessary (cf. sec. 260(5) Insolvency Act 1986).

---

43 Above at para. 9.6.

44 See for this above at para. 8.9.

45 On that, see above at para. 8.37.

46 For an example, see *Moises Gertner v. CFL Finance Ltd* [2018] EWCA Civ. 1781; *CFL Finance Ltd v. Bass* [2019] EWHC 1839 (Ch).

In **France**, consumer proceedings are conducted by the *commission de surendettement des particuliers*, Art. L. 712-1 et seq., 741-1 Code de la Consommation). The commission tries to facilitate a debt restructuring plan with the most important creditors if the debtor owns real estate (Art. 732-1 et seq. Code de la Consommation). The plan needs the consent of the creditors concerned, but silence qualifies as consent. If the plan is not accepted, the commission can order payment modifications for the next two years and impose a waiver for certain residual debts (Art. 733-1 et seq. Code de la Consommation). In hopeless economic cases, the *procédure de rétablissement personnel* under Art. L. 741-1 et seq. Code de la Consommation is available. The latter means are not arrangements with the creditors but rather settlements ordered by the commission. However, where the debtor has assets and the *procédure de rétablissement personnel* is followed by court-conducted liquidation proceedings under Art. L. 742-1 et seq. Code de la Consommation, the court can impose a debt restructuring plan in order to avoid the liquidation proceedings (Art. 742-24 et seq. Code de la Consommation). 9.33

In **Germany** it is mandatory to attempt a consensual solution, albeit in consumer insolvency proceedings only. A consumer insolvency procedure can only be opened if it is proven through a certification by a suitable person or agency that the debtor's attempt to reach an out-of-court agreement with their creditors about the clearance of debts has failed (§305(1)No.1 Insolvenzordnung). The debtor must also include a plan for the settlement of debts with the application to open insolvency proceedings to which the creditors have access and to which they can also object. The court only reaches its final decision about the application to open insolvency proceedings and opens them once this final attempt to reach an agreement with the creditors has also failed (§§305-311 Insolvenzordnung). 9.34

In the **USA**, the main feature of chapter 13 proceedings is the payment plan presented by the debtor. As these proceedings can only be commenced by the debtor, this is a voluntary solution avoiding liquidation proceedings. Pressure is put on the debtor to use this solution, since the court may dismiss an application for chapter 7 proceedings if granting such proceedings would be an abuse because the debtor has regular income which can be used to satisfy the creditors' claims in chapter 13 proceedings (§707(b)(1) Bankruptcy Code).[47] 9.35

---

[47] See above at para. 9.15.

4. *Simplified Liquidation Proceedings*

9.36 Differently from corporate insolvencies, regular insolvency proceedings are much too elaborate when it comes to consumer insolvencies. Since there are mostly only a few creditors and no or few assets, extensive formal liquidation proceedings are neither necessary nor fundable. Hence, where formal insolvency proceedings are unavoidable, a **reduced procedure** might be sensible. In small cases, neither creditors' committees nor creditors' meetings are useful. Although an Insolvency Practitioner, whose tasks also cover the registration of claims and the valorisation of assets in consumer insolvencies, is indispensable, written proceedings and reduction of expenditure are advisable.

9.37 Surprisingly, this topic is rarely addressed in **national laws**. However, in Germany, consumer insolvency proceedings are markedly simplified. This follows, firstly, from the fact that the debtor must supply the court with certification documenting income and estate, information about creditors, and obligations. Secondly, the court should be content with one creditors' meeting, can refrain from establishing a creditors' committee, and the proceedings are generally conducted as written proceedings (§5(2) Insolvenzordnung). Further, the possibility of debtor-in-possession proceedings is excluded in consumer insolvencies (§270(1)(3) Insolvenzordnung). In the US, nothing of the kind is at hand. Where the debtor has no regular income and is therefore not able to commence chapter 13 proceedings, liquidation proceedings under chapter 7 Bankruptcy Code are the only way. Statute does not provide for simplified proceedings, although in practice they are reduced to few steps, since the available assets are usually not distributable.[48] In England and Wales, bankruptcies for individuals are regulated separately from insolvencies for companies, but the main features of the proceedings are broadly the same, the most important exception being the discharge for individuals.[49] In France, however, consumer insolvencies are conducted by the *commission de surendettement des particuliers* in the first instance which is primarily tasked to avoid liquidation proceedings and to restructure the debtor's financial obligations.[50] It is an administrative rather than a regular

48 Cf. above fn. 42.

49 See for the latter above at para. 9.6.

50 Cf. above at para. 9.33.

insolvency procedure. Liquidation proceedings are an exception and are conducted in a simple manner on the basis of Art. L. 742-1 et seq. Code de la Consommation.

5. *Relation to Discharge*

The relationship between discharge and insolvency proceedings is an **important topic**, since most consumers enter insolvency proceedings in order to gain discharge rather than to be deprived of their estate (provided they have any at all). As we have seen above,[51] some jurisdictions (England and Wales, France) offer stand-alone discharge proceedings where insolvency proceedings are financially not feasible and therefore not reasonable. Others (Germany, USA) insist on insolvency or restructuring proceedings as a prerequisite for discharge, then financed by public funds. For details, reference can be made to para. 9.12 above. 9.38

For further reading: *Bork*, Einführung, §§33, 34, 36; *Fletcher*, Law of Insolvency, para. 3-001 et seq., 11-001 et seq.; *Tabb*, Law of Bankruptcy, §10.1 et seq. 9.39

[51] At para. 9.12.

CHAPTER 10
CROSS-BORDER INSOLVENCY LAW

In the tenth chapter, the cross-border aspects of insolvency proceedings will be introduced. We will learn about the issues, which typically arise where a debtor has assets, creditors, contracts, offices or other affairs abroad, and we will be informed about the rules regulating these issues. In particular, the questions as to international jurisdiction and the applicable law will be in our focus and recognition of foreign insolvency proceedings and decisions will be dealt with. Finally, we will learn about rules on cooperation and coordination of multiple proceedings. 10.1

I. BASICS

Increasingly, insolvency proceedings have **international connotations**. 10.2 Debtors have assets abroad, are obliged to foreign creditors, are engaged in contractual relationships with counterparties in other jurisdictions, or have other cross-border affairs, e.g. offices, branches, or subsidiaries in a different country. This not only holds true for entrepreneurs but also for consumers who order goods from abroad or own a holiday home in an foreign state. As soon as other jurisdictions are involved, we can speak of cross-border insolvencies and the rules that deal with this phenomenon can be consolidated as cross-border insolvency law.

A. ISSUES

Cross-border insolvency law deals with **typical problems**. The first 10.3 question concerns the number of proceedings: is there only one single set of insolvency proceedings or should there be separate proceedings in each jurisdiction involved? If there is only one single set of proceedings, which state has international jurisdiction to open such proceedings? What are the trans-border effects of "outgoing" domestic insolvency proceedings (e.g. does the seizure of the estate include assets located abroad)? Are "incoming" foreign proceedings recognised domestically, e.g. does a foreign Insolvency Practitioner have the power to dispose of assets located inland? Which law does apply to the insolvency proceedings (e.g. is the insolvency law of the opening state[1] applicable to security rights encumbering collateral located in another state)? Where there are multiple proceedings, how are they coordinated?

B. CODIFICATIONS

10.4 In searching for a codification of international insolvency law, a wealth of suitable material can be found. Internationally **binding laws**, which apply to more than one state, and thus do not constitute purely national law but rather transnational law, belong within the first group of laws to be depicted here. The first transnational law to be named is the European Insolvency Regulation (EIR[2]), which applies to all Member States of the European Union with the exception of Denmark. Alongside this, there are – among others – the Nordic Bankruptcy Convention, which applies to the Scandinavian countries of Denmark, Finland, Iceland, Norway, and Sweden, the Treaties of Montevideo, which were ratified by Argentina, Bolivia, Columbia, Paraguay, Peru, and Uruguay, the Havana Convention, which was signed by 15 South American states and is better known as the Code Bustamante, and finally the Uniform Act Organising Collective Proceedings for Wiping off Debts, which is binding for the 17 Member States of the OHADA (Organisation for the Harmonisation of Business Law in Africa).

10.5 A second group consists of **non-binding recommendations** for the legislature and for those involved in cross-border insolvency proceedings. A prominent example is the UNCITRAL Model Law on Cross-Border Insolvency,[3] which has been incorporated into the national law of

---

1 Henceforth, the meaning of "opening state" is the state where insolvency proceedings have been opened.

2 For details, see *Bork/Mangano*, European Cross-Border Insolvency Law; *Bork/van Zwieten* (eds.), Commentary on the EIR; *Brinkmann* (ed.), EIR; *Moss/Fletcher/Isaacs* (eds.), The EC Regulation on Insolvency Proceedings.

3 More by *Ho* (ed.), Cross-Border Insolvency.

41 states. In addition, different recommendations by international organisations should be mentioned, such as the Principles of Cooperation in Transnational Insolvency Cases among the NAFTA Countries (NAFTA Principles), which were formulated by the American Law Institute, or the Cross-Border Insolvency Concordat, which was created by the International Bar Association. Cooperation guidelines are helpful for practice, particularly the Global Principles for Cooperation in International Insolvency Cases (Global Principles) published by the American Law Institute in cooperation with the International Insolvency Institute, and the European Communication and Cooperation Guidelines for Cross-Border Insolvencies, presented by INSOL Europe.

National rules on international insolvency law belong to the third group. 10.6
Examples to be named include §335 et seq. Insolvenzordnung, which leans heavily on the European Insolvency Regulation, as well as chapter 15 of the US Bankruptcy Code, which builds upon the UNCITRAL Model Law. The United Kingdom had four legal regimes operating regarding cross-border insolvency cases. During the EU membership of the UK, in relation to other Member States of the EU, the EIR is applicable. In relation to Commonwealth states, s. 426 Insolvency Act 1986 is applied. And in relation to all other states, the provisions of the Cross-Border Insolvency Regulation 2006 apply, which incorporated the UNCITRAL Model Law into national English insolvency law. In addition, duties to cooperate can be derived from the common law. In France, however, cross-border insolvency law is not codified but handled on a case-by-case basis under general legal principles (*droit commun*) unless the EIR or bilateral treaties apply.[4] It is for this reason that French cross-border insolvency law will not be considered in detail in this chapter.

C. PRINCIPLES

In the first chapter, we have learned about the principles of insolvency 10.7
law,[5] which can be grouped into two groups: procedural and substantive principles. At this stage, a third group must be introduced, which

4 *Le Corre*, Droit et pratique des procedúres collectives, para. 093.091; extensively *Dammann/Sénéchal*, Le droit de l'insolvabilité international, para. 2038 et seq.

5 Above at para. 1.9 et seq.

comprises the **jurisdictional principles** of cross-border insolvency law and concerns itself with principles on the collision of rights, addressing the circumstances in which two sovereign states are involved in a cross-border insolvency case.[6] Modern international insolvency laws generally base themselves on the principles of unity and universalism (universality):[7] there should fundamentally be only one unified set of proceedings opened against an insolvent debtor (unity), which has worldwide scope (universalism). The latter applies in any case from the perspective of the state opening the proceedings, which demands worldwide application of its "outgoing" proceedings, while it is another story as to whether other affected states will recognise the "incoming" insolvency proceedings as requiring recognition. In addition, the principle of equality of states, which can be found in Art. 2(1) of the Charter of the UN, precludes a state from forcing worldwide application of its law on another, but the principle of mutual trust between states proposes that, if the insolvency law and the handling of the insolvency proceedings in the original state meet the required standards, the relevant state should be urged to recognise it. Regardless, the principle of cooperation and communication between the different official bodies taking part in the proceedings is generally recognised with regard to cross-border insolvency proceedings. The EIR acknowledges this principle, for example, in Art. 41 et seq. regarding the relationship between main and secondary insolvency proceedings and in Art. 56 et seq. regarding group insolvency proceedings; the UNCITRAL Model Law already recognises it in its Preamble, which names as its significant goal the encouragement of cooperation between procedural organs of the affected states, and also refers to it in Art. 25 et seq., which concerns itself extensively with the cooperation of courts and insolvency practitioners. In the context of international insolvency law, the principle of subsidiarity as well as the principle of proportionality also plug the gaps.

II. DETAILS

10.8 When insolvency proceedings have cross-border effects, **typical questions** arise. The first concerns international jurisdiction: the courts of which state are competent to open and to administer the proceedings?

---

6 Details in *Bork*, Principles of Cross-Border Insolvency Law, para. 1.29, 2.1 et seq.
7 Details below at para. 10.9 et seq.

The second question deals with the law applicable to the proceedings and its effects: are affairs and relationships abroad governed by the law of the opening state or is this law superseded by the local law? Finally, how about recognition? Are decisions of domestic insolvency courts recognised abroad and, if so, under which conditions? However, cross-border insolvency law is a very complex matter and a field of law of its own. In this book, only basic features can be addressed. For more detailed information, reference must be made to specialised literature.[8]

A. JURISDICTION

The matter of international jurisdiction is closely connected to two fundamental principles of cross-border insolvency law: unity and universalism (universality). The meaning of **unity** is that there shall be no more than one single set of insolvency proceedings governing the debtor's insolvency.[9] A logical consequence of this principle is that the opening of insolvency proceedings in one state hinders the opening of a second insolvency procedure in another state (which, by the way, is supported by the procedural principles of priority[10]). Although this principle is accepted in many regulations, significant exceptions can be found. A second set of proceedings is unavoidable if state B does not recognise the opening decision of state A. Another reason for two (or more) insolvency proceedings for the same debtor may arise from the complexity of the debtor's affairs abroad. In such cases, it may be reasonable not to include these affairs in the domestic insolvency proceedings of state A but to open another procedure in state B. For example, this is permitted in Art. 3(2), 34 et seq. EIR, which provide for so-called "secondary proceedings" in another Member State of the EU if the debtor possess an establishment within the territory of that other Member State.[11] Such secondary 10.9

8 See for European law the references above in fn. 2. Beyond, see *Dammann/Sénéchal*, Le droit de l'insolvabilité international; *Mélin*, La faillite internationale; *Sheldon*, Cross-Border Insolvency; *Wessels*, International Insolvency Law.

9 More in *Bork*, Principles of Cross-Border Insolvency Law, para. 2.2 et seq.

10 For this, see above at para. 1.10.

11 Similar provisions are Art. 28 et seq. UNCITRAL Model Law and in England and Wales Art. 28 et seq. Sch. 1 Cross-Border Insolvency Regulation 2006, in Germany §§354 et seq. Insolvenzordnung, in the US §§1528 et seq. Bankruptcy Code.

proceedings are conducted alongside the main proceedings, a distinction which is well known to the UNCITRAL Model Law[12] and many national laws.[13]

10.10 If there is, under the principle of unity, only one single set of insolvency proceedings these must necessarily encompass all the debtor's assets regardless of their location. This is why the principle of unity is regularly accompanied by the principle of **universalism,** according to which insolvency proceedings should have global scope and attach all the debtor's assets no matter whether they are situated inland or abroad.[14] However, this approach is formulated from the perspective of the opening state and we can call it "outgoing universalism". A different matter is the other state's willingness to recognise the effects of foreign insolvency proceedings on its own territory, be it automatically, or be it based on a court decision. If it does so, we can call that "incoming universalism". The principle of universalism – as opposed to the principle of territorialism, according to which insolvency proceedings have only domestic effects – is accepted by the UNCITRAL Model Law[15] and many national laws.[16] However, there are also exceptions, which correspond mainly to the exceptions to the principle of unity.[17] For example, where cross-border insolvency law provides for secondary insolvency proceedings, these affect only assets located in the state where the secondary proceedings are conducted whereas the main proceedings cover all other assets (i.e. all except those, which are subject to the secondary proceedings). Where such exceptions exist, we speak of "modified universalism".

10.11 An important feature of the two principles discussed above (but also of the principle of predictability[18]) is **jurisdiction**. While the UNCITRAL Model Law is silent on this matter, a leading example is

12 Art. 2 UNCITRAL Model Law.

13 See below in fn. 16.

14 For details, see *Bork*, Principles of Cross-Border Insolvency Law, para. 2.8 et seq.

15 Cf. Art. 5 UNCITRAL Model Law.

16 See for Germany §343 Insolvenzordnung, for the USA §1505 Bankruptcy Code; for France Cour de Cassation (chambre commerciale) – 21.3.2006 – 04-17869 = Bull. civ. 2006, IV, no. 74; for England and Wales Art. 5 Sch. 1 Cross-Border Insolvency Regulation 2006 and *Sturgeon Central Asia Balanced Fund Ltd (in liquidation)* [2019] EWHC 1215 (Ch).

17 For them, see above at para. 10.9.

18 Above at para. 1.10 and extensively *Bork*, Principles of Cross-Border Insolvency Law, para. 3.40 et seq.

given by Art. 3(1) European Insolvency Regulation, which – binding for parties and courts[19] – states: "The courts of the Member State within the territory of which the centre of the debtor's main interests is situated shall have jurisdiction to open insolvency proceedings ('main insolvency proceedings'). The centre of main interests shall be the place where the debtor conducts the administration of its interests on a regular basis and which is ascertainable by third parties. In the case of a company or legal person, the place of the registered office shall be presumed to be the centre of its main interests in the absence of proof to the contrary. That presumption shall only apply if the registered office has not been moved to another Member State within the 3-month period prior to the request for the opening of insolvency proceedings. In the case of an individual exercising an independent business or professional activity, the centre of main interests shall be presumed to be that individual's principal place of business in the absence of proof to the contrary. That presumption shall only apply if the individual's principal place of business has not been moved to another Member State within the 3-month period prior to the request for the opening of insolvency proceedings. In the case of any other individual, the centre of main interests shall be presumed to be the place of the individual's habitual residence in the absence of proof to the contrary. This presumption shall only apply if the habitual residence has not been moved to another Member State within the 6-month period prior to the request for the opening of insolvency proceedings." It follows from this wording that the Regulation, assisted by comprehensive case law,[20] refers basically to the "centre of main interests" (hereafter: COMI) and endeavours to assist the courts in determining the debtor's COMI. The COMI-concept is also addressed by the UNCITRAL Model Law[21] and many other national laws,[22] albeit for recognition purposes only and not

---

19 Cf. *CJEU* Case C-493/18 *UB v. VA, Tiger SCI, WZ and Banque patrimoine et immobilier SA*, ECLI:EU:C:2019:1046.

20 See the judgments of the CJEU Case C-341/04 *Eurofood IFSC Ltd.*, ECLI:EU:C:2006:281; *CJEU* Case C-1/04 *Susanne Staubitz-Schreiber*, ECLI:EU:C:2006:39; *CJEU* Case C-396/09 *Interedil*, ECLI:EU:C:2011:67.

21 Art. 2(b), 16(3), 17(2)(a) UNCITRAL Model Law. Cf. *Re Videology Ltd* [2018] EWHC 2186 (Ch).

22 See for England and Wales Art. 2(g), 16(3), 17(2)(a) Sch. 1 Cross-Border Insolvency Regulation 2006; for the USA §§1502(4), 1516(c), 1517(b) Bankruptcy Code and *In re Serviços de Petróleo Constellation S.A.*, 600 B.R. 237 (Bankr. S.D.N.Y. 2019).

in the context of international jurisdiction where many states rely on their regular insolvency law[23] or general civil procedural law.

10.12 **Example**: D S.A., a company with registered office in Luxembourg, is the subsidiary of an Italian Holding company. D S.A. is tasked to generate financial means for the group by borrowing money from banks and issuing bonds and to forward the money as a loan to other group companies. The directors of D S.A. move the office of the company from which they run the company to London (UK) and apply for administration proceedings. Before the High Court can decide upon this application, the shareholders dismiss the directors and appoint a new director who instantly moves the office to Düsseldorf and applies for insolvency proceedings in Düsseldorf. The court in Düsseldorf appoints a preliminary Insolvency Practitioner and orders preliminary measures, among others by binding transactions of the debtor company to the consent of the preliminary Insolvency Practitioner. This raises the question as to international jurisdiction. Since all states involved are members of the EU, Art. 3 EIR is applicable. Given that the directors of D S.A. are the only employees and that financial affairs can be dealt with from any office in the world, it must be conceded that D S.A. moved its COMI first from Luxembourg to London and then to Düsseldorf, thereby rebutting the presumption, which refers to the registered office in Luxembourg. Hence, the court in Düsseldorf has international jurisdiction under Art. 3(1) EIR. However, this would not have hindered the court in London to open insolvency proceedings, since the COMI of D S.A. was in London at the time of the application to the High Court and the subsequent COMI shift is irrelevant under the *perpetuatio fori* rule.[24] What *is* relevant, is the decision of the court in Düsseldorf to appoint a preliminary insolvency practitioner, since this is an opening decision (Art. 2 No. 7(ii) EIR), which is automatically recognised in all other EU Member States (Art. 19(1) EIR) and hinders further opening decisions under the *lis pendens* rule.[25]

---

23 In Germany the general rule for insolvency courts in §3 Insolvenzordnung is applied ("centre of the debtor's business activity"). The same holds true for France (reference to Art. R. 600-1 Code de Commerce: "centre of main interests").

24 *CJEU* Case C-1/04 *Susanne Staubitz-Schreiber*, ECLI:EU:C:2006:39.

25 *CJEU* Case C-341/04 *Eurofood IFSC Ltd.*, ECLI:EU:C:2006:281.

International jurisdiction is frequently regulated not only for the opening of insolvency proceedings but also for **annex procedures**. For example, according to Art. 6 EIR, the courts of the Member State within the territory of which insolvency proceedings have been opened shall have jurisdiction "for any action which derives directly from the insolvency proceedings and is closely linked with them".[26] Typical examples of such trials stemming from the insolvency proceedings are actions on transactions avoidance,[27] on directors' liability for wrongful trading,[28] on the allocation of assets to main and secondary proceedings,[29] and on the recognition of claims to the insolvency schedule.[30] 10.13

B. APPLICABLE LAW

A second set of issues concerns the law applicable to the insolvency proceedings. To begin with, insolvency proceedings are national proceedings conducted by national courts and must therefore be governed by national insolvency law, generally referred to as ***lex fori concursus***. This does not change automatically just because the debtor has assets or creditors abroad. It is therefore generally accepted not only under the principles of unity and universalism but also under the principle of predictability[31] that insolvency proceedings are conducted under the law of the opening state and that this also holds true for cross-border affairs. Corresponding rules are Art. 7 EIR, which explains in great detail which affairs are governed by the *lex fori concursus*. In Germany, §335 Insolvenzordnung states that, unless provided otherwise, the insolvency proceedings and their effects shall be subject to the law of the state in which the proceedings have been 10.14

26 See also Art. 2(d) UNCITRAL Model Law on Recognition and Enforcement of Insolvency-Related Judgments: "Insolvency-related judgment: (i) Means a judgment that: a. Arises as a consequence of or is materially associated with an insolvency proceeding, whether or not that insolvency proceeding has closed; and b. Was issued on or after the commencement of that insolvency proceeding; and (ii) Does not include a judgment commencing an insolvency proceeding."

27 Cf. Art. 6(1) EIR and CJEU Case C-339/07 *Seagon v. Deko Martium Belgium NV*, ECLI:EU:C:2009:83.

28 *CJEU* Case C-295/13 *H. v. H.K.*, ECLI:EU:C:2014:2410.

29 *CJEU* Case C-649/13 *Comité d'entreprise de Nortel Networks SA and Others v. Cosme Rogeau and Cosme Rogeau v. Alan Robert Bloom and Others*, ECLI:EU:C:2015:384.

30 CJEU Case C-47/18 *Skarb Pánstwa Rzeczpospolitej Polskiej – Generalny Dyrektor Dróg Krajowych i Autostrad v. Stephan Riel*, ECLI:EU:C:2019:754.

31 For details, cf. *Bork*, Principles of Cross-Border Insolvency Law, para. 3.47 et seq.

opened. The UNCITRAL Model Law is silent on this matter and so are many national laws, particularly those which are based on the Model Law. Yet the reason for this silence is that these laws take it for granted that official bodies apply their national law to both domestic and foreign assets, creditors, contracts, etc.[32]

10.15 However, many **special constellations** exist, which call the application of the *lex fori concursus* into question. For example, where a Swedish debtor has an employee (sales agent) in Italy and the employment agreement is governed by Italian law, it is not self-evident that this contract should be subject to (the rules on employment contracts in) Swedish insolvency law. The same holds true for collateral encumbered with security rights for the benefit of a foreign creditor, at least where the collateral is not located in the opening state. Other examples are tenancy agreements where the premises are located in another state, and transactions which are governed by foreign law but shall be challenged under the transactions avoidance law of the *lex fori concursus*. Many regulations, which address the problems of applicable law, provide for exceptions or modifications to the *lex fori concursus* and declare other legal regimes applicable.[33] This particularly holds true for the European Insolvency Regulation where Art. 8-18 provide for special rules on the applicable law. Some – not all – of these rules shall be introduced below as examples for typical exception provisions.

10.16 A very important and to some extent peculiar exception concerns ***rights in rem***. According to Art. 8(1) EIR, collateral which is encumbered with security rights and is located in another Member State is not affected by the opening of insolvency proceedings.[34] It is prevailing opinion in case law[35]

32 Cf. UNCITRAL, Legislative Guide on Insolvency Law, p. 69 para. 83 and Recommendation 31; for England *Dicey/Morris/Collins*, Conflict of Laws, para. 31-084 et seq.; for France *Dammann/Sénéchal*, Le droit de l'insolvabilité international, para. 2164 et seq.

33 However, French law only reluctantly accepts such exceptions, cf. *Dammann/Sénéchal*, Le droit de l'insolvabilité international, para. 2165 et seq.

34 Provisions similar to Art. 8(1) EIR can be found, for instance, in Germany (§351(1) Insolvenzordnung, albeit regarding foreign insolvency proceedings only) and Austria (§11(2) Insolvenzordnung; on this *Kodek*, The Treatment of Security Rights, IILR 2015, 10 et seq.).

35 See *CJEU* Case C-527/10 *ERSTE Bank Hungary Nyrt v. Magyar Állam and Others*, ECLI:EU:C:2012:417; *CJEU* Case C-557/13 *Hermann Lutz v. Elke Bäuerle*, ECLI:EU:C:2015:227.

and literature[36] that this insulates such collateral from any insolvency law, i.e. from the *lex fori concursus* as well as from the insolvency law of the state where the collateral is located (*lex situs*), and subjects it to the substantive law on security rights of the *lex situs*. This is justified with reference to the principles of predictability, efficiency and protection of trust. However, it is difficult to see how this can be upheld in light of the principles of universalism and equal treatment of creditors.[37] It is hardly convincing that secured creditors with collateral in another Member State are not affected by the insolvency proceedings at all and are treated differently from creditors with collateral in the opening state.[38] Similar deliberations are due for the rule on the right to **set-off** in Art. 9 EIR[39] (which can be seen as a special security right[40]) and for the rule on **reservation of title** in Art. 10 EIR.[41]

Example:[42] D, an Austrian company, has pledged shares in a Hungarian subsidiary as a security for a loan granted by the Hungarian bank C. After the opening of insolvency proceedings in Austria concerning D's estate, C files a lawsuit in Hungary against D seeking a declaratory judgment to the effect that it had a security right over the shares. The Hungarian court declines the request, arguing that, under Austrian insolvency law as the applicable *lex fori concursus*, actions against the debtor of insolvency proceedings are impermissible. Indeed, lawsuits regarding security rights must be filed against the Insolvency 10.17

---

36 Cf. (among others) Bork/van Zwieten-*Snowden*, EIR, para. 8.09 et seq.; Brinkmann-*Dahl/Kortleben*, EIR, Art. 8 para. 25 et seq.; *Fletcher*, Insolvency in Private International Law, para. 7.87; Moss/Fletcher/Isaacs-*Fletcher*, EIR, para. 4.11 et seq.; Sheldon-*Arnold*, Cross-Border Insolvency, para. 2.76.

37 More in *Bork*, Principles of Cross-Border Insolvency Law, para. 4.21, 6.12 et seq.

38 For criticism, see *Bork* (previous fn.); Bork/van Zwieten-*van Zwieten*, EIR, para. 0.49; *van Galen/André/Fritz/Gladel/van Koppen/Marks/Wouters*, Revision of the EIR, p. 52 at 5.6 et seq.; *Paulus*, Security Rights in Cross-Border Insolvency Proceedings, IILR 2014, 366, 369 et seq.; *Veder*, The Future of the European Insolvency Regulation, IILR 2011, 285, 289 et seq.; *Veder*, Security Rights, p. 338 et seq.; *Virgós/Garcimartín*, European Insolvency Regulation, para. 164; *Wessels*, International Insolvency Law, para. 10640b.

39 Similarly, §338 Insolvenzordnung. For details, see *Bork*, Principles of Cross-Border Insolvency Law, para. 6.43 et seq.

40 Cf. above at para. 5.49.

41 On the latter, see *Bork*, Principles of Cross-Border Insolvency Law, para. 6.70 et seq.

42 Following the *CJEU* Case C-527/10 *ERSTE Bank Hungary Nyrt v. Magyar Állam and Others*, ECLI:EU:C:2012:417.

Practitioner, not against the debtor. However, this is only true under national insolvency laws. As opposed to that, Art. 8 EIR exempts security rights from the application of each insolvency law whatsoever, provided the collateral (here: the shares) are situated in another Member State of the EU (here: Hungary) than the opening state (here: Austria). Hence, the pledge is treated as if insolvency proceedings would not exist and C's lawsuit against D is permissible.

10.18 As opposed to that, Art. 11 EIR, which assigns **purchase and tenancy agreements on immovables** to the law of the Member State within the territory of which the immovable property is situated,[43] is less problematic.[44] Although the policy of this rule is not clear, it can be justified under the principle of social protection,[45] albeit for tenancy agreements only where the tenant is a consumer, who deserves protection against "surprises from abroad", i.e. interference of foreign insolvency law in a domestic tenancy agreement. For all other contracts, there is no need and no justification for exempting them from the *lex fori concursus*. Similar deliberations are due for other norms, which assign certain contracts to the *lex contractus*, namely Art. 13 EIR,[46] which provides for the application of the *lex contractus* to **employment contracts** in order to protect employees against foreign (insolvency related) labour law.[47]

10.19 Finally, the exception for **transactions avoidance** should be mentioned. According to Art. 7(2) lit. m EIR, the transactions avoidance rules of the *lex fori concursus* are to be applied.[48] However, this is subject to Art. 16

---

43 See also §336 Insolvenzordnung.

44 Cf. *Bork*, Principles of Cross-Border Insolvency Law, para. 6.114 et seq.

45 See above at para. 1.11.

46 Similarly §337 Insolvenzordnung.

47 Details in *Bork*, Principles of Cross-Border Insolvency Law, para. 6.100 et seq.; see also *Fletcher*, Insolvency in Private International Law, para. 7.110; *Mélin*, La faillite internationale, para. 120; Sheldon-*Arnold*, Cross-Border Insolvency, para. 2.102; *Virgós/Garcimartín*, European Insolvency Regulation, para. 207; *Wessels*, International Insolvency Law, para. 10678, 10696.

48 Under the UNCITRAL Model Law, courts in some countries apply their own transactions avoidance laws. Other apply the transactions avoidance law of the foreign *lex fori concursus*; cf. for the UK *Galbraith v. Grimshaw*, [1910] AC 508; *UBS AG New York and others v. Fairfield Sentry Ltd (in Liquidation)* [2019] UKPC 20; for the USA *In re CIL Ltd.*, 582 B.R. 46 (2018); *In re Condor Insurance Ltd*, 601 F3d 319 (5th Cir. Miss. 2010); *In re Fairfield Sentry*, 485 B.R. 665 (S.D.N.Y. 2006); *In re Innternational Banking Corp. BSC*, 439 B.R. 614 (S.D.N.Y. 2010).

EIR, according to which the *lex fori concursus* "shall not apply where the person who benefitted from an act detrimental to all the creditors provides proof that (a) the act is subject to the law of a Member State other than that of the State of the opening of proceedings; and (b) the law of that Member State does not allow by any means of challenging that act in the relevant case".[49] The effect of this provision is that the benefitted person enjoys the application of the "most favourable" principle. If the detrimental act is not challengeable under the *lex fori concursus*, the creditor can keep what he or she has received. If it is challengeable, they get a second chance: they are permitted to overturn the challenge by proving that the act would be neither void nor voidable under any provision of the *lex causae*,[50] provided the *lex causae* is the law of a Member State of the EU. Hence, Art. 16 EIR grants a "safe harbour"[51] by permitting a defence against the application of the *lex fori concursus*. However, this is overprotective.[52] It has repeatedly been argued that protection of trust as granted by Art. 16 EIR is not justifiable, since the challenging of the act in question is a "foreseeable risk".[53] It is suggested that creditors who enter into transactions with a debtor (who is, in most cases, subject to insolvency proceedings shortly after the transaction) have to take into account the possibility that they cannot keep what they have received due to the debtor's national transactions avoidance law.

Example: C, the Luxembourg based only shareholder of the German D GmbH, grants a loan to her company. The loan agreement is governed by French law. Five months before the application for insolvency proceedings, D GmbH pays the loan back. After the opening of insolvency proceedings in Germany, the Insolvency Practitioner tackles the payment under German transactions avoidance law. This would be successful according to §135 Insolvenzordnung, which provides for the 10.20

49 Similarly, §339 Insolvenzordnung.

50 An example is, among others, the Italian case *Volare S.p.A. v. WLFC*, Tribunale di Busto Arsizio – 10.07.2012 – [2012] EICR(A) 350.

51 Bork/van Zwieten-*Garcimartín/Virgós*, EIR, para. 16.9.

52 Cf. *Bork*, Principles of Cross-Border Insolvency Law, para. 6.83 et seq.

53 Bork/Mangano-*Bork*, European Insolvency Law, para. 4.104; *Brinkmann*, Avoidance Claims in the Context of the EIR, IILR 2013, 371, 378; Hess/Oberhammer/Pfeiffer-*Veder*, European Insolvency Law, p. 577 et seq.; *Veder*, Security Rights, p. 315 et seq.; *Veder*, Party Autonomy, p. 267; *Veder*, The Future of the European Insolvency Regulation, IILR 2011, 285, 294 et seq.

avoidance of payments on shareholder loans.[54] However, since the loan agreement is governed by French law, C may prove that the payment is not voidable under French transactions avoidance law, which does not contain any rules on shareholder loans and requires the creditor's knowledge of the debtor's cessation of payments at the relevant time (Art. L. 632-2 Code de Commerce).[55]

C. RECOGNITION

10.21 It follows from the principles of universalism and cooperation and coordination[56] that "outgoing" insolvency proceedings, which claim to have worldwide effect, are expected to be recognised in all other affected jurisdictions. This is **necessary** in order to extend the effects of the opening decision to assets situated in another state and to enable Insolvency Practitioners to act on foreign soil. It goes without saying that the courts of state A have no power to produce legal effects on the territory of state B. Hence, it needs a recognition of foreign insolvency proceedings, either by statute or by court decision.

10.22 However, many states – examples are Norway or Switzerland – have decided to generally **refuse recognition**. They would not deny that insolvency proceedings have been opened abroad but they do not accept the legal consequences of such opening decision of a foreign court on their territory. Hence, where a foreign Insolvency Practitioner intends to (e.g.) sell assets located in such a state, he or she would not be recognised as being entitled to dispose of the assets. As a consequence, the Insolvency Practitioner needs a proxy of the debtor who may be obliged under the *lex fori concursus* to support and to cooperate with the Insolvency Practitioner and to make out the necessary documents.[57]

10.23 Conversely, most jurisdictions **grant recognition**, although there are many differences in the details, depending on the level of mutual trust

---

54 Cf. above at para. 6.46.

55 Above at para. 6.26.

56 See *Bork*, Principles of Cross-Border Insolvency Law, para. 2.52 et seq.

57 Cf. for Germany BGH, Beschl. v. 25.2.2016 – IX ZB 74/15 = NZI 2016, 365.

(among other factors).[58] On a procedural level, some regulations provide for automatic recognition by statute (albeit with the possibility of refusing recognition on application where certain conditions are met, the most important being questions concerning international jurisdiction of the foreign court or the public policy exception[59]). Examples include Art. 19 et seq., 32, 33 EIR and §343 Insolvenzordnung. Others require predetermined recognition proceedings and a recognition decision from the court, sometimes even on the condition that reciprocity is guaranteed.[60] Court decisions are primarily[61] required in those countries, which follow Art. 15 UNCITRAL Model Law, for example England (Art. 15 Sch. 1 Cross-Border Insolvency Regulation 2006) and particularly the USA (§§1504, 1505,[62] 1509, 1515 Bankruptcy Code[63]), where "Section 1509 of the Code, captioned 'Right of direct access', effectively establishes the bankruptcy court as a gatekeeper for a foreign representative's access to the U.S. courts, with recognition as the means to open the gate."[64] The court decision prerequisite is clearly deficient from a universalistic point of view, not only because it results in additional costs and expenditure of effort due to the recognition proceedings but also because it is a gateway to territorialistic *caveats* based on mistrust among states. Recognition of foreign proceedings by domestic courts is not a "rubber stamp exercise"[65]

58 See above at para. 10.7.

59 The latter entitles states to refuse recognition or enforcement "where the effects of such recognition or enforcement would be manifestly contrary to that State's public policy, in particular its fundamental principles or the constitutional rights and liberties of the individual" (Art. 33 EIR).

60 See *Yamauchi*, Should Reciprocity Be a Part of the UNCITRAL Model Cross-Border Insolvency Law?, 16 (2007) IIR, 145, 167 et seq.

61 Also in France, cf. *Dammann/Sénéchal*, Le droit de l'insolvabilité international, para. 2103 et seq., 2112 et seq.

62 This provision deviates from Art. 5 UNCITRAL Model Law, which provides for automatic recognition of foreign insolvency practitioners; see *Gilhuly/Posin/Malatesta*, Bankruptcy Without Borders, 24 (2016) ABILR, 47, 67.

63 Cf. *In re Iida*, 377 B.R. 243, 257 et seq. (9th Cir. B.A.P 2007); *In re Loy*, 380 B.R. 154, 164 (Bankr. E.D. Va. 2007); *In re OAS S.A., et al.*, 533 B.R. 83, 92 et seq. (Bankr. S.D.N.Y. 2015). For statistics on recognition of foreign proceedings in US courts, see *Gilhuly/Posin/Malatesta*, Bankruptcy Without Borders, 24 (2016) ABILR, 47 et seq.; *Westbrook*, 87 (2013) Am. Bankr. L. J., 247, 254 et seq.

64 *In re Millard*, 501 B.R. 644, 653 fn. 27 (Bankr. S.D.N.Y.). Cf. also *In re Ran*, 390 B.R. 257, 290 (Bankr. S.D. Tex. 2008); *Epstein/Markell/Nickles/Ponoroff*, Bankruptcy, p. 419; *Glosband/Kelakos/Lifland/McEvoy/Melnik/Seamon/Silverman*, Cross-Border Insolvency, p. 17.

65 *In re Basis Yield Alpha Fund (Master)*, 381 B.R. 37, 40 (Bankr. S.D.N.Y. 2008), citing *In re Bear Stearns High-Grade Structured Credit Strategies Master Fund, Ltd.*, 374 B.R. 122, 126/130 (Bankr. S.D.N.Y. 2007).

but opens the door for domestic courts to control foreign proceedings from scratch, which at least means checking whether they are procedurally fair and whether they contravene domestic laws or public policy.[66] However, this may be acceptable at least in relation to those foreign states where equal standards are not guaranteed by mutual binding laws, such as bilateral treaties or multilateral conventions.[67] On a substantive level, some courts may merely recognise that insolvency proceedings have been opened, while in other countries the court may recognise some or all of the worldwide effects of foreign proceedings (provided that the *lex fori concursus* claims that such worldwide effects exist).[68]

10.24 A different matter is the recognition of **judgments** closely related to insolvency proceedings.[69] In principle, this is a matter of recognition under international civil procedure law. However, some insolvency laws – encouraged by the UNCITRAL Model Law on Recognition and Enforcement of Insolvency-Related Judgments – include such judgments into their recognition rules. A leading example is Art. 32 EIR, which provides for automatic recognition of all judgments that concern the course and the closure of insolvency proceedings. This includes preliminary measures, the approval of a restructuring plan, and judgments deriving directly from the insolvency proceedings, which are closely linked with them (which refers particularly to judgments on transactions avoidance). In England, the Supreme Court is reluctant to accept the enforcement of foreign judgments on transactions avoidance.[70] Other countries recognise preservation measures ordered by the insolvency court in the same way as

---

66 For the USA, cf. *In re Compãnia De Alimentos Fargo, SA*, 376 B.R. 427, 434 (Bankr. S.D.N.Y. 2007); *In re Irish Bank Resolution Corp. Ltd.*, Case No. 13-12159 (Bankr. D. Del. 2014) para. 89; *In re Northshore Mainland Services, Inc.*, 537 B.R. 192, 207 (Bankr. D. Del. 2015); *JP Morgan Chase Bank v. Altos Hornos de Mexico, S.A. de C.V.*, 412 F.3d 418 (2nd Cir. 2005) para. 17.

67 Independent recognition proceedings are heavily supported by *Kolmann*, Kooperationsmodelle, p. 517 et seq., 527 et seq.; *LoPucki*, Courting Failure, p. 254 et seq. An overview of the opinions on this matter can be found in *Veder*, Bob's "Unvollendete"?, in: Tribute to Bob Wessels, p. 139, 145 et seq.

68 Examples: European Union, Art. 20(1) EIR; Germany, §§343, 335 Insolvenzordnung (cf. BGH, Urt. v. 24.06.2014 – VI ZR 315/13 = ZIP 2014, 1997); furthermore – post-Art. 20 UNCITRAL Model Law – England, Art. 20 Sch. 1 Cross-Border Insolvency Regulation 2006; USA, §1520 Bankruptcy Code and the resultant *ratio* of *In re Rede Energia S. A.*, 515 B.R. 69 (Bankr. S.D.N.Y. 2014).

69 For them, see above at para. 10.13.

70 *Rubin v. Eurofinance SA* [2012] UKSC 46.

they recognise the opening decision,[71] but cross-border insolvency laws are otherwise silent on the matter[72] and thereby rely on cross-border civil procedure law rather than on cooperation rules.

However, it should be highlighted that the recognition of judgments closely related to the conduct of insolvency proceedings, or at least the recognition of the insolvency proceedings themselves, frequently includes the recognition of decisions of the insolvency court sanctioning **compositions** such as insolvency plans or schemes of arrangement, especially if they are drafted in order to enable the reorganisation of the debtor's company. The wording of Art. 32(1) EIR expressly mentions compositions approved by the court which opened the proceedings, and this wording must be construed widely.[73] The UNCITRAL Model Law, although it does not mention compositions expressly, can be said to facilitate the recognition of insolvency plans under the general rules of Art. 21(1) ("any appropriate relief") and Art. 7 ("additional assistance"),[74] depending on the facts of the case in question and the limits of national law, and this is also true of national cross-border insolvency laws which are moulded in the image of the Model Law.[75] A third group of regulations accepts judgments sanctioning compositions as decisions terminating the proceedings, of which §343(2) Insolvenzordnung is a good example.[76] 10.25

The recognition of a foreign **discharge** goes without saying under the European Insolvency Regulation, which not only covers separate discharge proceedings under its Art. 1(1)[77] but also includes discharge decisions in insolvency proceedings through the automatic recognition of judgments closely related to them under Art. 32(1) EIR. Some national laws, however, 10.26

71 This holds true for Germany (§343(2) Insolvenzordnung), even if – following the distinction between recognition and enforcement – an execution judgment is necessary according to §353(2) Insolvenzordnung.

72 This is especially accurate regarding the UNCITRAL Model Law, as well as national laws of countries that have adopted the Model Law. However, for the exception of judgments approving compositions, see the following paragraph.

73 Bork/van Zwieten-*Oberhammer*, EIR, para. 32.12.

74 See also Art. X of the UNCITRAL Model Law on Recognition and Enforcement of Insolvency-Related Judgments.

75 Cf. for the UK *Cambridge Gas Transportation Corp v. Official Committee of Unsecured Creditors of Navigator Holdings Plc* [2006] UKPC 26; Sheldon-*Smith*, Cross-Border Insolvency, para. 6.104 et seq.; for the US *In re Metcalfe & Mansfield Alternative Investments*, 421 B.R. 685 (Bankr. S.D.N.Y. 2010); *In re Vitro S.A.B. de CV*, 701 F.3d 1031 (5th Cir. 2012).

76 For this interpretation, see BGH, Urt. v. 24.06.2014 – VI ZR 315/13 = ZIP 2014, 1997.

77 See also *Linna*, Cross-Border Debt Adjustment, 23 (2014) IIR, 20 et seq.

are more reluctant. While German[78] and American[79] courts recognise foreign discharge decisions consistently (only subject to the public policy exception), English law, for example, accepts a foreign discharge only if this is in accordance with the proper law of the contract pursuant to which the debt was incurred. Yet a debt will not be discharged where the proper law of the contract is not the law of the jurisdiction in which the proceedings are taking place, making the position of English law rather restrictive. This was decided early on by the Court of Appeal in *Gibbs v. La Societe Industrielle*,[80] which was criticised as constituting a "paradigm of territoriality",[81] but was confirmed in many other judgments.[82]

10.27 **Example**: German D GmbH is in financial turmoil because in four months a bond will become due and follow-up financing is not in sight. The directors of D GmbH develop a rescuing plan, which provides for a prolongation of the bond, for a cutback of the bondholders' claims, and for a reduction of interest rates. Since a minority opposes this plan, D GmbH commences administration proceedings in London (UK), claiming that the UK have international jurisdiction because the bond is governed by English law and the majority of bondholders are based in England. The Insolvency Practitioner starts a Scheme of Arrangement procedure,[83] which is eventually sanctioned by the

---

78 E.g. BGH, Urt. v. 14.01.2014 – II ZR 192/13 = NZI 2014, 238; BGH, Beschl. v. 18.09.2001 – IX ZB 51/00 = NJW 2002, 960.

79 The leading case is *Canada Southern R. Co. v. Gebhard*, 109 U.S. 527, 3 S. Ct. 363, 27 L. Ed. 1020 (1883). See also *Barclays Bank PLC v. Kemsley*, 992 N.Y.S. 2d 602 (N.Y. Sup.Ct. 2014).

80 *Gibbs v. La Societe Industrielle et Commercial des Metaux* [1890] 25 Q.B.D. 399, 406 (CA). Extensively on English law in this context *Dicey/Morris/Collins*, Conflict of Laws, para. 31R-092 et seq.; Sheldon-*Goldring*, Cross-Border Insolvency, para. 13.1 et seq.

81 *Tregear*, More than one way to skin a cat, 7 (2014) CRI, 51.

82 For example *Adams v. National Bank of Greece* [1961] AC 255, 287; *Joint Administrators of Heritable Bank plc v. Winding-up Board of Landsbanki Islands* [2013] UKSC 13; *National Bank of Greece and Athens v. Metliss* [1958] AC 509; *Global Distressed Alpha Fund v. PT Bakrie Investindo* [2011] EWHC 256 (Comm.). Most recently the Court of Appeal applied the rule in *Gibbs* in its decision *Gunel Bakhshiyeva (in her capacity as the foreign Representative of the OJSC International Bank of Azerbaijan) v. Sberbank of Russia and others* [2018] EWCA Civ. 2802 and the UK Supreme Court refused to hear an appeal against this decision.

83 Details above at para. 8.10.

High Court.[84] C, a German bondholder, files a lawsuit for full payment in Germany, claiming that the English insolvency proceedings and the Scheme are not recognisable in Germany. This would not be successful under the European Insolvency Regulation, since the insolvency proceedings were to be recognised under Art. 19(1) EIR.[85] The same holds true for the Scheme (Art. 32(1) EIR). However, after Brexit, the EIR is no longer applicable unless any exit treaties provide otherwise. As a consequence, German cross-border insolvency law applies, which is recognition-friendly but requires international jurisdiction of the English court under German cross-border insolvency law (§343(1)(2)No.1 Insolvenzordnung). Since D GmbH has its COMI (Art. 3 EIR[86]) and its centre of business activities (§3 Insolvenzordnung) in Germany, English courts have no jurisdiction under German law and neither the insolvency proceedings nor the Scheme are recognisable in Germany.

D. COOPERATION AND COORDINATION

10.28 Where there are **multiple proceedings**, coordination of these procedures is necessary.[87] There are four typical cases. First, there is only one single set of insolvency proceedings, opened in state A, but the debtor has assets in state B and the Insolvency Practitioner needs the support of the courts or enforcement institutions of state B to recover these assets. Second, concurrent insolvency proceedings are opened in two states, which do not apply the principle of universalism or do not recognise the competing proceedings. Third, main proceedings are opened in state A and secondary proceedings in state B. Fourth, a group of companies has group members in various jurisdictions and insolvency proceedings are

84 English courts are not very reluctant to confirm their international jurisdiction; in the context of Schemes of Arrangement see *Re NN2 NewCo Ltd and Politus BV* [2019] EWHC 1917 (Ch); *Re Syncreon Group B.V. and Syncreon Automotive (UK) Ltd* [2019] EWHC 2068 (Ch).

85 This holds true regardless of the fact that D GmbH's COMI was not in England, which cannot be examined on the recognition stage, *CJEU* Case C-341/04 *Eurofood IFSC Ltd.*, ECLI:EU:C:2006:281.

86 The European Insolvency Regulation is part of German insolvency law and also applicable in relation to Non-EU Member States; cf. *CJEU* Case C-328/12 *Schmid v. Hertel*, ECLI:EU:C:2014:6.

87 Extensively, *Bork*, Principles of Cross-Border Insolvency Law, para. 2.39 et seq.

opened for each group member in its COMI state. All these proceedings must be coordinated, at least in order to ensure that proceeds distributed in state A are taken into account when it comes to distributions in state B, since it must be guaranteed that all ordinary creditors are treated equally and that no creditor receives more than the full amount of his or her claim. Hence, it is necessary that the official bodies – courts[88] as well as Insolvency Practitioners – involved in multiple proceedings communicate and coordinate their actions where necessary.

10.29 **Rules** on coordination and cooperation can be found in many regulations. The European Insolvency Regulation provides for such rules in Art. 41 et seq. for the coordination of main and secondary proceedings and in Art. 56 et seq. for group insolvencies. Similarly, the **UNCITRAL** Model law aims at ensuring coordination and cooperation between the official bodies of multiple insolvency proceedings in various countries, which follows from its preamble and particularly from Art. 25 et seq.[89] Further, many "soft laws" endeavour to suggest and to support coordination and cooperation.[90] They all aim at promoting the efficiency and justice of the proceedings, particularly under the principles of equal treatment of creditors and best possible realisation of the debtor's assets by encouraging judges and Insolvency Practitioners in the jurisdictions concerned to communicate, to coordinate the proceedings, and to support the efforts of the other side where necessary and possible under domestic law.

10.30 **Examples**: A highly illustrative example is the cooperation of two bankruptcy courts in the USA and Canada in the *Nortel* case. The Nortel Networks group was a leading enterprise in the telecom market, with worldwide business activity and highly integrated subsidiaries in over 100 countries. On 14 January 2009, insolvency applications were lodged simultaneously in Delaware for the USA, in Toronto for Canada and in London for Europe, the Middle East, and Africa. Three mediation attempts on an international scale concerning how

88 On this, *Vallender/Nietzer*, Cooperation and Communication of Judges in Cross-border Insolvency Proceedings, in: Tribute to Bob Wessels, p. 127 et seq.

89 See also the UNCITRAL Practice Guide on Cross-Border Insolvency Cooperation, 2010.

90 Cf. above at para. 10.5.

to distribute the proceeds of 7.3 bn USD among the group's worldwide creditors failed. Finally, the courts in the USA and in Canada organised a 21-day joint trial with video conference calling facilities, facilitating the participation of all involved parties. Nearly 40 witnesses testified, deposition testimony of 130 witnesses was designated, and the parties admitted more than 2,200 exhibits into evidence. On 12 May 2015, the courts ultimately decided on the distribution of the proceeds simultaneously and reached the same conclusions, holding that the allocation of sales proceeds to all debtor entities should take place on a *pro rata* basis.[91]

Antwerp Bulkcarriers was a Belgian company facing Belgian insolvency proceedings.[92] The company owned a ship and American stevedores attached a lien under US maritime law to this ship. The ship sailed to Canada, where the stevedores opened a Canadian admiralty proceeding. The Belgian administrator sought for the ship to be turned over to him. The Canadian Supreme Court denied his application, the reason being that foreign bankruptcy law should "faithfully mirror the provisions of Canadian bankruptcy law", according to which "protection of secured creditors is a strong public policy in [Canadian] bankruptcy scheme". In the parallel case of *Holt Cargo Systems*[93] the Supreme Court ruled that "the need for such international cooperation in bankruptcy and insolvency has been evident for a very long time" but that "only some of the key components of the universalist approach have been reflected in Canadian law". "Given the almost infinite variations in circumstances that can occur 10.31

---

91 Canada: *Re Nortel Networks Corporation* [2015] ONSC 2987; confirmed in *Re Nortel Networks Corporation* [2015] ONSC 4170; *Re Nortel Networks Corporation* [2016] ONCA 332; *Re Nortel Networks Corporation* [2015] ONCA 681; USA: *In re Nortel Networks Inc.* 532 B.R. 494 (Bankr. D. Del. 2015). Extensively on this case *Harlang/Vininsky*, Nortel Networks, 34.8 (2015) ABIJ, 18 et seq.; *Peacock*, The Novel Cross-Border Bankruptcy Trial, 23 (2015) ABILR, 543 et seq.; *Tillman/Bullen*, Nortel, 28 (2015) Insolv. Int., 91 et seq. and 12 (2015) ICR, 202 et seq.; *Westbrook*, Nortel, 30 (2015) JIBFL, 498 et seq.

92 Following the Canadian case *Antwerp Bulkcarriers N. V. v. Holt Cargo Systems, Inc.* [2001] 3 S.C.R. 951; see also the illuminating analysis of this decision by *Pottow*, 104 (2006) Mich. L. Rev., 1899, 1922 et seq.

93 *Holt Cargo Systems Inc. v. ABC Containerline N.V. (Trustee of)* [2001] 3 S.C.R. 907.

in an 'international bankruptcy', the pragmatism of the 'plurality' approach continues to recommend itself. International coordination is an important factor, but it is not necessarily a controlling factor". This decision is a sad relapse to territorialism.[94]

10.32 ***For further reading***: *Bork*, Einführung, §38; *Fletcher*, Law of Insolvency, Chapter 28 et seq.; *Tabb*, Law of Bankruptcy, §1.27(e); *van Zwieten*, Principles of Corporate Insolvency Law, Chapter 15, 16.[95]

94 Cf. *Bork*, Principles of Cross-Border Insolvency Law, para. 2.64 et seq.
95 For France, see the references above in fn. 8.

LITERATURE

Boekraad, Gertjan, Over fixatie en verificatie van vorderingen, Tijdschrift voor Insolventierecht 2019/4, 18–30.

Bork, Reinhard, Creditors' Committees: An Anglo-German Comparative Study, Int. Insolv. Rev. 21 (2012), 127–141.

——, Einführung Einführung in das Insolvenzrecht, 9th ed., Mohr Siebeck, Tübingen 2019.

——, Principles of Cross-Border Insolvency Law, Intersentia, Cambridge 2017.

——, The "Protective Umbrella Procedure" – a New German Restructuring Tool, Insolvency Intelligence 25 (2012), 22–24.

——, Rescuing Companies in England and Germany, Oxford University Press, Oxford 2012.

Bork, Reinhard/Mangano, Renato, European Cross-Border Insolvency Law, Oxford University Press, Oxford 2016.

Bork, Reinhard/Voelker, Martin, The Anti-Deprivation Rule as an Anti-Avoidance Rule, Insolv. Int. 29 (2016), 65–75.

——, §91 InsO und die Anti-Deprivation Rule – ein Rechtsvergleich, KTS 2013, 235–261

Bork, Reinhard/Wiese, Jenny, Die Rechtsstellung des Insolvency Practitioner, Köln 2011.

Bork, Reinhard/van Zwieten, Kristin (eds.), Commentary on the European Insolvency Regulation, Oxford University Press, Oxford 2016.

Brinkmann, Moritz (ed.), European Insolvency Regulation, C. H. Beck/Hart Publishing/Nomos, München/Oxford/Baden-Baden 2019.

Brinkmann, Moritz, Avoidance Claims in the Context of the EIR, IILR 2013, 371–383.

Buccola, Vincent S. J. (Bankruptcy's Cathedral: Property Rules, Liability Rules, and Distress, available at https://ssrn.com/abstract=33538483353848, p. 1–50.

Buckley, Ross P., The Bankruptcy of Nations: An Idea Whose Time Has Come, 43(3) The International Lawyer, 2009, 1189–1216.

Carlsson, Philosophy in Bankruptcy, Michigan Law Review 85 (1987), 1341–1389.

Casey, Anthony J, The New Bargaining Theory of Corporate Bankruptcy and Chapter 11's Renegotiation Framework, https://ssrn.com/abstract=3353871, p. 1 et seq.

Chuah, Jason/Vaccari, Eugenio, Executory Contracts in Insolvency Law, Edward Elgar, Cheltenham 2019.

Clark, Robert Charles, The duties of the corporate debtor to its creditors, Harvard Law Review 90 (1976/1977), 505, 510.

Countryman, Vern, Executory Contracts in Bankruptcy, Part I: 57 (1973) Minn. L. Rev. 439–491, Part I: 58 (1974) Minn. L. Rev. 479–567.

Dammann, Reinhard/Sénéchal,Marc, Le droit de l'insolvabilité internationale, Joly, Issy-les-Moulineaux Cedex 2018.

Dicey, Albert Venn/Morris, John Humphrey Carlile/Collins, Lawrence Antony (eds.), Conflict of Laws, Sweet & Maxwell, 15th ed., London 2012.

Eidenmüller, Horst, What Is An Insolvency Proceeding?, working paper available at https://papers.ssrn.com/sol3/papers.cfm?abstract_id=2712628, p. 1–20.

Epstein, David G., Bankruptcy and Related Law, West Academy Publishing, 9th ed., St. Paul 2017.

Epstein, David G./Markell, Bruce A./Nickles, Steve H./Ponoroff, Lawrence, Bankruptcy: Dealing with Financial Failure for Individuals and Businesses, West Academic Publishing, 4th ed., St. Paul 2015.

Etzioni, Amitai, The Spirit of Community Rights, Responsibilities and the Communitarian Agenda, HarperCollins, New York 1993.

Faber, Dennis/Vermunt, Niels/Kilborn, Jason/Richter, Tomáš, Commencement of Insolvency Proceedings, Oxford University Press, Oxford 2012.

Faber, Dennis/Vermunt, Niels/Kilborn, Jason/van der Linde, Kathleen (eds.), Treatment of Contracts in Insolvency, Oxford University Press, Oxford 2013.

Faber, Dennis/Vermunt, Niels/Kilborn, Jason/Richter, Tomáš/Tirado, Ignacio (eds.), Ranking and Priority of Creditors, Oxford University Press, Oxford 2016.

Finch, Vanessa, The Measures of Insolvency 17 (1997) Oxford Journal of Legal Studies, 227–234.

——, Security, Insolvency and Risk: Who Pays the Price? 62 (1999) The Modern Law Review, 633–670.

Finch, Vanessa/Milman, David, Corporate Insolvency Law, 3rd ed., Cambridge University Press, Cambridge 2017.

Fletcher, Ian, Insolvency in Private International Law, 2nd ed., Oxford University Press, Oxford 2005.

——, The Law of Insolvency, 5th ed., Sweet & Maxwell, London 2017.

——, Spreading the Gospel: The Mission of Insolvency Law, and Insolvency Practitioners, in the Early 21st Century, [2014] J.B.L., 523–540.

Franken, M.J.M., Het Insolventiepassief, Wolters Kluwer, Deventer 2019.

van Galen, Robert/André, Marc/Fritz, Daniel/Gladel, Vincent/van Koppen, Frans/Marks, David/Wouters, Nora, Revision of the European Insolvency Regulation, Proposals by INSOL Europe, INSOL Europe, Nottingham 2012.

Gilhuly, Peter M./Posin, Kimberly A./Malatesta, Adam E., Bankruptcy Without Borders: a Comprehensive Guide to the First Decade of Chapter 15, 24 (2016) ABILR, 47–132.

Glosband, Daniel M./Kelakos, George M./Lifland, Burton R./McEvoy, Josefina F./Melnik, Selinda A./Seamon, Scott K./Silverman, Ronald J., Cross-Border Insolvency in the United States, American Bankruptcy Institute, Alexandria 2008.

Gross, Karen, Failure and Forgiveness – Rebalancing the Bankruptcy System, Yale University Press, New Haven and London 1997.

——, Taking community interests into account in bankruptcy; an essay, 72 (1994) Wash. U. L. Rev., 1031–1048.

Harlang, Robert/Vininsky, Mitch, Nortel Networks: A New Twist on Substantive Consolidation?, 34.8 (2015) ABIJ, 18–19, 66.

Heese, Michael, Die Funktion des Insolvenzrechts im Wettbewerb der Rechtsordnungen, JZ 2018, 179–191.

Hess, Burkhard/Oberhammer, Paul/Pfeiffer, Thomas (eds.), European Insolvency Law. The Heidelberg-Luxembourg-Vienna-Report, C. H. Beck/Hart Publishing/Nomos, München/Oxford/Baden-Baden 2014.

Ho, Look Chan, Cross-Border Insolvency, 4th ed., Global Law and Business, Horsell 2017.

Hynes, Richard M./Walt, Steven D., Bankruptcy Bounties, University of Virginia School of Law, Law and Economics Paper Series No. 2018-15, available at https://ssrn.com/abstract=3275490.

International Monetary Fund, Legal and Policy Development and Review Departments, "Proposed Features of a Sovereign Debt Restructuring Mechanism", 2003, available at http://www.imf.org/external/np/pdr/sdrm/2003/021203.pdf.

Jackson, Thomas, The Logic and Limits of Bankruptcy Law, Harvard University Press, Cambridge MA 1986, and Beard, Washington D. C., 2001.

Janger, Edward J., Predicting When The Uniform Law Process Will Fall: Article 9, Capture and the Race to the Bottom, 83 (1988) Iowa Law Review, 569–632.

Johnston, William/Werlen, Thomas/Link, Frederick, Set-Off Law and Practice, Oxford University Press, 3rd ed., Oxford 2018.

Kadner Graziano, Thomas/Bojārs, Juris/Sajadova, Veronika, A Guide to Consumer Insolvency Proceedings in Europe, Edward Elgar Publishing, Cheltenham, 2019.

Keay, Andrew/Walton, Peter, Insolvency Law, 4th ed., Lexis Nexis, Bristol 2017.

Kodek, Georg E., The Treatment of Security Rights – The Austrian Perspective, IILR 2015, 10–17.

Kolmann, Stephan, Kooperationsmodelle im internationalen Insolvenzrecht, Gieseking, Bielefeld 2001.

Konstantinov, Dmitry, Wrongful trading: Comparative Approach (England and Wales, Russia and the USA), BRICS Law Journal 2 (2015), 100–124.

Korch, Insolvenzrecht und Marktgesetze, ZHR 182 (2018), 440–481.

Krueger, Anne O., A New Approach to Sovereign Debt Restructuring, 2002, available at http://www.imf.org/external/pubs/ft/exrp/sdrm/eng/index.htm.

Le Corre, Pierre-Michel, Droit et pratique des procédures collectives, 10th ed., Dalloz, Paris 2019.

Legislative Guide on Insolvency Law, Part 1 and 2: see *United Nations Commission on International Trade Law.*

Linna, Tuula, Cross-Border Debt Adjustment – Open Questions in European Insolvency Proceedings, 23 (2014) IIR, 20–39.

LoPucki, Lynn M., Courting Failure: How Competition for Big Cases Is Corrupting the Bankruptcy Courts, The University of Michigan Press, Ann Arbor 2005.

Madaus. Stephan, Leaving the Shadows of US Bankruptcy Law: A Proposal to Divide the Realms of Insolvency and Restructuring Law, 19 (2018) Eur Bus Org Law Rev 615–647.

McBryde, William W./Flessner, Axel/Kortmann, Sebastian (eds.), Principles of European Insolvency Law, Kluwer, Deventer 2003 (new edition 2005).

McCormack, Gerard/Bork, Reinhard (eds.), Security Rights and the European Insolvency Regulation, Intersentia, Cambridge/Antwerp/Portland 2017.

McCormack, Gerard/Keay, Andrew/Brown, Sarah, European Insolvency Law – Reform and Harmonization, Edward Elgar Publishing, Cheltenham/Northampton 2017.

Mélin, François, La faillite internationale, Librairie Générale de Droit, Paris 2004.

Mokal, Rizwaan Jameel, The Search for Someone to Save: A Defensive Case for the Priority of Secured Credit, 22 (2002) Oxford Journal of Legal Studies, 687–728.

Moss, Gabriel, Scheme of arrangement: a recent example, Insolv. Int. 2003, 6.

Moss, Gabriel/Fletcher, Ian F./Isaacs, Stuart (eds.), The EC Regulation on Insolvency Proceedings, Oxford University Press, 3rd ed., Oxford 2016.

Müller, Hans-Friedrich, Insolvenzverfahren für souveräne Staaten – Ausweg aus der Schuldenkrise?, KTS 2013, 263–276.

Nsubuga, Hamiisi Junior, Corporate Insolvency and Employment Protection: A Theoretical Perspective, (2016) 4 NIBLeJ 4 (1-24).

Parry, Rebecca/Ayliffe, James/Shivji, Sharif (eds.), Transactions Avoidance in Insolvencies, 3rd ed., Oxford University Press, Oxford 2018.

Paulus, Christoph G., Security Rights in Cross-Border Insolvency Proceedings, IILR 2014, 366–374.

Paulus, Christoph (ed.), A Debt Restructuring Mechanism for Sovereigns: do we need a legal procedure? C. H. Beck/Nomos/Hart Publishing, München/Baden-Baden/Oxford/Portland 2014.

Peacock, Lauren L., The Novel Cross-Border Bankruptcy Trial, 23 (2015) ABILR, 543–570.

Piekenbrock, Andreas, Die Überschuldung als Eröffnungsgrund in Europa, KTS 2017, 333–363.

Pottow, John A. E., Greed and Pride in International Bankruptcy: The Problems of and Proposed Solutions to "Local Interests", 104 (2006) Mich. L. Rev., 1899–1949.

Principles of European Insolvency Law, see *McBryde/Flessner/Kortmann.*

Rault, Charlotte Julie, The legal framework of sovereign debt management, Nomos, Baden-Baden 2017.

Rogoff, Kenneth/Zettelmeyer, Jeromin, Bankruptcy Procedures for Sovereigns: A History of Ideas, 1976–2001, IMF Staff Papers 49 No. 3, available at https://www.elibrary.imf.org/view/IMF024/03375-9781589061224/03375-9781589061224/03375-9781589061224.xml.

Saint-Alary-Houin, Corinne, Droit des entreprises en difficulté, 11th ed., LGDJ, Issy-les-Moulineaux Cedex 2018.

Schermer, Barry, Response to Professor Gross: Taking the Interests of the Community into account in Bankruptcy, 772 (1994) Wash. U. L. Rev., 1049 et seq.

Schillig, Michael, Deepening Insolvency – Liability for Wrongful Trading in the United States?, 30 (2009) Company Lawyer 298–303.

Scott, Robert E., Through Bankruptcy with the Creditors' Bargain Heuristic, 53 (1986) 53 U. Chi. L. Rev., 690–708.

Sheldon, Richard (ed.), Cross-Border Insolvency, Bloomsbury Professional, 4th ed., Haywards Heath 2015.

Snijders, Jurian, Fixatiebeginsel en partijautonomie, Een kwart eeuw, Wolters Kluwer, Deventer 2016, 367–382.

Steffek, Felix, Insolvenzgründe in Europa – Rechtsvergleich, Regelungsstrukturen und Perspektiven der Rechtsangleichung, KTS 2009, 317–353.

Tabb, Charles Jordan, Law of Bankruptcy, West Academic Publishing, 4th ed., St. Paul 2016.

Tillman, John/Bullen, Matthew, Nortel: Cross-Border Decisions Points the Way to Distributions, 28 (2015) Insolv. Int., 91–93.

Tregear, Francis, More than one way to skin a cat: universalism will trump territoriality where possible, 7 (2014) CRI, 51–52.

United Nations Commission on International Trade Law, Legislative Guide on Insolvency Law, Part 1 and 2, United Nations Publications, New York 2005.

——, UNCITRAL Model Law on Cross-Border Insolvency Law with Guide to Enactment and Interpretation, United Nations Publications, New York 2014.

——, UNCITRAL Model Law on Recognition and Enforcement of Insolvency-Related Judgments, New York 2018.

——, UNCITRAL Practice Guide on Cross-Border Insolvency Cooperation, United Nations Publications, New York 2010.

Vallender, Heinz/Nietzer, Eberhard, Cooperation and Communication of Judges in Cross-border Insolvency Proceedings, in: Santen, Bernhard/van Offeren, Dick (eds.), Perspectives on International Insolvency Law: A Tribute to Bob Wessels, Kluwer, Deventer 2014, 127–138.

Veder, Michael, Bob's "Unvollendete"?, in: Santen, Bernhard/van Offeren, Dick (eds.), Perspectives on International Insolvency Law: A Tribute to Bob Wessels, Kluwer, Deventer 2014, 139–150.

Veder, Michael, Cross-Border Insolvency Proceedings and Security Rights, Kluwer Legal Publisher, Deventer 2004.

Veder, Michael C., Party Autonomy and Insolvency, in: Westrik, Roel/van der Weide, Jeroen (eds.), Party Autonomy in International Property Law, sellier, München 2011, 261–276.

Veder, Michael, The Future of the European Insolvency Regulation – Applicable law, in particular security rights, IILR 2011, 285–297.

Virgós, Miguel/Garcimartín, Francisco, The European Insolvency Regulation: Law and Practice, Kluwer Law International, The Hague 2004.

Warren, Elisabeth, Bankruptcy Policy, 54 (1987) U. Chi. L. Rev., 775–814.

Wessels, Bob, International Insolvency Law, Kluwer, 3rd ed., Deventer 2012.

——, International Insolvency Law Part I – Global Perspectives on Cross-Border Insolvency Law, Wolters Kluwer, 4th ed., Deventer 2015.

Westbrook, Jay Lawrence, An Empirical Study of the Implementation in the United States of the Model Law on Cross Border Insolvency, 87 (2013) ABLJ, 247–271.

——, Nortel: the cross-border insolvency case of the century, 30 (2015) JIBFL, 498–499.

Yamauchi, Keith D., Should Reciprocity Be a Part of the UNCITRAL Model Cross-Border Insolvency Law?, 16 (2007) IIR, 145–179.

van Zwieten, Kristin, Goode on Principles of Corporate Insolvency Law, Sweet & Maxwell, 5th ed., London 2018.

INDEX

ABOUT THE AUTHOR

Prof. Dr. Reinhard Bork is Professor of Law at the University of Hamburg, Germany, where he holds the Chair for Civil Procedural Law. He has held the position of Dean of the Law Faculty, was Robert S. Campbell Visiting Fellow at Magdalen College Oxford twice, and is currently also Professor for International Insolvency Law at Radboud University Nijmegen, the Netherlands. He has previously served as a judge at the Upper State Court (Court of Appeal) in Hamburg, the Commercial Law Division. He has considerable experience as an arbitrator in national and international cases.

www.ingramcontent.com/pod-product-compliance
Ingram Content Group UK Ltd.
Pitfield, Milton Keynes, MK11 3LW, UK
UKHW021845100926
8556IPUK00019B/1053

9 781780 689838